Dr Johnson's Dictionary

Dr Johnson's Dictionary

The Extraordinary Story of the
Book that Defined the World

HENRY HITCHINGS

JOHN MURRAY

Text © Henry Hitchings 2005

First published in Great Britain in 2005 by John Murray (Publishers)
A division of Hodder Headline

The right of Henry Hitchings to be identified as the Author of the Work has been
asserted by him in accordance with the Copyright, Designs and Patents Act 1988.

1 3 5 7 9 10 8 6 4 2

A CIP catalogue record for this title is available from the British Library

ISBN 0 7195 6631 2

Typeset in 10.75/13 Monotype Bembo by
Servis Filmsetting Ltd, Manchester

Printed and bound by
Clays Ltd, St Ives plc

Hodder Headline policy is to use papers that are natural, renewable and recyclable
products and made from wood grown in sustainable forests. The logging and
manufacturing processes are expected to conform to the environmental regulations of the
country of origin.

John Murray (Publishers)
338 Euston Road
London NW1 3BH

To my parents

Contents

CONTENTS

Dr Johnson's Dictionary

Adventurous

1. He that is inclined to adventures; and, consequently, bold, daring, courageous

2. Applied to things; that which is full of hazard; which requires courage; dangerous

On 15 April 1755 the first great dictionary of English was published. Samuel Johnson's giant *Dictionary of the English Language* was an audacious attempt to tame his unruly native tongue. In more than 42,000 carefully constructed entries, Johnson had mapped the contours of the language, combining huge erudition with a steely wit and remarkable clarity of thought.

In doing so, Johnson had fashioned the most important British cultural monument of the eighteenth century. Its two folio volumes tell us more about the society of this period – lustily commercial, cultivated but energetic, politically volatile yet eager for consensus – than any other work. They document the copious vitality of English and its literature, and Johnson's spirit – by turns humorous, ethical and perceptive – presides over every page.

The appearance of the *Dictionary* marked the end of a heroic ordeal. Johnson had begun work on it full of bluff confidence; he thought he would get the job done in less than three years. It was not long, however, before he began to buckle beneath the magnitude of the task. His labours were absorbing, yet painful; he would eventually characterize them as a mixture of 'anxious diligence' and 'persevering activity'. When the trials of compilation overtook him, so too did the black despondency that blighted his adult life. Johnson had to wrestle not only with the complexities of the English language, but also, as we shall see, with the pangs of personal tragedy.

Although a tirelessly productive author, Johnson considered himself disgracefully lazy – believing that only Presto, a dog belonging to his friend Hester Thrale, might truly be thought lazier. His diaries are full of self-recrimination: assurances that he will work harder, along with detailed schedules to ensure that he do so. His schemes of work suggest at once a schoolboy's hunger for self-improvement and a schoolboy's slender acquaintance with the realities of what can actually be achieved. Yet if Johnson's self-flagellating self-encouragement is striking, so too are his working habits – hardly those of a diligent professional. 'Whoever thinks of going to bed before twelve o'clock is a scoundrel,' he was wont to claim. His nights were as often spent in jovial company as in the prison house of learning.

It is surprising, given Johnson's oscillation between sociability and melancholia, that the *Dictionary* ever got written at all. Surprising, too, that it is so good. Johnson's ability to complete the job despite the distractions he faced affords us a crucial insight into his character: the methods he employed, the means he used to deal with his depressions and disappointments, suggest the very essence of his working mind, the special character of his achievement.

The *Dictionary* captures, and to some degree pre-empts, its age's passion for organization. The ambitious ordering of the arts was reflected in a vast range of manuals, taxonomies and histories – of painting, of poetry, of music, and of the nation. At the same time the desire to 'stage' knowledge – for both entertainment and public benefit – was evident at festivals such as the Shakespeare Jubilee, and in assembly rooms, theatres, lecture halls, or new institutions such as the British Museum and the Royal Academy.[1] Like the colossal *Encyclopédie* of the Frenchmen Diderot and d'Alembert, which distilled the essence of the Continental Enlightenment, the *Dictionary* was a *machine de guerre*. It would become an instrument of cultural imperialism, and its publication was a defining moment in the realization of what was in the eighteenth century a brand new concept, namely Britishness.

The authority of Johnson's work has coloured every dictionary of English that has since been compiled. In the second half of the eighteenth century, and for most of the nineteenth, it enjoyed totemic status in both Britain and America. When British speakers of English refer today to 'the dictionary', they imply the *Oxford English Dictionary*, while Americans incline towards *Webster's*. But for 150 years 'the dictionary' meant Johnson's *Dictionary*. To quote the editor of the Supplement to the *OED*, 'In the whole tradition of English language and literature the *only* dictionary compiled by a writer of the first rank is that of Dr Johnson.'[2] Unlike other dictionaries, Johnson's is a work of literature.

Its influence has been especially profound among writers. As a young man Robert Browning read both its folio volumes in their entirety in order to 'qualify' himself for a career as an author. He was not the first to use them in this way. The eighteenth-century historian William Robertson read the *Dictionary* twice, while Henry Thomas Buckle, the reviled author of a once celebrated *History of Civilization in England*, worked through it diligently in order to enlarge his vocabulary, and Thomas Jefferson treated it as an anthology of quotations. In the 1930s, Samuel Beckett could add his name to the roll of revisionary users, gleaning from its pages a crop of strange terms – 'increpation', 'inosculation', 'to snite'.[3]

Johnson's was *the* dictionary in the eyes of authors as various as Keats and Shelley, Byron and Wordsworth, George Eliot and Mary Wollstonecraft, Carlyle, Ruskin, the Brontës and Trollope, Jeremy Bentham and John Stuart Mill, Samuel Smiles, George Gissing, Matthew Arnold, and Oscar Wilde. Even though they had more recent dictionaries at their disposal, Hawthorne and Poe deferred to the authority of Johnson. Emerson thought Johnson a 'muttonhead' at definition, but consulted him all the same. Johnson's *magnum opus* was the dictionary for Darwin (he cites it in an essay on flowers) and for James Clerk Maxwell, who noted regretfully that it did not contain the word 'molecule'.

Sometimes the *Dictionary*'s power could have startling results. In the summer of 1775 the toast of British high society was Omai, a young man brought back from Tahiti by Tobias Furneaux, a member of Captain Cook's party. Quick to learn chess, Omai was rather less successful in his command of English, but apparently, having gathered from the *Dictionary* that 'to pickle' meant 'to preserve', he saluted Lord Sandwich, the Admiral of the Fleet, with the hope that 'God Almighty might pickle his Lordship to all eternity'. The story may be apocryphal, but it illustrates quaintly the expansive afterlife of Johnson's text.

Even its detractors could not escape its influence. More than sixty years after the *Dictionary*'s publication, Samuel Taylor Coleridge agitated about its deficiencies in *Biographia Literaria*, yet when he coined the verb 'to intensify' he conceded that, while puzzling over its application, he had checked to see if it was in Johnson. Thirty years later, *Vanity Fair* testified to the work's enduring power. When Becky Sharp leaves her 'Academy for Young Ladies', she is presented with a miniature copy of the *Dictionary* by its principal, Miss Pinkerton: 'the Lexicographer's name was always on the lips of this majestic woman, and a visit he had paid to her was the cause of her reputation and her fortune'. Becky is not impressed. 'And just as the coach drove off,' writes Thackeray, 'Miss Sharp put her pale face out of the window, and actually flung the book back into the garden.' The gesture is a symbolic overthrow of traditional, masculine authority, and of Englishness (Becky speaks French 'with purity and a Parisian accent', and adores Napoleon). It is signal evidence of what Johnson's great work had come to embody.

The achievement of the *Dictionary* made Johnson a national icon. But, as his reputation grew, public attention focused on the man – a constellation of quirks and quotable effusions – more than on his works. Soon after his death, in December 1784, the first biography was published. Many more followed, most notably James Boswell's, which appeared in 1791.

These accounts, and Boswell's in particular, have ensured that Johnson has become a magnet for reverent affection. This affection has been inspired by his memorable aphorisms ('Patriotism is the last refuge of a scoundrel', 'No man but a blockhead ever wrote, except for money') and bizarre mannerisms (collecting orange peel, pausing to touch every lamp post as he walked down Fleet Street, blowing out his breath like a whale). Readers recall with amusement his definition of oats – 'a grain, which in England is generally given to horses, but in Scotland supports the people' – and his vast appetite – he called himself 'a hardened and shameless tea-drinker', and Hester Thrale, who likened him to both an elephant and a haunch of venison, reckoned he often ate seven or eight peaches before breakfast. His biographers have taken pleasure in charting the minute byways of his existence: his opinion of cucumbers, the precise number of bottles of port he drank, the size of his breeches, the names of his cats. Yet more broadly, the affection for Johnson stems from a peculiarly English or Anglophile fondness for anyone who can be thought of as a 'character', and it tends to be most deeply felt by those who prefer tangible truths to abstract notions – a preference that Johnson's life and work repeatedly manifest.[4]

Accordingly, we associate Johnson with carousing, with the vigorous talk of the Club and the coffee house, and with sexual unhappiness. He made a bad marriage, to a woman twenty years his senior; he talked, in his own phrase, 'for victory', battering his combatants with learning, lancing them with finely judged critique; and he loved a glass of punch (or '*poonsh*', as he would have said, in his Staffordshire accent). We enjoy his stout good humour, his warm intelligence, his robust humanity; and we are morbidly intrigued by the long shadows of his melancholy.

Yet Johnson's true achievement is, before anything else, that of a great writer – an original stylist, an important philosopher of travel, a founding father of the modern art of biography, a Christian moralist well equipped to understand an increasingly secular world. He is a poet and playwright, a novelist, a preacher and essayist, a translator, journalist and political commentator, a reviewer and critic, a bibliographer, historian and philologist. The *Dictionary* draws together many of the skills of these trades: more than any of his famous dicta, it illuminates the machinery of his mind. Its creation was a voyage not so much of self-discovery as of self-invention.

The 1750s were the most fecund period of Johnson's creative life. In addition to the *Dictionary*, he produced a large body of essays, mainly of a philosophical or moral cast. The best of these appeared in the *Rambler*, a twice-weekly periodical. The *Rambler* was almost entirely written by Johnson, and its title became one of his many sobriquets. But this popular image of Johnson – as a rover or wanderer, a digressive amateur, a peddler of confused and inconsequential narratives – belittles him. Far more fitting is the image conjured up by the title of another magazine to which he contributed at this time, the *Adventurer*.

Johnson's notion of adventure was intellectual, not physical: although he aspired to visit Poland, Iceland and the Baltic, and even spoke wistfully of going to see the Great Wall of China, his real business lay in voyages of the mind. In one of the best essays in the *Adventurer*, published in October 1753, he describes the importance of grand projects. Whoever devises them, he tells us, 'unites those qualities which have the fairest claim to veneration, extent of knowledge and greatness of design'. The danger he or she faces lies in 'aspiring to performances to which, perhaps, nature has not proportioned the force of man'. Such performances are characterized by 'rash adventure and fruitless diligence'.[5] Wittingly or not, Johnson has achieved a self-portrait. The *Dictionary* is exactly this kind of undertaking, completed in defiance of circumstance and probability.

Amulet

An appended remedy, or preservative: a thing hung about the neck, or any other part of the body, for preventing or curing some particular diseases

To understand the significance of the *Dictionary* as an event in Johnson's life, we must step back to trace the route by which he arrived at the task. Johnson's own philosophy of biography was that it should 'often . . . pass slightly over those performances and incidents which produce vulgar greatness, to lead the thoughts into domestic privacies, and display the minute details of daily life'.[1] The private Johnson is the early Johnson, and it is worth examining his beginnings. It is customary to concentrate on his mature years. After all, this period is often referred to as 'The Age of Johnson'. But the lustre of metropolitan life and its exalted fruits were not Johnson's birthright. In later years he would sit at the centre of literary London, yet his origins were humble, parochial and by no means propitious.

The journey began in Lichfield on 18 September 1709, with Johnson's birth. His parents were Michael, a local bookseller then in his fifties, and Sarah, a woman already past forty.* They had been married a little over three years, and Samuel was their first child. According to his own account the birth was difficult: 'I was born almost dead, and could not cry for some time.'[2]

Michael Johnson was a prominent local figure, and in the year his son was born he held office as sheriff of Lichfield. Later he served as a town councillor and senior bailiff. He seems to have been a popular man, though not a practical one. When he attempted to extend his

---

* In the eighteenth century the term 'bookseller' denoted someone whose activities combined retail and publishing. London was the centre of the British book trade, and provincial booksellers often found it commercially expedient to operate as printers, as bookbinders, as distributors of newspapers, and even as vendors of patent remedies.

business to include the manufacture and sale of parchment, the venture almost ruined him.★ Little is known of his background or early life, save that he came from the tiny Derbyshire village of Cubley, was the son of a man variously described as a 'day-labourer', 'cottager' and 'yeoman',[4] and served his apprenticeship under a London bookseller called Richard Simpson, who kept shop at the Three Trouts in St Paul's Churchyard.

Michael's antecedents were modest, and he was ambitious to expand his commercial interests in order to leave behind more than he had inherited. In part this was a reaction to his wife's better connections: Sarah's father, Cornelius Ford, was a landowner, 'a little Warwickshire Gent' who had in 1649 set up in some style, and at a cost of £750, in a house called Haunch Hall at King's Norton in the west Midlands.[5] Yet it was Mr Ford who introduced the couple; he made Michael's acquaintance when he bought some divinity books from him, approved of his interest in Sarah, and settled £430 on her when she married.

The birth of the Johnsons' first child cemented their social position. Michael, as sheriff and now a father, installed in a solid new fifteen-room house in the middle of the city, could imagine himself a local heavyweight and – for the time being – Sarah's equal. The two men they chose as their son's godparents were Lichfield worthies. Richard Wakefield, a lawyer and bibliophile, was the local coroner. Samuel Swynfen was a physician who, despite owning a substantial property outside town, lodged with the Johnsons in order to be near his patients. In October 1712 the household was enlarged by the arrival of a second son, Nathaniel. While Johnson, who throughout his life favoured diminutive forms, referred to his brother as 'Natty', the little existing evidence suggests their relationship was anything but affectionate.

The environment in which the boys grew up was narrow.

★ Having failed to serve an apprenticeship as a tanner, Michael was not legally entitled to trade as such, and his doing so landed him in court. He also faced trial for not paying his taxes. Even his core business was unsuccessful. He seems, for instance, to have been an incompetent binder of books. One of his best customers, Sir William Boothby, complained repeatedly of his poor handiwork: 'Your books do open very ill so that it is troublesome reading [-] pray mend this great fault.'[3]

Lichfield is a small city close to the very centre of England, about fifteen miles north of Birmingham, in the county of Staffordshire. In the early eighteenth century it was busy but provincial, with a population of less than 4,000. (At the time of the first national census, in 1801, the figure stood at 4,842; today it is 30,000.) Johnson was born in an upstairs chamber at his parents' house on Breadmarket Street, close to the local grammar school and the city's dominant feature, its fine, three-spired twelfth-century cathedral. Throughout his life he expressed affection for his birthplace. Its natives were, he claimed, 'the most sober, decent people in England, [and] the genteelest in proportion to their wealth'. Moreover, they 'spoke the purest English' – a typically proud claim.[6] He often returned, and in his sixties, travelling to Scotland with Boswell, stayed overnight at the inn next to his childhood home, the Three Crowns, where he encouraged his companion to try a real Staffordshire oatcake – an experience that prompted Boswell to recall one of his friend's most pungent dictionary definitions: 'It was pleasant to me to find, that oats, the food of horses, were so much used as the food of people in Dr Johnson's own town.'

Johnson described Lichfield as 'a city of philosophers: we work with our heads, and make the boobies of Birmingham work for us with their hands'. It is a place rich in its cultural associations. Joseph Addison's father was dean of Lichfield. David Garrick, comet of the London stage, was brought up there. Both, like Johnson, are buried in Westminster Abbey. The antiquarian Elias Ashmole was the son of a local saddler, and was born in Breadmarket Street; his collection, bequeathed to Oxford University, became Britain's first museum. Others have more oblique associations with the city. The stalls in the cathedral were carved by George Eliot's uncle, Samuel Evans, the original of Seth in *Adam Bede*, and, in the years after Johnson left, a half-timbered property on Beacon Street was home to the botanist and physician Erasmus Darwin, an intimate of Wedgwood and Rousseau, and grandfather of Charles Darwin.

Johnson's attachment to his birthplace is evident in the *Dictionary*. He explains, in the entry under 'lich' ('a dead carcass'), that Lichfield was named after the Christians once martyred there, and that its name literally means 'the field of the dead'. His etymology seems spurious:

the city's name probably derives from the Celtic *luitcoit*, meaning 'grey wood', or from the related Roman name for the area, Letocetum. But Johnson chooses a more graphic explanation, and the decision to offer one at all is a mark of his fondness for the city. Then, in a characteristic, albeit muted, autobiographical gesture, he salutes his former home with the words *Salve magna parens* ('Hail, great parent'). The phrase, an echo of a line in Book II of Virgil's *Georgics*, is a clear reminder both that Johnson is a proud Lichfield man and that he is the *Dictionary*'s author. The pride he takes in his provincial roots is an important trait: he would never assimilate himself to the polite felicities of the upper middle class, and the *Dictionary* would testify to the strength of his self-image.

Johnson's early years were uncomfortable. He was a sickly child: blind in one eye, partially deaf, and scarred by the glandular disease known as scrofula, all as a result of being put out to a wet-nurse, Joan Marklew, whose milk was infected with tuberculosis. It is surely no coincidence that his entry in the *Dictionary* for 'scrofula' includes a single illustrative quotation, from Richard Wiseman's *Seven Chirurgical Treatises* (1676): 'If matter in the milk dispose to coagulation, it produces a *scrofula*.' Scrofula can be contracted in other ways, but Johnson could not dissociate the disease from the way he personally picked it up. Under 'nurse', his first definition is 'a woman that has the care of another's child', and he quotes Sir Walter Ralegh's *History of the World*: 'Unnatural curiosity has taught all women, but the beggar, to find out *nurses*, which necessity only ought to commend.' Again there is a hint of criticism. The criticism is Ralegh's, not Johnson's, but it is striking that he chose to excerpt this quotation and reproduce it in the *Dictionary*.★

The consequences of Mrs Marklew's infected milk were lasting. Johnson was required in infancy to have an 'issue' cut in one arm to allow fluid to drain away – the word is defined in the *Dictionary* as 'a vent made in a muscle for the discharge of humours'. The operation, performed without anaesthetic, must have been gruesome. Johnson

---

★ A third quotation on this theme can be found under 'putrid', where he records the physician John Arbuthnot's observation that 'If a nurse feed only on flesh, and drink water, her milk, instead of turning sour, will turn *putrid*, and smell like urine.'

insisted he had felt no distress during the procedure, being preoccupied by 'having my little hand in a custard',[7] but it appears the issue needed to be kept open until he was six years old, and this will have been a source of inconvenience, not to say embarrassment. He endured other problems besides: there is evidence that he had a painful operation performed on the lymph glands in his neck, and a throwaway reference in his diary some sixty years later suggests that he was struck down with smallpox.[8]

Johnson's ill health necessitated a trip to London when he was a child of just two. Popular wisdom held that an infant could be cured of its ailments if touched by the monarch. Sir John Floyer, a Lichfield resident who had once been the personal physician of Charles II, recommended this remedy to Johnson's parents, and the child was duly taken by his mother to be touched. The journey took two and a half days – in a stuffy coach, with no suspension, on a bone-breakingly uneven road. When at last they arrived in the capital, mother and child lodged with one of Michael's acquaintances in the book trade, John Nicholson, in Little Britain, a part of town that Washington Irving was to describe as 'the heart's core of the city' and 'the stronghold of John Bullism'.[9] Johnson's memories of the trip were limited. However, he did retain a solemnly confused recollection of meeting a lady in diamonds wearing a long black hood. This was Queen Anne, and Johnson wore for the rest of his life the 'touchpiece' she gave him – a thin gold amulet bearing on one side an image of the archangel Michael, and on the other that of a ship in full sail.

The amulet was his breastplate, a barricade against infection, but it could not suppress the language of his genes. By the time he was eight years old he was showing symptoms of a nervous disorder akin to Tourette's syndrome, though of course no such diagnosis was available. His health seems to have improved by his teens, yet his appearance never fully recovered; his features were rutted with scars, the lasting marks of his trauma.

Early experience conditions adult life; childhood is the precinct in which we learn the rituals of maturity. Johnson's early pain taught him fortitude. It also taught him resilience. But there were other teachers besides. He seems, for instance, to have learned a thing or two about pugilism from his father's younger brother, Andrew, who had some reputation as a prizefighter, and to have been stirred, by stories of another athletic uncle, to experiment with reckless feats of climbing – an early metaphor for his gravity-defying ascent through the world of English letters. He told Hester Thrale how this uncle, while on a journey, had passed a spot where a stone had been erected to commemorate a man who had made a fantastic leap there. He then recalled what followed: 'Why now, says my uncle, I could leap it in my boots; and he did leap it in his boots.'[10] Johnson inherited this enthusiasm for physical challenges. In his seventies, returning to Lichfield, he looked for a rail he had enjoyed jumping as a boy; having found it, he removed his coat and wig, and jumped over it – twice.

Apple

1. The fruit of the apple tree
2. The pupil of the eye

From an early date Johnson's intellectual interests were fostered in the family bookshop. It was there that he learned the geography of both company and solitude – in the society of his father's customers, and in the privacy of his reading. In 1706 Michael bought the library of the late William Stanley, ninth earl of Derby, which comprised almost 3,000 volumes. The expense of doing so was considerable, and Michael's acquisitive instincts seem again to have outstripped his commercial abilities, for Johnson observed that some of the Earl's books were still to be found on his father's shelves almost forty years later. The one valuable consequence of Michael's disappointment was that the house on Breadmarket Street resembled a free library, the shelves of which Samuel could roam at will. He would assure Boswell that a good strategy for instilling in children a love of learning was to give them this freedom: 'I would put a child in a library (where no unfit books are) and let him read at his choice.'

Johnson learned to read early, tutored by his mother and then at a kindergarten on Dam Street, not much more than 100 yards from the family home. His kindergarten teacher was Ann Oliver, a shoe-maker's widow who owned a small confectionery business; fifteen years later, when he went up to Oxford, she made him a leaving present of some gingerbread. Dame Oliver was superseded by Thomas Browne, another shoemaker, who also lived in Dam Street and, according to his pupil, 'published a spelling book, and dedicated it to the Universe; but, I fear, no copy of it can now be had'.

In due course Johnson proceeded to the local grammar school, where, after the fashion of the age, he had Latin and Greek thrashed into him by violent schoolmasters. His records of his youth betray little admiration for these men; he describes one, Edward Holbrooke, as 'peevish and ill-tempered', and another, John Hunter, as 'wrong-headedly severe'.[1] In the *Dictionary*, 'school' and 'schoolhouse' are defined as a 'house of discipline and instruction'; one should note the sequence – tellingly, the discipline precedes the instruction.* The skills so purgatorially acquired in school were more profitably employed at home, and reading was an instrument of therapy and a salve for his discomforts.

The young Johnson was what Coleridge liked to call a 'library cormorant', a rapacious creature nesting among books. He dived upon his reading matter haphazardly. When he heard that Petrarch had been 'the restorer of poetry', the meaning of the words was not altogether clear (why had poetry needed restoring?), but the name lodged in his mind. Not long afterwards, while searching the high bookshelves of his father's shop to see if Natty had left any apples there to dry, he knocked a copy of Petrarch's *Works* from its shelf. Distracted from his quest, he forgot about the apples and read the book instead.

The Italian scholar-poet is not the sort of writer one could expect a small boy, even in the early eighteenth century, to select for himself, but Johnson, supplied with the book by accident, could not put it down. For the rest of his life he would maintain an aversion to children's literature and a strong belief that readers should read as their fancies and fortunes take them. 'A child', he told Boswell, 'should not be discouraged from reading anything that he takes a liking to from a notion that it is above his reach.' That turn of phrase – 'above his reach' – seems in this case peculiarly apposite.

Johnson's childhood was no idyll of scholarly precocity. Reading was, as it is for so many unhappy children, a retreat from the wretchedness of family life. The image of childhood Johnson later presents is unsentimental: 'One cannot love *lumps of flesh*, and little infants are nothing more'; 'no attention can be obtained from children without the affliction of pain'; 'a boy of seven years old has no *genius* for anything except a peg-top and an apple pie'. In a poignant

---

* Johnson also quotes Shakespeare's Jack Cade, who in *The Second Part of King Henry VI* condemns Lord Say to death because 'Thou hast most traitorously corrupted the youth of the realm in erecting a *grammar school.*'

moment he would reflect that 'Poor people's children never respect them. I did not respect my own mother, though I loved her: and one day, when in anger she called me a puppy, I asked her if she knew what they called a puppy's mother.'[2] It is easy to be contemptuous of children and their pleasures when, like the adult Johnson, one has never had children of one's own. Moreover, it is natural to recall isolated episodes of discord more vividly than extended periods of comfortable passivity. Still, little that Johnson ever had to say about his early years belies the impression that he was an unhappy child, and that books afforded a vital escape from this curdled domesticity.

Another anecdote of Johnson's childhood, presented by Hester Thrale, suggests his intense engagement with the books through which he thumbed. 'He was just nine years old', she tells us, 'when having got the play of Hamlet to read in his father's kitchen, he read on very quietly till he came to the Ghost scene, when he hurried up stairs to the shop door that he might see folks about him.'[3] His communion with the text was so complete that he took it for reality, and in those words 'got the play . . . in his father's kitchen' there is a nice suggestion of the accidental, unpurposed nature of his reading. He believed that 'what we read with inclination makes a much stronger impression', but in practice he often read without design, and it was this kind of reading that nourished and sustained the extremities of his erudition.★

★ Under 'childish' he quotes from Milton: 'When I was yet a child, no *childish* play / To me was pleasing; all my mind was set / Serious to learn and know.'

Bookworm

1. A worm or mite that eats holes in books, chiefly when damp

   'My lion, like a moth or *bookworm*, feeds upon nothing but paper, and I shall beg of them to diet him with wholesome and substantial food' – *The Guardian*

2. A student too closely given to books; a reader without judgement

Johnson's childhood reading was formidable – wide, and deep. Yet it was directed to no particular end: he read for pleasure, and to learn, but without a clear sense of the rewards of learning. This changed in his seventeenth year when, at the invitation of a cousin, he spent nine months away from Lichfield.

This generous cousin shared the name of Johnson's grandfather Cornelius Ford; inevitably, Johnson preferred to call him 'Neely'. Ford, who was thirty-one, had been a fellow of Peterhouse College, Cambridge, but was now settled at Pedmore in Worcestershire. He had spent a good deal of time in London, was acquainted with the leading poet of the day, Alexander Pope, and struck Johnson as 'a man of great wit and stupendous parts'.[1] Although a parson, he was not averse to the tavern life; Hester Thrale rather censoriously describes him as 'a man who chose to be eminent only for vice'.[2] A more tolerant portrait is offered by William Hogarth, in his *Midnight Modern Conversation*: a clergyman, believed to be Ford, sits peaceably amid a crowd of drunks, his frothy wig a touch askew, surrounded by twenty-three empty wine bottles. Yet, even if Ford was usually a little more temperate than his friends, city living had proved costly. In order to be able to pay off his extensive debts he had recently married the daughter of a prosperous ironmaster. Now retired from the clamour of Hogarth's London, he was the first worldly man of letters Johnson encountered, and half a century later, in his life of the minor poet Elijah Fenton, Johnson would pay his cousin qualified tribute, reflecting that his abilities 'instead of furnishing convivial merriment to the voluptuous and dissolute, might have enabled him to excel among the virtuous and wise'.[3]

Ford was an example of a brilliant man who had squandered his talents: Johnson intended to rise above such profligacy. Yet the worldly parson afforded his young relative a sense of the real possibilities open to a man of learning. The time Johnson spent with his

William Hogarth, *Midnight Modern Conversation*, 1733. Parson Ford is in the centre, wig askew

well-connected cousin fomented an awareness of the scholarly opportunities offered by the great universities and the social ones afforded by the nation's vibrant capital. Ford pressed him to read more widely in his native tongue, and it was during his time at Pedmore that Johnson became familiar with the work of the poets Samuel Garth and Matthew Prior, the playwright William Congreve, and Addison's suave essays – all of which he would draw on extensively when he came to compile the *Dictionary*. He also experimented with translating substantial works from Greek and Latin, and with writing his own poetry.

Johnson's stay at Pedmore was both escape and education. It removed him from the cramped familiarity of Lichfield, and inspired fresh ambitions. When the time came for him to return to Breadmarket Street, the transition was not easy. Severe Mr Hunter refused to let him back in to the grammar school, and his father's debts continued to mount. The openness of Pedmore had been corrupting: Johnson was now much more keenly aware of the constrained atmosphere of his family home. Relations between his parents had never been easy, and material anxiety injured them further: his father regarded his mother as an illiterate, and chastised her for spending excessive sums on tea, while she made little secret of her contempt for his financial misadventures. 'A family', Johnson would later write, 'is a little kingdom, torn with factions and exposed to revolutions.'[4] He sounds like King Lear, but his family life was a chapter of mostly prosaic disappointments. One of his most humane modern biographers, John Wain, himself a native of Staffordshire, vividly imagines this:

> Today, when we make our decorous pilgrimages to the house . . . , climbing up the polished wooden stairs and peering into the small but beautifully proportioned rooms, it seems commodious enough. But when it had to house a book business with miles of shelves, the four Johnsons and their two or three servants, and all the clutter with which human beings surround themselves, there must have been times when it was bursting at the seams. All three of the Johnson males were large; when they squeezed past each other on the stairs, or in the narrow spaces between crowded bookshelves, they must have seemed like mastiffs in a terrier's kennel.[5]

Johnson retreated from this confinement whenever he could. Sometimes he visited the home in nearby Sadler Street of his friend Edmund Hector, whose sixteen-year-old sister was the object of his first adolescent crush. Sometimes he went to the Cathedral Close to discuss politics with Gilbert Walmesley, a favoured customer at his father's shop and a well-known local figure. Walmesley held a sinecure as the 'inspector' of a lottery; the security of this undemanding job allowed him to be the patron of talented local youths, and the bookseller's ungainly son was his favourite. When not with Walmesley or Hector, Johnson would visit Theophilus Levett, the controversial Jacobite who had succeeded Johnson's godfather Richard Wakefield as coroner and town clerk, or a local apothecary, John Marten. Their homes were congenial to intelligent debate in a way that his own was not. Yet most often he retreated into books. Influenced by his cousin Ford and by his Lichfield mentors, he metamorphosed from an undiscriminating bookworm into a mature, discerning reader, still wide-ranging in his tastes, but with more refined powers of judgement and a keener sense of literature's possibilities.

Commoner

1. One of the common people; a man of low rank; of mean condition

5. A student of the second rank at the university of Oxford; one that eats at the common table

Not long after his stay with Cornelius Ford, Johnson was unexpectedly able to continue his education, at Oxford. This was made possible by a legacy to Sarah; her cousin Elizabeth Harriotts died in February 1728, leaving her not only a pair of 'flaxen' sheets and pillow cases, but also the substantial sum of £40. At the same time, one of Johnson's friends from Lichfield Grammar School, Andrew Corbet, who had come into a considerable amount of money following the death of his mother, promised to subsidize Johnson's expenses in order to have with him a 'companion in . . . studies'. Corbet's promise would later dissolve, but in October 1728 Johnson followed him – on horseback – to Pembroke College, an institution to which he was tied through his godfather Samuel Swynfen and a cousin, Henry Jesson, who were both Pembroke alumni.

Johnson spent a little over thirteen months at Pembroke. It was a small institution, founded in the early seventeenth century, and consisted of a single quadrangle, with only forty or fifty students in permanent residence. It had no chapel, and social life revolved around the hall. Johnson played draughts in the summer common room, and the odd informal game of cricket in the commoners' garden.[1] He lived in rooms above the gatehouse, two flights up, which afforded a fine view of Christopher Wren's Tom Tower across the road at Christ Church. His proximity to the college gate meant that he was often to be found loitering there, a sort of dishevelled custodian; his servile manner suggested poverty, and on one occasion another student, William Vyse, made him the somewhat insulting gift of an old pair of shoes. His tutor was William Jorden, a lugubrious man who was viceregent of the college, but whose main business at this time was looking for an undemanding position in the Church. Johnson professed 'love and respect' for him, yet was sufficiently unimpressed with his methods to prefer sliding on the ice in the nearby meadows.

Although he eagerly followed a course of lectures in logic and ethics given by a Christ Church tutor, Edmund Bateman, Johnson's tuition was most often self-administered. He took to Oxford more than 100 volumes from his father's shop – at that time a large personal library for a student. Significantly, a third of these were not scholarly works, but literary ones, to be read for pleasure: Milton, Pope, Dryden, Prior, the poetic physician Sir Richard Blackmore, the Latin poets Ovid and Catullus, and an edition of Addison in four volumes. He continued his habit of seizing on whatever came his way: when he found Jonathan Richardson's *Theory of Painting* lying on the stairs he carried it back to his room and wolfed it down. It was during this period, too, that he encountered William Law's recently published *A Serious Call to a Devout and Holy Life*, a book that was to have a profound influence on him – and that would later play a significant role in his reinforcement of moral principles in the fourth edition of the *Dictionary*. Moreover, as would increasingly become his wont, he devised for himself an exhaustingly ambitious plan of study, announcing that 'I bid farewell to Sloth, being resolved henceforth not to listen to her siren strains.'[2] Despite occasional professions to the contrary, he now believed that learning should be schematized, and that one of the duties of the scholar was to organize his knowledge – to produce a map of his reading, both projected and achieved. Yet, as one biographer has justly observed, 'his college period was one of absorption, not production'.[3] He was not ready to convert the rich materials he was assembling into a work that would be worthy of his name.

Johnson's time at Oxford is characterized by Boswell as a period of 'dejection, gloom, and despair'. Boswell implies that poverty prevented Johnson from entering fully into college life. At first this seems unlikely, as the annual cost of his studies, excluding incidental expenses, would have been little more than £20, an amount that Sarah's inheritance ought to have covered for more than a single year. Yet Boswell's version of events is based on Johnson's, and it is true that Johnson finally settled his college account only in 1740. Perhaps, in spite of the frugal habits learned at home, he found it hard to economize when he was away, or, more likely, he resented the privations (in particular, the social privations) that were the reward of financial prudence; for, then as now, university education is a social experience as much as an intellectual one, and the inability to play a full part in the social lives of his peers will have discomfited Johnson far more than any uneasiness about academic standards, resources or curriculum. Certainly he was confident in retrospect that his time at Oxford was unhappy. When he learned that William Adams, one of his Pembroke contemporaries, recalled his having been a 'gay and frolicksome fellow', he was at pains to correct the impression: 'I was rude and violent. It was bitterness which they mistook for frolic.'

All the same, Johnson retained an attachment to his old university, and to his old college. In the *Dictionary* he notes the Oxford phenomenon of 'battels' (retrospective payment for meals and lodging, rather than payment in advance – a system summed up by Johnson as 'to feed on trust'). He also notes, with further shades of autobiography, the Oxford term 'commoner' ('a student of the second rank' – in other words one, like him, without the benefit of a scholarship). There seems to be no reticence here about undergraduate life, and the *Dictionary*, though its entries occasionally mock the pomposity of university students and the introspection of academia, betrays at least a hint of nostalgia for collegiate existence. Moreover, it seems likely that Johnson would have returned to Oxford in 1730, and that he might have been awarded one of Pembroke's Ossulston scholarships, had it not been for two particular concerns: his unwillingness to take the statutory oath of allegiance to the monarch, and his father's declining health. Here we have a clue to Johnson's real unhappiness: circumstances beyond his control curtailed his education, and he was again forced to return to the pinched and narrow world of Breadmarket Street.

Darkling

Being in the dark; being without light: a word merely poetical

Johnson withdrew from student life because his father, Michael, was dying, but the first death to convulse his world was unexpected: though not yet forty, Cornelius Ford passed away in August 1731 – as a result, it seems, of overexerting himself in a Covent Garden brothel. Less surprisingly, Michael followed in December, after a long period of illness. We know little of Johnson's reaction. However, shortly before his father's death an incident occurred which he later confessed had 'ever since lain heavy on my mind'. His father, still anxious about his business, asked Johnson to go to Uttoxeter to look after a book stall he usually set up there on market days. Johnson refused. He could be forgiven for not wishing to ride fifteen miles to tend the stall, which had never been a success. But although at the time he disdained the idea, he later repented the decision. 'Pride was the source of that refusal,' he admitted, 'and the remembrance of it was painful.' In consequence, fifty years later, when he was not far from death himself, he did penance, taking a post-chaise to Uttoxeter and 'going into the market at the time of high business, uncovered my head, and stood with it bare an hour before the stall which my father had formerly used, exposed to the sneers of standers-by and the inclemency of the weather'.[1]

This episode suggests that Johnson felt guilty about neglecting his father's affairs, but in fact he took close care of them, and his immersion in family matters meant that he did not venture far from Lichfield for several years. Having inherited only £20 from his father, he tried hard to revive the ailing family business. But his efforts came to nothing, and in an attempt to secure a source of regular income he looked for a job as a schoolmaster. He worked for four months as an usher in a school at Market Bosworth in Leicestershire. The school's patron was Sir Wolstan Dixie, an irascible man who liked to settle arguments with his fists, and Johnson was expected to serve as his chaplain. Boswell relates that Dixie was a disagreeable taskmaster, a man of 'intolerable harshness', who made Johnson's life one of 'complicated misery'. We may infer the true harshness of Dixie's character from his reaction, in later life, to the discovery that his daughter Ann was enjoying secret assignations with a young man in Bosworth Park. Instead of speaking to his daughter or her suitor, Dixie set mantraps throughout the surrounding area. One of these traps was activated soon afterwards – by Ann, who died of her wounds.

The experience of working for Dixie, unpleasant though it was, did not deter Johnson from applying for several other teaching jobs. Each time, he was rejected. In a typical episode, he was passed over for a job at Solihull because it was feared his 'way of distorting his face . . . may affect some young lads'. His alarming appearance disqualified him from any work for which he might have to project an image of gentlemanly respectability. Yet he still aspired to teach, and had therefore to be familiar with the standard textbooks of the day, many of them the same rather dated works from which his own fearsome masters had once declaimed. It was evident that new resources were needed; Johnson's brief career as a schoolmaster would translate into a lifelong commitment to ennobling the art of education.

While scouting around for further employment, Johnson had several pet projects in hand. One was a translation of an account of Abyssinia by the Portuguese missionary Jeronimo Lobo. Johnson spent a good deal of time at the Birmingham lodgings of his old schoolfriend Edmund Hector, which were in the house of a bookseller, Thomas Warren. He contributed to a local newspaper that Warren had set up, and it was Warren, probably spurred on by Hector, who persuaded Johnson to press ahead with his version of Lobo's *Itinerario*. It was actually a translation of a translation: Lobo's original had been rendered into French in 1728, and it was from the French that Johnson worked – often giving dictation while lying in bed. Still, this was Johnson's first published book. The material may now seem desiccated, but he planned it with a view to commercial advantage, not academic praise. It earned him the less than magnificent sum of five guineas, and was not enthusiastically received. Yet it can be seen as a template for his later work. His greatest skill, exhibited even at this early stage in his career, was not for original composition. Rather, it was for capitalizing on other people's work – for editing and abridging, for improving and explaining, for paraphrase and critique.

The translation of Lobo's *Voyage to Abyssinia* was published in February 1735. The year was a momentous one, for it saw Johnson's personal life change dramatically, with his marriage to Elizabeth Porter. Elizabeth, known as 'Tetty', was a woman of limited accomplishments, a fading blonde forty-six years old to his twenty-five. He initially got to know her through her husband, Harry, a Birmingham woollen-draper, who belonged to the social circle of the ever-encouraging Hector. When Harry Porter died, in September 1734, at the early age of forty-three, Johnson appears to have swooped upon his widow. She was impressed by his attentions, and 'saw Othello's visage in his mind'.[2] They were married at Derby the following July, in St Werburgh's church.★

Derby was not the most obvious place for the marriage. It is possible that Johnson had an ancestral connection with St Werburgh's – a Richard Johnson had been the local vicar in the early years of the previous century. More likely, however, it was the couple's desire to escape the opprobrium of Tetty's family and friends that drove them so far from Birmingham. Opponents of the match suspected Johnson was after the Porters' money. Tetty's brother-in-law, Joseph Porter, had promised to settle a handsome annuity on her if she would break off the engagement. It is possible, too, that Tetty's eldest child, nineteen-year-old Lucy, was the original object of Johnson's affections, and that she doubted the depth of his interest in her middle-aged mother.

Certainly it was a strange conjunction. Johnson was a scruffy, poor and awkward young man, a bibliophile and a scholar; Tetty was un-educated, flighty and encumbered with three children (in addition to Lucy there were two boys, Jervis Henry and Joseph, aged sixteen

---

★ It is of passing interest that Harry Porter's sister had in 1726 become the second wife of Johnson's 'wrong-headedly severe' schoolmaster John Hunter.

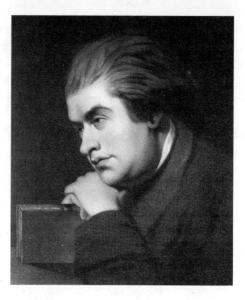

Johnson in his thirties, from a mezzotint by George Zobel

Elizabeth Johnson (Tetty) by an unknown artist. This rather improbable likeness hints at how little we really know about Johnson's wife

and ten).* Those who knew them as a couple have left behind no more than a thimbleful of details about their marriage: Johnson is supposed to have had great respect for his wife's judgement, and she to have had an interestingly quick sensibility, but biographers have tended, in the absence of hard facts, either to sentimentalize the relationship or to present it as the result of a youthful aberration on Johnson's part – a hollow alliance whose rituals he learned to discharge by rote. Johnson consistently maintained that 'it was a love marriage upon both sides'. We have no concrete reason to doubt him, but Tetty's friends and family, with the exception of the mollified Lucy, remained sceptical.

Nevertheless, the marriage took place, and married life encouraged Johnson to new designs. He felt morally compelled to provide for his wife and stepchildren, but the £600 that Tetty brought to the marriage helped to fund schemes he could not otherwise have achieved. Not long after they wed, the couple rented a house at Edial (pronounced 'Edjal'), a tiny village three miles west of Lichfield.† Urged on by Gilbert Walmesley, Johnson established a school there using Tetty's money. His academic credentials, though sufficient to convince Walmesley of his potential as a teacher, seem to have convinced few others, and he had considerable trouble attracting pupils. Legend has it that there were only three: David Garrick, Garrick's brother George, and another boy, Lawrence Offley. In fact as many as eight boys may have enrolled, but twice that number would have been needed to make the school a going concern. Moreover, Garrick's account of his time at Edial suggests that Johnson had difficulty commanding the respect of his students, who were troubled – true to the earlier predictions of the governors at Solihull – by his 'oddities of manner and uncouth gesticulations', yet also saw fit to mock his inept attempts at lovemaking, which they were able to observe through his bedroom keyhole.

---

* Following the marriage, Lucy lived with her mother and stepfather until they left Lichfield; Jervis refused to have anything to do with his stepfather and elected to pursue a career at sea; and Joseph was cared for by his father's relatives, though he later came to terms with his mother's second marriage.

† Just how small Edial was may be inferred from the fact that in 1666 only sixteen local residents were deemed liable to pay hearth tax, while the population even in the middle of the nineteenth century was scarcely 200.

The school at Edial folded after a single year, and in the early part of 1737 Johnson decided to move to London. He would leave Tetty behind, in her daughter's care; it was understood that she would join him once he had found himself something resembling steady work. He had recently completed a tragedy, *Irene*, which he wished to present on the London stage. More immediately, he thought he could earn money by churning out topical articles. It may seem strange to think that a young man seeking to earn a living should have expected to do so as an author – one would have to be exquisitely naive to entertain such a plan today – but Johnson stood to benefit from the increasing rampancy of print culture.

It was only in the first part of the eighteenth century that it became possible for an author who wrote for readers to earn a living by his pen. I say 'who wrote for readers' because playwrights (Shakespeare, for instance) and the beneficiaries of patronage (such as Ben Jonson) had long been able to make a living from their creative efforts. It was in the 1720s with Defoe – himself in the later stages of a career which had hitherto been buoyed by the bounty of patrons – that writers first started to make money solely by finding an audience of paying readers, and it was then that the literary marketplace came into being, as indeed did the most commercially appealing form of literature, the novel.

During this period the book trade was revolutionized. Censorship diminished, and copyright came into being. Moreover, the early years of the eighteenth century gave rise to a galaxy of new phenomena that included the printed handbill, printed receipts, printed tickets, printed advertisements, and posters. At the same time there was a surge in the production of political pamphlets, broadsides, books for children, and even street maps. Alexander Pope satirized the rage for print in his poem *The Dunciad* (1728–43); he mockingly suggested that its democratizing power had brought 'the Smithfield Muses to the Ear of Kings'. Johnson echoed Pope's sentiments, complaining that 'so widely is spread the itch of literary praise, that almost every man is an author, either in act or in purpose'.[3] In a calmer moment, he reflected that 'It is strange that there should be so little reading in the world, and so much writing.'

In the *Dictionary* Johnson would mock the prevailing culture and its ephemeral productions in his definition of 'grubstreet': 'Originally the name of a street in Moorfields in London, much inhabited by writers of small histories, dictionaries, and temporary poems; whence any mean production is called *grubstreet*.' In his entry under 'biographer' he would quote Joseph Addison: 'Our Grubstreet *biographers* watch for the death of a great man, like so many undertakers, on purpose to make a penny of him.' As these quotations suggest, the atmosphere was one of cynical opportunism. Addison's friend Sir Richard Steele, the father of modern journalism and author of the thrice-weekly *Tatler*, once invited the poet Richard Savage to join him for lunch, and then dictated a pamphlet because he needed ready money to pay for the meal. This kind of throwaway effort was symptomatic of what Johnson referred to as an 'epidemical conspiracy for the destruction of paper'.[4]

Grub Street lay in the poor parish of St Giles's Cripplegate, close to the open sewers of Moorfields and the lunatic asylum at Bedlam, but it was not so much a geographical space as a state of mind. It is likely that Johnson never set foot in Grub Street proper, yet its metaphoric significance was as powerful for him as for any writer of his age. 'Grub Street' was shorthand for the pains and perils of authorship: poverty and sickness, dirt and disease, plagiarism and backbiting. In *The Dunciad* Pope depicts its inhabitants, swarming like locusts, sucking life from the ordure all around them, clamorous in self-applause, exhausted by 'purgings, pumpings, blankettings and blows'.

Lord Macaulay, ready as ever with a flush of gorgeous hyperbole, evokes the circumstances of the Grub Street authors:

> Sometimes blazing in gold-laced hats and waistcoats; sometimes lying in bed because their coats had gone to pieces, or wearing paper cravats because their linen was in pawn; sometimes drinking champagne and Tokay with Betty Careless; sometimes standing at the window of an eating-house in Porridge Island, to snuff up the scent of what they could not afford to taste; they knew luxury; they knew beggary; but they never knew comfort.

He goes on, 'They looked on a regular and frugal life with the same aversion which an old gypsy or a Mohawk hunter feels for a stationary abode . . . They were as untameable, as much wedded to their desolate freedom, as the wild ass. They could be no more broken in to the offices of social man than the unicorn could be trained to serve and abide by the crib.'[5]

Hideous though this sounds, it was to something like the sodality of Grub Street that Johnson aspired when he planned his move to the capital. If he was more scrupulous and intellectually rigorous than the usual gaggle of hacks, he sought all the same to benefit from the encouragement of the profit-hungry booksellers, from the appetites of a newly ravenous society of readers, and from associating with other authors. He would later write, in the *Rambler*, that 'Among the numerous requisites that must concur to complete an author, few are of more importance than an early entrance into the living world . . . Argumentation may be taught in colleges . . . but . . . the powers of attraction, can be gained only by a general converse.'[6]

The ambitions kindled by his mentors could be satisfied only in the capital. It is resonant, then, that the sole *Dictionary* illustration of 'fortune' in the sense 'the chance of life; means of living' is a short sentence from Swift: 'His father dying, he was driven to London to seek his *fortune*.' We should note, too, Johnson's quotation under 'improvement' from the preacher Robert South: 'I look upon your city as the best place of *improvement*: from the school we go to the university, but from the universities to London.' This is what he now, belatedly, chose to do.

To decamp

To shift the camp; to move off

Johnson set out from Lichfield on 2 March 1737, accompanied by his former pupil David Garrick. Johnson's intentions were clear; Garrick, ostensibly planning a career in the law, secretly hoped to conquer the London stage. Their resources were meagre, and, according to Johnson's not entirely serious account, by the time they arrived they had only fourpence between them – enough for a couple of pints of beer each. They initially lodged with a corset-maker, Richard Norris, who lived in Exeter Street, near the Strand, and they took their meals at the Pineapple in New Street.★ Johnson later told of how he 'dined . . . very well for 8d., with very good company', explaining that 'it used to cost the rest 1s., for they had wine; but I had a cut of meat for 6d., and bread for a penny, and gave the waiter a penny.' Dredging up memories of his early days in London, he entered in his diary a cryptic scrap which reads, 'Norris the staymaker – fair Esther – w. the cat – children – inspection of the hand – stays returned – lodging – guinea at the stairs – Esther died – ordered to want nothing – house broken up – advertisement – eldest son – quarrel.'[1] We can only guess what this might mean, but in these tiny shards there is an intriguing glimpse of the unknown Johnson, a new-fledged city-dweller.

The life of the tavern and the coffee house compensated for the inadequacies of many Londoners' accommodation, and Johnson was no exception. He would later recount to Boswell how an Irish painter had told him that a man was able to live in London on £30 a year 'without being contemptible': he could rent a garret for eighteen

---

★ The chief feature of Exeter Street at that time was the Exeter Change, which consisted of an assortment of small shops. In Johnson's later years, it would serve as home to an exotic and dangerous menagerie run by one Gilbert Pidcock.

pence a week, and could set up an unofficial office in a coffee house by spending as little as threepence a day. This, broadly, was Johnson's way of life during the next decade, although he found he needed more than an annual £30. His home was a place to lay his head, and most of his time was spent elsewhere. He did not remain for long with Mr Norris; in the course of his forty-seven years in London, he resided at as many as eighteen different addresses, and in the early years he moved especially often, usually for financial reasons.

Johnson's opinion of London seems to be enshrined in his well-known judgement that 'When a man is tired of London, he is tired of life.' But like many adoptive Londoners he found his sense of the capital's delights tempered by feelings of confusion and estrangement. These feelings are encapsulated in his poem *London*, published anonymously in 1738. *London* is a bold performance, sufficiently satirical that on the title page the name of the publisher, Robert Dodsley, is deliberately misspelled, in order to give the impression that it is a piracy. Its mordant presentation of contemporary politics was calculated to advertise Johnson's talents – a sort of poetic calling card – but it also testifies to his disquiet in this new environment. There are pointed references to a variety of London types – the 'fiery fop', the 'frolick drunkard, reeling from a feast', the 'female atheist [who] talks you dead', sycophants and lottery-farmers, prowling attorneys, the 'relentless ruffians' who set ambushes for the unwary, and the 'warbling eunuchs' who strut upon the London stage. The most famous couplet expresses the resentment of a poor, unheralded writer:

> This mournful truth is ev'rywhere confessed,
> SLOW RISES WORTH, BY POVERTY DEPRESSED.

The poem was sufficiently successful that a second edition was required within a week, and a fourth the following year. Johnson, however, had to make do with a payment of ten guineas. There were compliments and plaudits, but these could not put food on the table or pay for a clean shirt, and his straitened circumstances meant that his feelings about London were not as unequivocally positive as they would later become.

Even so, the metropolis excited him. London was a thrillingly busy commercial centre, undergoing extraordinary flux. Its allure drew every imaginable ethnic and social group, and the result was a cultural melting pot as well as a consumer paradise, inflamed by the capitalism of Empire. By mid-century its population had climbed to 700,000. Yet even then it was cluttered with the remnants of medieval life, and when Johnson arrived in the 1730s the city was quite primitive. For instance, there was just one bridge across the Thames.★ Only in 1761 was the process of pulling down the city's medieval gates begun. Traitors' heads were displayed at Temple Bar – as late as 1746 Horace Walpole records that 'spy-glasses' could be had for 'a half-penny a look'. Soldiers were ritually flogged in St James's Park (where in 1763 Casanova was shocked to see men urinating in the bushes, though pleased to see them running races in the nude). The city's green spaces, rather than being its 'lungs' as they are today, proved hospitable to sewage, robbers and cattle.

Furthermore, much of what we now consider central London was undeveloped farmland: Paddington was a village, Tottenham Court Road was bordered by unkempt fields where paupers sifted cinders, and Islington was known chiefly as a place where cows were kept – though Johnson would later go there to take its 'good air'. This was the London of Canaletto, who lived in the city throughout the years Johnson spent on the *Dictionary*, yet it was not uncommon for livestock to be found roaming the streets, and occasionally a hapless pedestrian would be gored by an ox. Pavements had not been introduced, and in an age where the chief means of transport was still the horse the roads were glutted with excrement. The city was in the process of expanding to the east and west, and many of the new buildings were conceived on a grand scale, but despite the Georgian rage for *grands projets* it was a place of narrow streets and dark corners, grey fogs and sunless days. The German physicist Georg Christoph Lichtenberg, who visited London in 1770 and again in 1774, reported having to write by candlelight at half-past ten in the morning. In the 1730s it was worse than Lichtenberg could have imagined.

Londoners were coarse, robust and opportunistic – a fact that

---

★ A second, Westminster Bridge, was begun in 1738. It cost £389,500, and was opened in November 1750. Blackfriars Bridge followed in 1769, at a cost of a further £153,000.

foreign visitors remarked in tones of awe and horror. Johnson was struck by this aspect of the city's character whenever he returned from spending time elsewhere; after one trip back to the Midlands, he reflected that the fascination of the capital lay in its 'diversity of good and evil'.[2] The largest city in Europe, its population was increasing at an alarming rate, with new arrivals drawn by the promise of better wages and greater opportunities. Proximity breeds familiarity, then competition, then contempt, and among the increasingly proximate Londoners of the eighteenth century the threat of violence was frequent. Five years after he published *Tom Jones* (1746), Henry Fielding conducted an *Enquiry into the Causes of the late Increase of Robbers*. He identified the 'irregularity of buildings' as one problem, but felt that at root it was a question of the innate criminal tendencies of the city's lower orders.[3] These, such as they were, cannot have been improved by the bestial public entertainments of the day. One of the most popular forms of amusement was watching executions. Others included cockfighting, bull-baiting and attending freakshows. Criminality was visible in many guises: housebreaking, common robbery, pickpocketing, confidence tricks, racketeering, embezzlement and kidnapping, as well as more arcane offences like filing coins, barratry (spreading false rumours) and vagabonding (begging under false pretences). Petty criminals, sentenced to stand in the pillory, were frequently pelted with stones, vegetables and dead animals by passers-by quite ignorant of their crimes. At hangings, the relatives of the condemned would lurk on the periphery, hoping to resuscitate them if the hangmen failed to complete their duties; but surgeons, permitted a quota of ten corpses a year for dissection, would attack them in order to prevent revival.

The vicious and despairing character of contemporary Londoners is suggested in the evocative names of now-disappeared streets and neighbourhoods: Cutthroat Lane, Labour in Vain Yard, Little Sodom, Melancholy Walk. It is suggested, too, in the wealth of contemporary slang for miscreants and their crimes: an 'angler', for instance, was a thief who sat on a roof and used a fishing rod to hook the possessions of pedestrians passing below; a 'plumper' was a professional perjurer, who would testify to the truth of a false story; 'stealing the beaver', a crime among milliners, consisted of substituting cheap fabric for the more expensive material ordered by customers; and a 'moon-curser' was a boy who, having been employed to lead the way down dark streets with a lamp, steered his employers straight into the hands of muggers (or 'footpads' as they were known).[4]

In a letter dating from 1743, the poet William Shenstone notes that pickpockets 'make no scruple to knock people down with bludgeons in Fleet Street and the Strand, and that at no later hour than eight o'clock at night'. Shenstone admitted he went to the theatre less often than he would have liked, for fear of being attacked. The piazza at Covent Garden was considered especially treacherous: robbers descended on their victims 'in large bodies, armed with couteaus'. Shenstone's concerns were widely shared. Johnson felt able to tramp the streets at night, knowing that his bulk would deter most assailants, but on one occasion he was set upon by four men in the street, and although he managed to overpower them all, he got into the habit of carrying a cudgel with him when he went out after dark.

From the outset, Johnson was keenly aware of the city's hazards. Even before he moved to London he had been a reader of the *Gentleman's Magazine*, a popular new monthly. There was no better guide to London life, nor any more accurate barometer of public feeling. The issues from 1737 contain complaints about the frequency of riots and the prevalence of suicides, a report of an armed raid at the Drury Lane playhouse, and a consideration of the different kinds of mob, alongside pieces proposing a cure for being bitten by a mad dog and warning of the perils of drinking tea. They remind us, too, that in the year of Johnson's arrival Dick Turpin was the talk of the town; he had achieved such notoriety that a bounty of £100 had been placed on his head. With no proper police force, the city was a Mecca for villains like Turpin. Law enforcement was minimal, and legalized violence existed in forms such as the press gang. Brothels were common, prostitutes ubiquitous. James Boswell would later delight in the range of options, from *poules de luxe* at fifty guineas a night to 'the civil nymph . . . [who] will resign her engaging person . . . for a pint of wine and a shilling'.[5] Perhaps unsurprisingly, he suffered at least nineteen bouts of venereal disease. Yet in this he was not unusual.

Much of London's criminality was fuelled by alcohol, or by a thirst for it. The city's precincts did not stretch even as far as Knightsbridge, but were home to 5,875 alehouses and 8,659 brandy shops.[6] Gin, often referred to as 'Madam Geneva' (and sometimes as 'Kill-Grief'),

William Hogarth, *Gin Lane*, 1751

was a national obsession. It had first arrived in England in the 1680s, along with William of Orange. Fifty years later, as many as one in ten London properties was a gin shop. According to official records, nearly 7 million gallons were consumed in 1730, and this figure

excludes the vast quantities of low-grade gin sold from wheelbar-
rows, which was often adulterated with turpentine.[7] The sale of
spirits was officially prohibited in 1736, but the measure was so
unsuccessful that prohibition was lifted seven years later, and a more
pragmatic approach resulted in the Gin Act of 1751, which increased
duties and restricted sales. As far as Johnson was concerned, the gin
shops were the greatest blemish on London's commercial landscape,
although for the poor, he admitted, gin and tobacco were among the
very few 'sweeteners' of existence.

No one better captured the city's toxic character than William
Hogarth. In mapping its moral geography, the artist, who had been
brought up in the shadow of St Bartholomew's Hospital, depicted a
gutter society polluted with vice and fuelled by cheap drink. Johnson
respected both his moral designs and his commercial savvy. Hogarth's
most celebrated etching, which appeared in 1751, is entitled *Gin
Lane*; no artistic fantasy, it is a piece of documentary evidence. Yet
every bit as expressive of the discontents of London life is his *The
Enraged Musician* of ten years before: its cacophonous cast includes a
screaming baby in the arms of a ballad-monger, a sow-gelder blowing
a horn, a screeching parrot and yelping dog, an itinerant oboist, and
a boy battering a drum. Even at its best, London was a raucous, jangling Babel.

While it was possible for a Londoner or a visitor to escape the
clutches of intoxicated robbers and avoid witnessing a cockfight, no
one could fail to notice the city's seediness, dirt and crime. Yet the
instability was no hindrance to creative endeavour: London was a
hive of literary activity. Forty years later Johnson would assert that
'when a man knows he is to be hanged in a fortnight, it concentrates
his mind wonderfully', and, by much the same token, the perennial
possibility of being savaged or gulled meant that Londoners threw
themselves into their labours with a concentrated energy. In Tobias
Smollett's novel *The Expedition of Humphry Clinker* (1771), his gouty
anti-hero Matthew Bramble complains that Londoners are 'impelled
by some disorder of the brain, that will not suffer them to be at rest',
and Johnson drew from his surroundings just such a mad determination to be busy. 'Those who are content to live in the country are
fit for the country,' he declared. As far as he was concerned, the city

had a 'wonderful immensity', and 'the full tide of human existence is at Charing Cross'.

Exhilarated by his new environment even as it distressed him, Johnson quickly set about finding an outlet for his literary ambitions. An encounter with a bookseller called Wilcox proved bruising: when Johnson was asked how he planned to make his living and replied 'by my literary labours', Wilcox surveyed his muscular frame and sug-

William Hogarth, *The Enraged Musician*, 1741

gested, 'Young man, you had better buy a porter's knot.'[8] But Johnson was not reduced to working as a porter; instead, he secured employment in the Clerkenwell offices of the *Gentleman's Magazine*.

Its editor was Edward Cave, another native of the west Midlands. The son of a cobbler from Rugby, he had moved as a young man to London and, after a spell working for a timber merchant, was apprenticed as a printer. In January 1731 he started the magazine, a long-cherished project. It was the first important publication of its kind in Britain, and proved successful: by the time Johnson joined, its circulation had risen to 10,000. It was in fact the first periodical to be styled a 'magazine', a detail Johnson would respectfully note in the *Dictionary*, explaining that the word, which had originally meant 'storehouse', had 'of late . . . signified a miscellaneous pamphlet, from a periodical miscellany . . . published under the name of . . . Edward Cave'.

Johnson's employer appears to have had little ability as a writer, but he was a skilled director of others' efforts, continually dreaming up new features, and quick to identify pieceworkers who were capable of penning them. Johnson's fluency of composition meant that he was well suited to the mechanical work the magazine required. Initially, his role was sub-editorial; one of his jobs was editing the accounts of parliamentary debates written by Cave's reporter, the Scotsman William Guthrie. Within a couple of years Guthrie had graduated to other work, and Johnson assumed sole responsibility for writing up the debates. His reports were a tissue of fact and fiction. Boswell records Johnson's telling him that 'sometimes . . . he had nothing more communicated to him than the names of the several speakers, and the part which they had taken in the debate'.★

The semi-fictional accounts of debates in parliament that Johnson wrote for Cave were an education in working to order. They taught him how to draw disparate materials together into an organic whole; how to work at speed (he would sometimes turn out as many as 10,000 words in a day); how to construct and balance arguments; how to reconcile or juxtapose dissonant points of view; and, above all, how to make the most of an unpromising task. His work on the *Gentleman's Magazine*, and on the debates especially, accustomed him to the vicissitudes and duties of a life of writing, an existence that combined studious drudgery with occasional opportunities for creative flair.

★ Johnson was left to supply the speeches himself, and this he did with no little aplomb. In the process he glamorized the rhetoric of even the most uncharismatic of parliamentarians. Years later the actor Samuel Foote praised in his hearing a speech by Pitt, claiming its superiority to any of the orations of Demosthenes. Lest Foote get too carried away in his eulogy, Johnson felt it necessary to interrupt: 'That speech I wrote in a garret in Exeter Street.'

Johnson's contributions were richly various. He was capable of turning his hand to a remarkably wide range of tasks. In order to drum up interest in his planned translation of Paolo Sarpi's *History of the Council of Trent* (later abandoned after he had established that another man named Johnson had long been busy with the same project), he put together a short biography of Sarpi. Pleased with this experiment, he wrote several more brief lives, including one of Sir Francis Drake. He helped Dr Robert James, another Lichfield acquaintance, who would later achieve fame for his wildly successful and rather dangerous Fever Powder, with his plans for a *Medicinal Dictionary*, and provided him with a dozen biographies of physicians. At the same time he was publishing political pamphlets, critical essays (notably a sixty-four-page study of *Macbeth*) and poetry.

London furnished Johnson with plenty to write about, and with fresh collaborators. However, he had yet to fix on a single project that could draw together his skills and synthesize the many strands of knowledge he had accumulated. This was what he wanted – a substantial enterprise which would put him on a par with the Renaissance scholars he admired. He would wait ten years for such a project to be conceived.

To dissipate

2. To scatter the attention

'This slavery to his passions produced a life irregular and *dissipated*' – Johnson's *Life of Savage* (1744)

Of all Johnson's writings from the 1740s, the most immediately attractive is the biography he wrote of his friend the volatile poet Richard Savage. Johnson probably met Savage through Cave, and by the end of 1738 the two men were inseparable. Savage was Johnson's principal guide through the underworld of literary London. His personality was alternately magnetic and repulsive. An able but immodest writer, he occasionally contributed to the *Gentleman's Magazine*, and knew the dark side of city living as well as any author of the age. He was a gifted mimic and perennial seducer, a compulsive role-player, and a depressive. Infamously, he claimed to be the bastard child of the Countess of Macclesfield, aspired to the position of Poet Laureate, and set up as a 'Volunteer Laureate' when he was denied it. Worse, he had killed an unemployed man called James Sinclair in a coffee-house brawl, and had been spared the gallows only after appealing for a royal pardon. Johnson describes him as 'compassionate by nature and principle', yet notes that when provoked 'he would prosecute his revenge with the utmost acrimony', and that 'very small offences were sufficient to provoke him'. 'Violence' and 'unclouded gaiety' were the two moods between which he veered:[1] he sounds, all in all, a dangerous yet charming fantasist, and a thoroughly unsuitable companion for a young writer.

Johnson's *The Life of Mr Richard Savage* contains a good deal of autobiographical material, suggestive of the circumstances he knew during his early years in London. Among the *Life*'s most memorable passages is Johnson's description – one serpentine sentence – of his friend's nocturnal wanderings:

He lodged as much by accident as he dined, and passed the night sometimes in mean houses, which are set open at night to any casual wanderers, sometimes in cellars, among the riot and filth of the meanest and most profligate of the rabble; and sometimes, when he had not money to support even the expenses of these receptacles, walked about the streets till he was weary, and lay down in the summer upon a bulk, or in winter, with his associates in poverty, among the ashes of a glass-house.[2]

Was Johnson one of these 'associates in poverty'? He does not say so, and he was not exactly a pauper at this time, but, as Richard Holmes suggests in his sharply imagined study *Dr Johnson and Mr Savage*, 'he is rhetorically present'; the immediacy of the writing argues familiarity with the situation.[3] Boswell was certainly of this opinion, and claimed that Savage, 'habituated to the dissipation and licentiousness of the town', steered Johnson into dreadful 'indulgencies' – for which we are, I think, to read 'sexual indiscretions'.

Certainly Johnson's association with Savage damaged his relationship with Tetty, who had recently moved down from Lichfield. It seems to have caused a temporary separation, during which she lived at an address in Castle Street, near the Tower of London. The rift did not last, but Savage led Johnson astray. 'He never contributed deliberately to spread corruption amongst mankind,' Johnson protested unconvincingly, before conceding that it was 'impossible to pay him any distinction without the entire subversion of all oeconomy, a kind of establishment which, wherever he went, he always appeared ambitious to overthrow'.[4] It requires little imagination to see how aggrieved Mrs Johnson must have been by her husband's dalliance with a man so contemptuous of domestic harmony.

The unlikely friendship shocked most who knew Johnson, yet it ended abruptly in July 1739, when Savage left London to pursue a life of supposedly innocent pleasures in Wales; and it was put beyond repair when he died in a Bristol jail four years later, having been imprisoned over an £8 debt. The friendship is of greatest interest now for the light it sheds on Johnson's wilderness years, the period between his arrival in London and his signing up to write the *Dictionary*. We see a vulnerable, suggestible young man, restless and confused, eager to socialize with other writers and be accepted as a writer himself. In Savage's mercurial life Johnson saw an allegory of all human existence. Its vicissitudes 'tested men's dreams and hounded down their weaknesses'.[5]

Savage's story was a caution to Johnson. By the time he came to write the *Dictionary*, it might easily have been forgotten, but Savage's meagre poetic legacy is commemorated among the illustrative quotations. One of the eight words under which he appears is 'lone', in the sense 'having no company'; the line quoted is 'Here the *lone* hour a blank of life displays.' Two others under which his work can be found – significant given his tendency to flitter between extravagance and self-loathing – are the words 'to squander' and 'suicide'. Johnson defines 'suicide' as 'self-murder; the horrid crime of destroying one's self'. Although Savage did not kill himself, he might as well have done; his erratic behaviour alienated everyone he knew. The first quotation Johnson provides is a miniature fragment from Savage's poem *The Wanderer*: 'Child of despair, and *suicide* my name'. The other, more arresting, comes from Samuel Richardson's novel *Clarissa*: 'To be cut off by the sword of injured friendship is the most dreadful of all deaths, next to *suicide*.'

Savage's departure from London did not immediately cause Johnson to return to a more regimented course of life. With financial worries mounting – Tetty had been forced to sell a silver cup his mother had bought for him as an infant – he spent the winter of 1739 back in the Midlands, looking into various opportunities in schoolmastering. He failed to secure a job as the headmaster of a school at Appleby in Leicestershire, and diverted himself by visiting Lichfield friends such as Gilbert Walmesley. During his stay he spent quite some time in the company of Walmesley's sister-in-law, Molly Aston, an accomplished poet and wit – a woman very different, in other words, from Tetty. Johnson's thoughts of his marital difficulties and limited achievements as a writer were eclipsed for a time by the pleasures of good company. Yet he knew that these were diversions, and his stay in the Midlands, enjoyable though it was, reminded him of precisely what he had hoped to achieve by moving to London, and of the urgent need – for reasons both financial and psychological – to fulfil those hopes. When he returned to the capital and to the *Gentleman's Magazine*, his productivity increased.

Of the projects that occupied him during the next few years, the most important was also the least pleasurable. He was employed by Thomas Osborne, a prominent but peculiarly ignorant bookseller based in Holborn. Osborne had paid £13,000 for the huge library of Robert and Edward Harley, the first and second earls of Oxford. The library comprised almost 50,000 books, at least a quarter of a million pamphlets, and more than 7,000 volumes of manuscripts. Osborne engaged Johnson and William Oldys, formerly Edward Harley's personal librarian, to catalogue the collection. Osborne seems to have been another difficult employer, and he and Johnson had occasion to quarrel, perhaps on account of Johnson's unnecessarily minute (and time-consuming) care in bibliographical matters, but probably because Johnson spent more time reading the books than cataloguing them. Boswell writes that 'It has been confidently related . . . that Johnson one day knocked Osborne down in his shop, with a folio, and put his foot upon his neck.' Johnson countered this popular story with the explanation that 'he was impertinent to me, and I beat him. But it was not in his shop: it was in my own chamber.' Their differences notwithstanding, Johnson's work for Osborne was profitable: it not only acquainted him with a vast number of rare and valuable books, but also gave him cause to think carefully about the means and methods of organizing and classifying knowledge, of categorizing books and itemizing their contents.

Over the next few years Johnson slowly built his reputation, mainly by word of mouth, and by the mid-1740s he was earning more than £100 a year – a modest though not derisory amount. However, a large part of this income was paid to the doctors who ministered to his increasingly sickly wife. The couple's rapprochement was costly: the doctors' visits came to as much as a guinea a time, and Tetty's deteriorating condition meant that at least a quarter of Johnson's income was channelled in this direction. The physician Robert Levet, who met Johnson in 1746, would later tell Hester Thrale that Tetty was 'always drunk and reading romances in her bed, where she killed herself by taking opium'.[6] Garrick no more charitably described her 'swelled cheeks of a florid red, produced by thick painting, and increased by liberal use of cordials'. He also poked fun at her 'flaring and fantastic' attire.

44

Whatever the truth of these portraits, Johnson was anxious for Tetty's health and was bound to provide for her. He needed to augment his income. He needed, above all, regular and substantial work. Thanks to the growing reputation of the *Gentleman's Magazine*, and to an increasing awareness among the more astute London book-sellers of Johnson's part in it, this was not an unlikely prospect, and early in 1746 he was approached by Robert Dodsley, the publisher of *London*. Dodsley's proposal was a simple but daunting one: that Johnson compile a modern, authoritative English dictionary.

English

Belonging to England; thence English is the language of
England

The eighteenth century was seized by a rage for order, manifest in a
range of new phenomena: the price tag, standardized weights and
measures, the proliferation of signposts on public highways, the
increased use of account books and calendars. Crafts metamorphosed into technologies. Collectorship thrived as never before. The
vogue was for organizing, structuring and methodizing. Works of
reference became both fashionable and necessary – classic examples
include David Hume's six-volume *History of England* (1754–62) and
the first *Encyclopaedia Britannica* (1768–71). There are linguistic clues
to this new culture: the expression 'to look something up' first
entered the language in 1692, when it was employed by the antiquarian Anthony Wood.

One key aspect of the movement was an obsession with seeking
out origins – of philosophies, beliefs and political systems; of
scientific principles and natural phenomena; and of language, in all
its ramifications. The new historians of ideas, like the innovators and
adventurers, were continually required to come up with names for
the things they invented or discovered. Scientists and *philosophes*
needed specialized and specific vocabulary with which to articulate
their fresh visions of the world. Writers of all kinds were becoming
more analytical and technical. The growth of Empire insinuated
officialdom into the language, and required Britishness, in its many
guises, to be codified, in order to be exportable. Imperialism is in part
a feat of rhetoric: to eighteenth-century imperialists, literal and
otherwise, it was clear that a standardized English would be a price-
less administrative tool, as well as a triumphant realization of that still
very new idea, Britishness.

To the burgeoning society of eighteenth-century Britain, the lack of a major dictionary was a source of embarrassment. After all, other, supposedly lesser, European powers had dictionaries. The French had founded the Académie française in 1635, and the Florentines the Accademia della Crusca as early as 1582: both were set up expressly to create dictionaries. Their work was slow. One member of the Académie française, Antoine Furetière, complained, 'When a committee is made up of five or six people, one of them is reading, another is delivering his opinion, two are gossiping together, one is asleep, and one is diverting himself by leafing through one of the Dictionaries on the table.'[1] Furetière was thrown out of the Académie for attempting the obvious short cut of writing a dictionary on his own. Those who remained took fifty-five years to produce their *Dictionnaire*; the Florentine Accademia took thirty over its *Vocabolario*.

Nevertheless, the job got done, and there were plenty of English savants who sensed the urgent need for a comparable work. In 1664 the recently established Royal Society formed a committee for improving the language. Twenty-two men strong, it made no substantial progress, and soon disbanded. But the quest continued. One of the committee's members, the Poet Laureate John Dryden, complained bitterly about the practice of 'corrupt[ing] our English Idiom by mixing it too much with French'. Daniel Defoe joined the fray in his *Essay upon Projects* (1697), lamenting the proliferation of lewd terms, which he considered the 'Vomit of the Brain', and proposing an academy akin to those on the Continent. A few years later Jonathan Swift broke the habit of a lifetime and sided with Defoe. His *Proposal for Correcting, Improving and Ascertaining the English Tongue* (1712) excoriated fashionable slang and sloppy usage – much of it perpetrated by 'illiterate Court Fops, half-witted Poets, and University Boys'.[2] Like Dryden and Defoe, he argued that 'Some method should be thought on for *ascertaining* and *fixing* our Language for ever.' The 'method' they all had in mind was an authoritative dictionary. One of those who made a start on such a work was Joseph Addison, seduced by the possibility of being paid as much as £3,000, but his duties as Under-Secretary of State hampered his progress, and so did ill health. When he gave up, his inchoate materials appear to have passed into the hands of his friend Ambrose Philips, who in 1720 published his own *Proposals for Printing an English Dictionary in Two Volumes in Folio*. But thirty years after Swift's *Proposal* a British Academy still seemed a remote prospect, and so did the dictionary such an institution might have produced. In the very year that Johnson began his task, the robust Anglican bishop William Warburton was still mournfully reflecting, in the preface to his new edition of Shakespeare, that 'We have neither Grammar nor Dictionary, neither Chart nor Compass, to guide us through this wide sea of words.'

We should be clear that there *were* English dictionaries before Johnson. In fact over the previous 150 years there had been more than twenty. The first dictionaries for English-speakers appeared in the sixteenth century. Sir Thomas Elyot's Latin–English dictionary appeared in 1538, and in 1598 John Florio published a huge Italian–English dictionary, which included quotations for the purpose of illustration. By the time Florio's *Worlde of Wordes* came out, the desirability of a simple English dictionary had been bruited by Richard Mulcaster, the esteemed and outspoken headmaster of the Merchant Taylors' School. In 1582 Mulcaster drew up what he termed a 'generall table' of 8,000 words 'we commonlie use', and reflected that 'It were a thing verie praiseworthy . . . if som one well learned . . . would gather all the words which we use in our English tung . . . into one dictionarie, and . . . wold open unto us therein, both their naturall force, and their proper use.'[3] He was the harbinger of a new kind of linguistic philosophy that gained currency in the seventeenth century. Its central principle was that a language could be devised – or even recovered – which would embody the very order of existence.

Mulcaster's encouragements to would-be lexicographers bore fruit in 1604, with the publication of Robert Cawdrey's *A Table Alphabeticall*. Cawdrey, who like Mulcaster was a schoolmaster, created a small lexicon 'for the benefit & helpe of Ladies, Gentlewomen, or any other unskillfull persons'. It contained no words beginning with *W*, *X* or *Y*, and was restricted to a mere 2,449 definitions, but it was a start – the first monolingual English dictionary. As the century continued, more works of its kind appeared. These were for the most part glossaries of 'hard words', intended as tools to help readers grasp the meaning of technical, obscure, foreign or even obsolete terms that they were likely to come across in books or in modish company. The names of their authors – John Bullokar, Elisha Coles, Thomas Blount and Henry Cockeram (who was the first of them to call his work a 'dictionary') – are now largely forgotten. The dictionaries themselves were either scrappy or overspecialized. None was satisfactory. The early English lexicographers failed to give a sufficient sense of language as it appeared *in use*. All proceeded by plagiarizing the work of their predecessors; they had little time for rigorous methodology.

The fantastic exception was John Wilkins's *Essay towards a Real Character and Philosophical Language* (1668). Wilkins, who was bishop of Chester, suggested a new orthography, akin to shorthand, as well as a more logical system of word formation. Thus for instance *de* was his word for 'element'; *deb* was the first of the elements, fire; *deba* was a type of fire, a flame; while *det* signified an 'appearing meteor', and *deta* a specific type of this, namely a rainbow. As Steven Pinker has pointed out, Wilkins's words 'are packed tight with information' and 'the slightest slip of the tongue or pen guarantees misunderstanding'.[4] The system's artificialities were hard to learn – even Wilkins could get confused, muddling up his own terms for 'tulip' and 'barley' – and the 'philosophical language' did not catch on. But he was the more thorough kind of innovator, pursuing his ends from a variety of angles, and among the *Essay*'s incidental features was an 'Alphabetical Dictionary', co-authored with another bishop, William Lloyd. A pivotal principle here was that all words used for the purposes of definition had themselves to be defined. Furthermore, this was a descriptive lexicon, which sought to record the true breadth of English. The 'Alphabetical Dictionary' received scant attention, but Wilkins, a sort of one-man philological avant-garde (who also developed a transparent bee hive that allowed honey to be removed without inconveniencing the bees), exerted a lasting influence. This can be seen, for instance, in the widely adopted Stenographic Soundhand conceived in the nineteenth century by Sir Isaac Pitman. We know that Johnson admired Wilkins's work, and in the *Dictionary* Wilkins is quoted frequently.

Most of Wilkins's contemporaries lacked his reformative vision, and were preoccupied with explaining hard words, but in the early part of the eighteenth century the hard-word glossaries went out of fashion, and the scope of dictionaries expanded.* The best work of this period was the *Universal Etymological Dictionary* compiled by Nathan Bailey, a schoolmaster from Stepney. First published in 1721, Bailey's dictionary went through thirty editions over the next eighty-one years. It was more useful and wide-ranging than its predecessors, but its definitions were often poor: 'cat' was 'a creature well known', 'to get' was defined simply as 'to obtain', 'cool' meant 'cooling or cold', 'black' was 'a colour', 'strawberry' 'a well known fruit', and 'to wash' meant 'to cleanse by washing' (although 'washing' was not defined). It was also full of bizarre digressions, red herrings and cack-handed attempts to explain popular sayings. For instance, Bailey explains the maxim 'A cat may look upon a king': 'This is a saucy proverb, generally made use of by pragmatical persons, who must needs be censuring their superiors, and take it by the worst handle, and carry it beyond its bounds: for the peasants may look at and honour great men, patriots, and potentates, yet they are not to spit in their faces.' We're none the wiser about cats for reading this, and not much wiser about their relationship to kings. The *Universal Etymological Dictionary* had more uses than limitations, but its limitations were unmistakable.

The need for a new English dictionary was therefore a matter both of national prestige and philological necessity. As Johnson would later put it, 'languages are the pedigree of nations', and at this time Britain's pedigree needed to be advertised. Educationalists since Mulcaster had been arguing that spelling should be standardized. The developing print culture demanded clearer standards of correctness. Furthermore, a new and authoritative dictionary would help readers accurately interpret both the statutes and the Scriptures.

Piecing together a dictionary that could fulfil these roles was the sort of task that appealed to Johnson's pedagogic instincts, as well as to his pride and ambition. He was keen to channel his energies into

---

* In the *Dictionary* Johnson defines 'glossary' as 'a dictionary of obscure or antiquated words', reminding us that he is explicitly trying to create something different from this.

something more permanent than the hack work he did for Cave. Yet he was not the one who initiated the project. Indeed, he seems originally to have been reluctant to take it on. It was dauntingly large. It was hardly in keeping with his poetic ambitions (he still hoped to mount a production of his verse drama *Irene*). In any case, he would have preferred at this time to assemble an edition of Shakespeare. But the publisher Jacob Tonson claimed a monopoly right in Shakespeare's plays, and Johnson had to abandon this plan.

Robert Dodsley by Edward Alcock, *c.* 1760

Robert Dodsley was the principal mover in persuading Johnson to redirect his attentions. Dodsley had been closely associated with Pope, who had drawn up plans for a dictionary, or for a canon of exemplary authors, and he therefore had at his disposal some useful preliminary materials. Boswell records Dodsley's brother James telling him that Johnson was one day sitting on a bench in Robert's shop, when Robert suggested that a new dictionary would be 'well received by the public'. 'Johnson seemed at first to catch at the proposition, but after a pause, said, in his abrupt decisive manner, "I believe I shall not undertake it."' When Johnson later offered his own account, the story was different. In October 1779, nearly a quarter of a century after his masterwork was published, he told Boswell that 'Dodsley first mentioned to me the scheme of an English Dictionary; but I had long thought of it.' There is a hint in these words of the self-applause of hindsight. But whether inspired by Dodsley's urgings or by his own latent ambitions, Johnson warmed to the design, and the two men soon agreed on the desirability of such a work.

Entrance

1. The power of entering into a place

2. The act of entering

3. The passage by which a place is entered; avenue

4. Initiation; commencement

5. Intellectual ingress; knowledge

6. The act of taking possession of an office or dignity

7. The beginning of any thing

Infused with a sense of bright new possibilities, Johnson plunged himself into the task. His first move was to work up a 'Short Scheme for Compiling a new Dictionary of the English Language'. Its nineteen pages, completed on 20 April, convinced Dodsley that he was the right man for the job. However, the project was too large to be underwritten by Dodsley alone, and he joined forces with a number of other booksellers. These were Andrew Millar, a Scot who had a reputation as a hard-headed deal-maker; the Knapton brothers, John and Paul, whose reputation was similar; Thomas Longman, who was the principal shareholder in Ephraim Chambers's popular *Cyclopaedia* (1728), a dictionary of the arts and sciences; Longman's partner Thomas Shewell; and Charles Hitch, who had been a keen though critical admirer of the poem *London*.[1]

We should not underestimate Dodsley's role in fostering the project. It was this ambitious and shrewd man, who had started his working life as a footman to the society wit Charles Dartiquenave (and had been the model for Fielding's Joseph Andrews), who persuaded Johnson to take the project on. He provided him with Pope's notes. He superintended the consortium of booksellers. He would solicit the patronage of the influential Earl of Chesterfield – of whom we shall hear more later. He diligently publicized the *Dictionary*, especially in his own magazine the *Museum*. Furthermore, his own studious work as a compiler meant that he had both materials and ideas to share with Johnson: his *Select Collection of Old Plays* had begun to appear in 1744, and in 1748 he would commence publication of a giant anthology of verse, *A Collection of Poems by Several Hands*. He was, or would soon become, the publisher of many of the period's most important writers: Pope, Richardson, Defoe, Laurence Sterne, Edmund Burke, Oliver Goldsmith and Thomas Gray.

In short, Dodsley embodied the remarkable power of the big eighteenth-century booksellers. Without the support of booksellers, a project on this scale could not be accomplished. Johnson recognized this: the prospect of undertaking a large work under Dodsley's aegis was overwhelming attractive. Accordingly, he committed himself to the job, signing the contract over breakfast at the Golden Anchor near Holborn Bar, on 18 June 1746. He was to be paid 1,500 guineas (£1,575), in instalments.[2]

At this point it is worth stepping aside to say something about money, in order to put the figure of £1,575 into proper perspective. By mid-century a gentleman could live quite well on £300 a year, and £50 was enough for a family of four if they were prepared to be abstemious. When Boswell moved from Scotland to London in 1762, his father made him an annual allowance of £200. An income over £500 was enough for one to be considered wealthy. The Duke of Cumberland, who led the King's troops at the battle of Culloden, earned almost £4,000 a year as head of the army. And what did money buy? A penny was enough to get drunk on, if you were prepared to let low-quality gin pass your lips; it also bought a pint of good beer, or a cup of coffee. A shilling bought dinner at a steakhouse or a pound of Parmesan cheese, while £1 was sufficient for a pair of silk stockings or a dozen French lessons, and a man's suit of respectable cut and cloth might cost £10. In 1762 Boswell found lodgings in Downing Street for forty guineas a year. A house in one of the grand new Mayfair squares could be rented for ten times that amount.[3]

Johnson's £1,575 was a considerable sum, then – perhaps equivalent to £150,000 today. But the contract required him to meet all his incidental expenses, and it would be wrong to imagine that he was suddenly rich. His deal with the booksellers brought him much-needed security, and that was all.

Soon after signing the contract, Johnson moved to 17 Gough Square, a minute's walk north of Fleet Street, in order to be near his printer, William Strahan, who had just opened premises at 10 Little New Street. Strahan was another Scot, originally from Edinburgh,

William Strahan by Sir Joshua Reynolds, exhibited 1783

and five and a half years Johnson's junior. Boswell characterizes him in terms of 'wealthy plumpness and good animal spirits'. Of the wealth we can be sure: in 1766 he paid £5,000 for a one-third share in the patent as King's Printer, and then spent another £2,000 on a new printing house in East Harding Street. The position was a lucrative one, generating net annual profits of several thousand pounds for each partner, and he was able to employ a staff of more than sixty.

Even before these developments, Strahan's business was at the heart of eighteenth-century book production, but the *Dictionary* was a dauntingly large commission. It demanded rigorous management, and Strahan found himself having to allay the tensions between Johnson and his commercially sensitive paymasters. A work on the scale of the *Dictionary* could not be printed all at once. Even though a busy printer would hold a couple of tons of type, neither he nor any other would have held sufficient type to be able to set up so vast a work in its entirety. The job had to be performed in instalments. This was a source of vexation on both sides, for Johnson and the shareholders soon differed sharply in their senses of what might constitute a sufficiently definite schedule. Strahan was the intermediary between them.

During the years in which Johnson worked on the *Dictionary*, Strahan was his paymaster, acted as his unofficial banker, franked his letters, and even periodically provided him with breakfast. Johnson visited frequently; he found his printer good and generous company. Strahan was a warm host, and an unaffected one. He and his wife had an impressive library of unusual books; occasionally these were lent to Johnson, and we know that one of the volumes he borrowed was a recent treatise on the tranquillizing powers of opium by a Scottish doctor called George Young. Besides, there were more immediately analgesic rewards to be had from visiting the Strahans' home. In the courtyard stood a lime tree which Johnson, in moments of abstraction, liked to hug.

It was near the Strahans at 17 Gough Square that Johnson lived throughout his work on the *Dictionary*. The square took its name from Richard Gough, a successful wool merchant who, some fifty years before, had envisaged it as an elegant quadrangle of bourgeois dwellings. By the time Johnson relocated there it was less respectable, and his annual rent was a modest £30. The house, which still stands, is one of a very few of its age to survive in the City of London, and the only one of Johnson's eighteen London homes to have done so. A solidly built William and Mary property, five bays wide and five storeys high, it now houses a small, well-run museum, cowering behind the offices of the American investment bank Goldman Sachs. In the cobbled square outside there is a modern statue of Johnson's cat Hodge, for whom he loved to buy oysters. The life-size bronze, shaded by an acacia tree, shows Hodge sitting at stroking height on the *Dictionary* – a perpetual reminder of Johnson's magisterial achievement, and of his more affectionate side.[4]

Johnson's house at 17 Gough Square, drawn and etched by William Monk and published in *Monk's Calendar*, 1931

The house itself has had several different incarnations since Johnson vacated it. It has served as both a printworks and a hotel. Thomas Carlyle, writing in 1832 of having 'lately discovered' Gough Square, told how he had found Johnson's former home occupied by an 'elderly, well-washed, decent looking man'. The property struck him as 'stout' and 'old-fashioned'. Its garden, to which Johnson must occasionally have retired when exhausted by his work, was fittingly described as 'somewhat larger than a bed-quilt'.[5]

By modern standards 17 Gough Square is fairly spacious. There are only three bedrooms, but the proportions of the rooms and landings are generous. A steep staircase leads to the garret where Johnson worked – a long gallery with oak beams. Visitors can now see only a reconstruction of the room, as the original fabric was damaged by fire during the Second World War. Yet we can imagine Johnson staring from his garret window towards St Paul's, dowsing for inspiration.★

Today the outlook is straitened, the skyline interrupted by office buildings. In Johnson's day it would have been less cramped, but the surrounding area was a maze of dark alleys. The neighbourhood was densely populated with booksellers, along with a motley assortment of other tradesmen – wig-makers, watchmakers, mercers and chand-lers. The street names are suggestive: Shoe Lane, Wine Office Court, Printer Street, Gunpowder Alley. The quick pulse of commercialism was matched by a brisk conviviality. There were taverns and coffee houses, chop houses and pie shops; of the taverns, Johnson favoured the Mitre and the Old Cheshire Cheese, both on Fleet Street. There was a seedy side to the neighbourhood, too. It was known for its pros-titutes, and for the shotgun marriages solemnized by debt-ridden clerics incarcerated in the Fleet Prison. Johnson spoke euphemisti-cally of the area's 'animated appearance'; it was often the scene of riots and public protests.

The garret at 17 Gough Square was the centre of Johnson's world. The room was ideal for his purposes – more office than study, and blessed with good light. Johnson equipped it with long trestle tables, giving it at first the appearance of a counting house, where clerks could finick over their papers. Yet within no time it became a sort of backstreet abattoir specializing in the evisceration of books. Johnson presided over the scene from an odd three-legged chair; traumatized volumes lay all around. 'A man will turn over half a library to make one book,' he reflected. His choice of verb is telling; he makes the process sound like a cross between a treasure hunt and a house clear-ance. And in this case, as we shall see, he turned over several libraries.

★ In the *Dictionary* Johnson quotes the following lines of Swift's:

> On earth the god of wealth was made
> Sole patron of the building trade;
> Leaving the arts the spacious air,
> With licence to build castles there:
> And 'tis conceiv'd their old pretence,
> To lodge in *garrets*, comes from thence.

Johnson's garret quickly took on an appearance of philosophic squalor, but it is worth remembering a few of the shortcomings of the eighteenth-century house that were not unique to 17 Gough Square. Until the reign of Queen Victoria, houses were lit with either lamps or candles. The candles tended to gutter, and posed a serious fire hazard (in later years Johnson, when he troubled to wear a wig, would scorch it by getting too close to his light). They also smelt: only the rich could afford beeswax candles, and most people's were made of animal fat. The atmosphere was smoky – houses were heated by burning coal, and cooking was usually done over a fire. Soot got everywhere. So did fleas: the first King George had found it necessary to employ his own dedicated 'bug destroyer'. Drainage was primitive: the majority of London houses were served by leaky cesspits, and, although water closets became increasingly common as the century progressed, the sanitary arrangements were by modern standards crude. The drainage system we today take for granted was an innovation of the Victorian period: Georgian waste pipes were made of elm, and oozed at their iron joints. The proximity of glue-makers, blacksmiths and paintworks thickened the air with noxious odours. Eighteenth-century houses were often dangerously unhygienic, as well as dark and cold. Gough Square was no exception.

Although their new home was an improvement on previous arrangements, the Johnsons did not entertain. Tetty's recurrent ill health, exacerbated by the urban filth, meant that visitors were discouraged. Johnson preferred to leave the house in order to socialize; when he remained at home, confident that he would receive no callers, he could rise late, heave himself upstairs, and pursue his work in a state of perfect dishevelment. A maid was often in attendance, and probably a cook as well, but all such arrangements were irregular. On one occasion, when Tetty's son Jervis turned up unannounced after a spell at sea, the maid was so unused to dealing with visitors that she neglected to ask him in; when she returned from telling her mistress that Jervis was at the door, he had gone. Indeed, it seems that the only other people to cross the threshold of 17 Gough Square with any regularity were Johnson's newly recruited helpers, a clutch of Grub Street's poorest citizens.

Factotum

A servant employed alike in all kinds of business

Johnson understood that compiling the *Dictionary* would be not just intellectually exacting, but a physical labour too. The work would have a secretarial dimension: there would be large books to be lugged; a multitude of quotations would require painstaking transcription; quires of paper would have to be cut up into copy slips. His thoughts on the nature of writing convey the impression that he considered it something to set oneself to 'doggedly', to persevere at, to achieve 'by slow degrees'. He would playfully give one sense of the word 'dull' as 'not exhilarating; not delightful; as, *to make dictionaries is dull work*'. And so it could be; but those who accomplished it were heroic. 'There is not so poor a book in the world that would not be a prodigious effort were it wrought out entirely by a single mind,' he told his erudite companions at the Turk's Head Club, on one of the first occasions when Boswell sat with him. The Herculean endeavours of the professional author were to be a recurrent theme of their friendship, and the *Dictionary* shaped his sense of them. It called for all the skills of the writer, but also for those of the editor, the explicator, the anthologist and the hod-carrier, the book-muncher, the pagemaker and the cultural steeplejack, and was as many as a dozen labours rolled into one.

In order to alleviate the inevitable drudgery of this work, Johnson employed six amanuenses, who attended to some of its more menial and mechanical aspects. No more than four were with him at any one time, but he was seldom without at least one in the first four years, and dispensed with their services only when money was short and there was truly nothing they could usefully do. There was from the start a tacit understanding that the amanuenses would keep Johnson company, and that he would keep them out of trouble – for it is clear that all six were accustomed to poverty, and that Johnson's decision to employ these particular men was partly motivated by charity. He rotated them as his needs (or theirs) dictated, and offered accommodation to those who could not afford lodgings elsewhere. The amanuenses were his servants, but also his companions – dogsbodies with the status of intimates, hirelings who doubled as friends. Their presence in the background is a reminder of the giant effort of compilation.

We know disappointingly little of these six. Their imprint is seldom discernible in the pages of the *Dictionary*. Yet, although Johnson took sole responsibility for the most difficult parts of the work, their contribution should not be underestimated: without his brood of helpers he would have struggled.

The first to be recruited was Francis Stewart, the son of an Edinburgh bookseller. Johnson hired Stewart the same day he signed the contract with the booksellers, and paid him a healthy advance against a proposed wage of twelve shillings a week. Stewart had previously worked as a journalist, and apparently helped Johnson with a number of definitions pertaining to the sleazier side of city life – an assortment of 'low' terms that included the jargon of popular card games. One suspects that Johnson, who was no card-player, would not have known that 'vole' was slang for a deal, and would not automatically have defined 'whist' as 'a game at cards, requiring close attention and silence'. One suspects, too, that he was nodding to his helper's experience when he defined 'above-board' as 'In open fight; without artifice or trick. A figurative expression, borrowed from gamesters, who, when they put their hands under the table, are changing their cards'; and the impression is reinforced when he adds, as if in a judicial aside, that 'It is used only in familiar language.'

Johnson, who habitually referred to Stewart as Frank, described him to Boswell as 'an ingenious and worthy man'. He spoke in similar terms of Robert Shiels, another Scot who worked for him at this time. Shiels was a hack writer whose principal achievement was his *Lives of the Poets*, a five-volume work which appeared in 1753. He was engaged to write it on the strength of an elegy he had composed for the poet James Thomson, whose *The Seasons* was one of the most popular works of the age. Shamefully, Shiels was denied credit for the *Lives*; the publisher paid Theophilus Cibber, a disreputable playwright who was languishing in a debtors jail, ten guineas for the right to use his name. This was done in the hope that a gullible public would take the 'Mr Cibber' of the title page for Theophilus's father, Colley Cibber, who was at that time Poet Laureate. The fraud became widely known, but Shiels reaped no benefit: he died of consumption at Christmas that year. His name survives most lastingly in an episode recorded by Boswell. Johnson is assessing the abilities of Thomson. 'His fault', he argues, 'is such a cloud of words sometimes, that the sense can hardly peep through.' He switches then to reminiscence: 'Shiels . . . was one day sitting with me. I took down Thomson, and read aloud a large portion . . . and then asked, – Is not this fine? Shiels having expressed the highest admiration. Well, Sir, (said I,) I have omitted every other line.' The anecdote, small as it is, shows us Johnson enjoying a moment of genial banter with one of his helpers. Such interludes were necessary: even the most deadening work can be illuminated by a flash of fraternal good humour.

The camaraderie of the garret was amplified by two Scottish brothers, the Macbeans. The elder of them, Alexander, was experienced in the more leaden aspects of lexicography. He had worked on the fourth and fifth editions of Ephraim Chambers's *Cyclopaedia* in the 1740s, and had assembled materials for a military dictionary – a project Johnson had proposed to Cave as early as 1738. Macbean brought to the team a patiently acquired knowledge of what it meant to put a work of reference together. In later life he turned this knowledge to personal advantage, organizing the library of Archibald Campbell, third duke of Argyll, and writing a book about the geography of the ancient world. To this Johnson subscribed a preface, despite his reservations: 'I have lost all hope of his doing anything properly, since I found he gave as much labour to Capua as to Rome.' (Johnson was right to be concerned. In the third century BC Capua was a strategic location on the Appian Way, and became Hannibal's base in Italy; the Roman siege of Capua was a key event in the Second Punic War. But the city merited no more than a few paragraphs, and Macbean's priorities sound dotty.) Still, Macbean's limitations as an author did not damage Johnson's regard for him as a man. In his final months he wrote to Hester Thrale that the recently deceased Macbean 'was very highly esteemed' by all at Gough Square, and that he 'was one of those who, as Swift says, *stood as a screen between me and death*'.[1] This sounds like more than the standard exaggeration of elegy; no evidence survives of how Macbean interposed between his master and his Maker, but we know that he and his colleagues did much to allay Johnson's melancholy.

Macbean's contribution to the *Dictionary* is more palpable than that of any of his colleagues. He is cited as an authority for the definition of 'to maunch', a Scottish term meaning 'to eat much', for 'sorn' ('a kind of arbitrary exaction or servile tenure'), and for the etymology of 'loord' ('a drone'). He even managed to insinuate his own work into the *Dictionary*: under 'salubrious' and 'scale' there are quotations bearing his name. Remarkably, in the case of 'scale' he succeeded in smuggling a sliver of his inept poetry into the text without Johnson's noticing. But the imposture was evidently discovered, for the quotation is omitted from the revised fourth edition.

The elder Macbean was joined by his brother William, of whom less is known, and by a fifth Scot, an even more shadowy figure known to posterity only as 'Mr Maitland'.★ Working alongside them was a single Englishman, V. J. Peyton. The fact that he is known by his initials rather than his first name indicates the paucity of information he left behind. He seems, however, to have had a flair for languages, and in the years after the *Dictionary* he published a history of English and a guide to its grammar. Johnson's friend Giuseppe Baretti maintained that Peyton was 'a fool and a drunkard', adding that 'I never saw so nauseous a fellow.' Baretti was prone to extremes of opinion and emotion, so perhaps we should not take this too seriously, but a graphologist would find much to discuss in Peyton's shaking handwriting. In May 1758 he assigned the copyright in his book of French grammar to a Mr Nourse; his script is that of an infirm, old or drunk man. Yet the initial *P* of his name is executed with a self-conscious flourish.[3] What is certain is that Peyton, in common with his fellow amanuenses, knew extreme poverty. When his wife fell ill he sat starving by her bed, and when she died he soon after succumbed to a fever. He left insufficient funds to pay for either

---

★ More shadowy still is a possible seventh amanuensis, a Mr Stockton, to whom Johnson refers – as 'Mr Stockton who writes for me' – in a letter to Dodsley from December 1746.[2]

burial, and his old employer, generous to the last, met the expenses. In a letter to Mrs Thrale, Johnson poignantly reflects that 'Such miscarriages when they happen to those on whom many eyes are fixed, fill histories and tragedies[,] and tears have been shed for the sufferings, and wonder excited by the fortitude of those who neither did nor suffered more than Peyton.'[4]

A question to conclude: why were so many of the amanuenses Scots? Johnson's published writings suggest he thought little of 'North Britons', and Boswell, a Scot himself, records plenty of his barbs against them ('Much may be made of a Scotsman, if he be *caught* young', 'The noblest prospect which a Scotchman ever sees, is the high road that leads him to England'). All the same, London was by mid-century full of capable young men from across the border who had ventured to the capital in the hope of forging careers as authors, and Johnson, a perennial supporter of nascent literary talents, allowed his prejudices to be mastered by his sympathies.[5]

To gather

1. To collect; to bring into one place; to get in harvest

2. To pick up; to glean; to pluck

Johnson was glad to have his posse of helpers, but before he could direct their efforts he had to resolve a host of sticky questions. How does one compile a dictionary from scratch? Is it a matter of thinking of words, and then of their definitions and the means of illustrating them? Or of finding the illustrations and working back from there? Should you seek out existing resources, in order to cannibalize their juicier parts, or ignore all such precedents, choosing instead to be dispassionate and to begin with the cleanest of clean slates? What kind of words need to be included, and what can safely be left out? Should one incorporate the technical terms of chemistry and engineering, zoology and jurisprudence? Does one need to define everyday words like 'water' and 'chair', with which readers will presumably be familiar?

Johnson began the *Dictionary* with no convenient English model to hand. Of his predecessors, only Bishop Wilkins had thought carefully about how best to compile a dictionary, and his thinking had been directed towards peculiarly artificial ends. Yet Johnson, already familiar with a vast range of dictionaries from cataloguing the Harleian library, re-examined the efforts of his predecessors. Their misadventures gave him clues about the difficulties of his task, even if they did not provide him with a robust methodology.

Having completed this research, Johnson produced a map of his intentions. In August 1747 he published a 'plan' of the work, addressed in deferential terms to Philip Dormer Stanhope, fourth earl of Chesterfield. The *Plan of an English Dictionary* built on the 'scheme' he had presented to Dodsley the previous year. In its original form it was a thirty-four-page pamphlet, intended to establish Johnson's authority as a lexicographer. It did this by showing the degree of thought he had expended on the project, and also by enlisting the 'vicarious jurisdiction' of Chesterfield. At the same time it was designed to warn off rival lexicographers, by showing the seriousness of Johnson's ambitions. The bibliophile Thomas Birch, a perceptive commentator, thought it 'an ingenious performance', but noted that 'the style is too flatulent'.[1] From the moment the *Plan* appeared, critics were queuing up to pass judgement. It certainly is rhetorical, but plenty remains once its windy courtesies are subtracted.

Johnson begins by observing that lexicography has an unhappy reputation. It is 'generally considered as drudgery for the blind, as the proper toil of artless industry'. He shrugs this traditional view aside. He notes that the word 'dictionary' has 'long conveyed a very miscellaneous idea'. This too he rebuffs, emphasizing that other people's failures are not going to deter him. Instead, he quickly gets down to discussing the practicalities of his task. 'In the first attempt to methodize my ideas,' he writes, 'I found a difficulty, which extended itself to the whole work', for 'It was not easy to determine by what rule of distinction the words of this dictionary were to be chosen.' He stresses the need to select 'the words and phrases used in the general intercourse of life, or found in the works of those whom we commonly style polite writers'. Yet he has another mission in mind: the dictionary's 'chief intent' must be 'to preserve the purity, and ascertain the meaning of our English idiom'.

He goes on to propose certain key principles. 'It seems necessary to the completion of a dictionary, designed . . . for popular use, that it should comprise, in some degree, the peculiar words of every profession.' However, 'it will be proper to print those [words] which are incorporated into the language in the usual character, and those which are still to be considered as foreign, in the Italick letter'. He promises to rationalize spellings, although he will 'make no innovation without a reason sufficient to balance the inconvenience of change'. He suggests that he will give guidance on correct pronunciation. He remarks that 'The difference of signification in words generally accounted synonymous, ought to be carefully observed', and that 'the strict and critical meaning ought to be distinguished from that which is loose and popular'. 'My idea of an English dictionary', he explains, is one 'by which the pronunciation of our language may be fixed, and its attainment facilitated; by which its purity may be preserved, its use ascertained, and its duration lengthened'.

At this point, amid all the talk of ascertaining and preserving, he seems optimistic about his chances of understanding and ordering the chaos of the language's copiousness. Perhaps we can hear a note of anxiety (he describes what 'ought' to be done, rather than what will be done), but the general tone is confident. Reiterating the importance of his labours, he states that 'one great end of this undertaking is to fix the English language'. For a modern reader, the verb 'to fix' has two obvious senses: 'to mend' and 'to fasten securely'. For Johnson, as the relevant *Dictionary* entry attests, it usually meant the latter. Despite his natural tendency to legislate, his first aim was not to revise the language with interventionist, pontifical zeal, but to record and fortify its present condition.

The *Plan* shows Johnson thinking intently about the difficulties facing him as a lexicographer, and about the particular difficulties of English. For instance, he notes that 'many words written alike are differently pronounced', and that 'our inflexions . . . admit of numberless irregularities', citing as an example of the latter the plurals of 'fox' and 'ox' – 'foxes' and 'oxen'. As Johnson discerned, even at this early stage, English poses some peculiarly stubborn problems. The most intractable of these are an irregular spelling system that was marshalled – and then quite casually – only in the fifteenth century; a profusion of synonyms, and an abundance of polysemy (the phenomenon whereby a single word can have numerous meanings); a large number of words adopted from other languages; a fascinating variety of regional pronunciations and dialect terms; and the vast and ever-thickening jungle of its idioms. Yet to Johnson it still seemed possible to stabilize the language, by cataloguing these difficulties. It would be hard, he knew, but not hopeless.

When Johnson discusses the present raggedy state of English, his writing has a distinctly moral cast. He personifies the language, describing it as 'licentious' and 'inconstant'. He stresses that, by tracing etymologies and not accepting any word 'of which no original can be found', 'we shall secure our language from being overrun with *cant*, from being crowded with low terms, the spawn of folly or affectation'. This imagery suggests he thinks of himself as a reformer – and not just as a linguistic reformer, but as a social one too: a moral policeman in linguist's clothing. It is no surprise to find Johnson setting himself up as an arbiter of standards. However, the accent he places on stability, while consistent with his own political instincts, was probably exaggerated in order to win the patronage of Lord Chesterfield. The *Plan* is a document with an agenda. Chesterfield was obsessed with propriety of usage, with the disciplinary strictures of *politesse*, and with embalming or even bettering the language. At this stage it doubtless seemed prudent to mask any concerns about the likelihood of doing so, and to proffer instead this swollen rhetoric, complete with an assurance that English would be sent to school.

Linguistic conservatives like Chesterfield were afraid that unchecked changes in general usage would cause the English of the eighteenth century to become as bewildering to its inheritors as the language of Chaucer was to them. They were correct, of course, in seeing that their language was in flux. Then and now, the engines of this change include international commerce and travel, which involve contact with other languages; shifts in political doctrine or consensus; translations, which frequently preserve the idiom of their originals; fashion (in Johnson's age, the nascent cult of sensibility), whose adherents require a special figurative language to articulate their refined and rarefied perspectives; and advertising, which uses foreign terms to connote mystique. These transfusions are what keep a language alive, but this is a modern view. Chesterfield could not begin to see that change was a force for the good. With time, Johnson's conservatism – the desire to 'fix' the language – gave way to a radical awareness of language's mutability. But from the outset the impulse to standardize and straighten English out was in competition with the belief that one should chronicle what's there, and not just what one would like to see.

Johnson professes himself daunted by the task that lies before him: 'I am frighted by its extent, and, like the soldiers of Caesar, look on Britain as a new world, which it is almost madness to invade.' Chesterfield is his Caesar, but, speaking with the grandeur of the general rather than his mere foot soldiers, Johnson hopes that 'though I should not complete the conquest, I shall, at least, discover the coast, civilize part of the inhabitants, and make it easy for some other adventurer to proceed further, to reduce them wholly to subjection, and settle them under laws'. The language of this passage is constitutional: equating himself with the Roman colonists, he apparently aspires to the formalism of Roman law. But the political significance is easily overplayed; in truth, the passage is tinged with an essential quality of Johnson's that is all too often forgotten – a playful good humour.

In private, Johnson maintained that he could complete the job quickly. 'I have no doubt that I can do it in three years,' he supposedly told his friend William Adams. When Adams objected that the French Academy's forty members had taken forty years (in fact, as we know, they took fifty-five), Johnson shrugged this scepticism aside: 'Sir, thus it is. This is the proportion. Let me see; forty times forty is sixteen hundred. As three to sixteen hundred, so is the proportion of an Englishman to a Frenchman.'

Johnson's boast that he could complete the task in three years was one he tried to substantiate. But his actual work on the *Dictionary* quickly proved the inadequacy of his original plans. Of the many hazards that impeded his progress, the most awkward was a crisis of philological conscience: his desire to accomplish the job at speed was countered by a sense of the moral importance of the work and the philosophical difficulties of rationalizing language. In the Preface he eventually contributed to the finished volumes, he would reflect that 'The English dictionary was written with little assistance of the learned, and without any patronage of the great; not in the soft obscurities of retirement, or under the shelter of academic bowers, but amidst inconvenience and distraction, in sickness and sorrow.' This smartly formulated sentence makes light of many discontents.

If we read Boswell's account of Johnson's labours, we are persuaded that the process of compilation was, for all its longueurs, largely untroubled. Boswell writes that 'The words, partly taken from other dictionaries, and partly supplied by himself, having been first written down with spaces left between them, he delivered in writing their etymologies, definitions, and various significations. The authorities were copied from the books themselves, in which he had marked the passages.' He imagines Johnson 'tugging at his oar', 'engaged in a steady course of occupation'. 'Steady' is hardly the right word for

Johnson's approach, and Boswell's description of Johnson's working methods is straightforwardly inexact. We should remember that Boswell did not know Johnson until eight years after the *Dictionary*'s completion. By the time they met, Johnson's fame was assured, chiefly by this giant work, and he had interred the dark memory of the difficulties attending its compilation. Boswell was too callow, or maybe too lazy, to probe its real history. In any case, Johnson was not much disposed to talk about his past. As he told the guests at a dinner hosted by Sir Joshua Reynolds, 'A man cannot with propriety speak of himself, except he relates simple facts; as, "I was at Richmond", or . . . "I am six feet high."' The rodomontade of lavish self-recall was a vice he left to others. So Boswell never learned the true details of the making of the *Dictionary*. He blithely suggests that Johnson began by drawing up a word-list, and that he then came up with the definitions before finally sniffing out appropriate illustrations.

There is something fishy about this explanation. Imagine beginning with a giant word-list and then scouring your bookshelves for examples of the words' various meanings. You would give up in despair. I know, because I have tried it. I selected words at random from Johnson's *Dictionary* and then looked for appropriate illustrative passages. The first word that presented itself was 'scarecrow' ('an image or clapper set up to fright birds'). Right away I set about trying to find it, dipping in and out of several books that promised to contain a suitable example. I looked in my copy of Jane Austen's *Persuasion*, because I remembered Sir Walter Elliot's complaint that the men in Bath resembled scarecrows; but I was unable to locate the reference. Then I looked in my collected Shakespeare – wasn't there something about scarecrows in *King Lear*? I searched fruitlessly, and cursed myself for not owning *The Wizard of Oz*. Eventually I found 'scarecrow', appropriately enough, on the opening page of a translation of Sten Nadolny's *The Discovery of Slowness*. In true Johnsonian style, the book fell off a high shelf as I was reaching for another. Time elapsed: fifty frantic minutes. This just for a single, imperfect illustration of one word. The *Dictionary* Johnson produced contains approximately 110,000 quotations in support of 42,773 entries, and he used only half the quotations he collected. Were I to continue my experiment, many words would prove easier to locate (one wouldn't struggle to find a quotable example of 'and'), but, assuming I could improve my average 'find time' to, say, thirty minutes, the task would take me more than 50,000 hours. If I worked for twelve whole hours a day, I'd spend eleven and a half years compiling my dictionary. And by contemporary standards it would be pathetically inadequate.

Johnson did not work this way. In fact his first move *was* to plunder lists of words from Nathan Bailey's dictionary, and from Robert Ainsworth's recent Latin *Thesaurus*, and he later consulted these and similar works to ensure that he had not missed out anything important. His use of these sources is amply documented in the finished volumes.[2] But this was a method he discarded. Instead, once the *Plan* was written, he chose to apply himself to the 'perusal' of English writers. In the opening paragraph of the *Plan* he stereotypes the lexicographer's work as 'beating the track of the alphabet with sluggish resolution'. Johnson disengaged from this tradition by starting with books, not with the alphabet. The word-list would be generated by the illustrations, rather than preceding them.

In order to find his corpus of materials he read a huge variety of texts. Some he chewed over and digested, others he merely tasted; some he inspected out of curiosity, and others he read with great care. Among the authors he chose were a good number he had never previously examined: he later confessed to Boswell that he had not read any of Bacon's works until he began the *Dictionary*. He was a 'curious' reader; and he defines this adjective, with an appropriate degree of psychopathology, as 'addicted to enquiry'. We may think of Johnson as a sort of butterfly-collector, gathering specimens of usage out in the wild and then arranging them systematically at a later date.

Johnson's reading was not the stuff of gentlemanly leisure. One should not imagine him sequestered in some Elysium of scholarly bliss. His early biographer Sir John Hawkins, a sour but usually reliable source, describes Johnson's personal library as 'copious but . . . miserably ragged' – more charity shop than *bibliothèque*, then.[3] Boswell paints much the same picture: when he visited Johnson in 1763 he found his quarters full of 'good books', but noted with regret that 'they are all lying in confusion and dust'. Nothing seems to have dissuaded Johnson from this negligent treatment of his library. Another visit by Boswell found the lexicographer 'busy putting his books in order': he was wearing 'a pair of large gloves, such as hedgers use'. Moreover, Johnson could not afford all the books he needed. He was obliged to beg and borrow. His agricultural way with reading matter dismayed first-time lenders and discouraged them from further loans. He claimed that his scribbled notes could be removed by being rubbed with breadcrumbs, but no one was convinced. His old pupil Garrick, now the darling of the London stage, owned a fine set of rare Shakespearean quartos. Johnson borrowed these. When they were returned, Garrick lamented their near-ruin. Later, when Johnson requested to see them again, Garrick refused.

The imagery that attaches to Johnson's reading habits is notably visceral: surgical perhaps, but veering towards butchery. He spoke to Boswell of ripping the heart out of a book 'like a Turk'. Boswell's uncle characterized Johnson's reading as 'Herculean'; the biographer adapted this, attributing to his relative a description of Johnson as a 'robust genius, born to grapple with whole libraries'. Frances Reynolds, sister of Sir Joshua, remarked that he read 'with amazing rapidity'. Fanny Burney recalled seeing him read a work called *De Veritate Religionis* – 'over which he seesawed at . . . a violent rate', like an oversized jockey spurring on his unhappy mount. His Quaker sparring partner Mary Knowles, with whom he liked to argue about women's rights, thought he knew how to read 'better than anyone': 'he gets at the substance of a book directly; he tears the heart out of it'. Boswell records Johnson keeping a volume wrapped up in the tablecloth on his lap while eating – 'to have one entertainment in readiness when he should have finished another'. In this he resembled 'a dog who holds a bone in his paws in reserve, while he eats something else which has been thrown to him'. Boswell concedes that this image is 'coarse' (one might add 'contemptuous'), but it attests graphically to Johnson's manners as a reader. And he was aware of his crude habits; he once gave Hester Thrale a handsome copy of Demosthenes, explaining that it was 'too fine for a Scholar's talons'.[4]

This rough treatment of books was not so very unusual. In an age when the availability of printed reading matter dramatically increased, the fetishization of books as aesthetic treasures diminished. Johnson saw books not as objects of reverence, but as the packages of ideas. They were resources, and existed to be exploited.

Higgledy-piggledy

A cant word, corrupted from *higgle*, which denotes any confused mass, as higglers carry a huddle of provisions
together

In the first instance, the achievement of the *Dictionary* is an achievement of reading. Johnson traversed the literature of the previous 200
years – sometimes ploughing, sometimes grazing – and marked as he
did so words that warranted inclusion, as well as the passages that contained them.★

We can hardly consider this a rigorously systematic approach, and
Johnson's early work on the *Dictionary* proceeded haphazardly. When
he identified a passage suitable for quotation, he underlined with a
black lead pencil the word he meant it to illustrate, marked the beginning and end of the passage with vertical strokes, and wrote the initial
letter of the chosen word in the margin. Working in pairs, the
amanuenses would then go over the books Johnson had marked.
Each time one of them came to a marked passage he would transcribe
it on to a quarto sheet and strike out the marginal letter. Six different
kinds of crossing out can be discerned in the extant copy texts – only
thirteen of Johnson's marked-up texts survive – and one may reasonably assume these correspond to the six amanuenses, although we
lack the evidence to associate any of the cross-out strokes with a particular amanuensis.[1]

The quotations were set out in columns, and, once full, the
quarto sheets were cut up into slips, each bearing a single quotation.
These copy slips were kept in bins, and arranged in alphabetical
order by the amanuenses. As work proceeded, the juggling of copy

---

★ Samuel Parr, who composed the epitaph for Johnson's statue in St Paul's Cathedral,
collected books with a view to writing Johnson's biography. There were so many that
he saw he could never do the job properly: 'It would have contained a view of the
literature of Europe.'

S E C T. I.

Of gaining clear and diſtinct Ideas.

THE firſt Rule is this, /*Seek after a clear and diſtinct Conception of Things as they are in their own Nature, and do not content yourſelves with obſcure and confuſed Ideas, where clearer are to be attain'd.*/

There are ſome Things indeed whereof diſtinct Ideas are ſcarce attainable, they ſeem to ſurpaſs the Capacity of the Underſtanding in our preſent State; ſuch are the Notions of *Eternal, Immenſe, Infinite*, whether this *Infinity* be applied to *Number*, as an infinite Multitude; to *Quantity*, as infinite Length, Breadth; to *Powers* and *Perfections*, as Strength, Wiſdom, or Goodneſs infinite, *&c.* /Tho' Mathematicians in their Way demonſtrate ſeveral Things in the Doctrine of *Infinites*, yet there are ſtill ſome inſolvable Difficulties that attend the Ideas of *Infinity,*/ when it is applied to Mind or Body; and while it is in Reality but an *idea ever growing*, we cannot have ſo clear and diſtinct a Conception of it as to ſecure us from Miſtakes in ſome of our Reaſonings about it.

There are many other Things that belong to the material World, wherein the ſharpeſt Philoſophers have never yet arrived at clear and diſtinct Ideas, ſuch as the particular *Shape, Situation, Contexture, Motion of the ſmall Particles of Minerals, Metals, Plants, &c.* whereby their very Natures and Eſſences are diſtinguiſhed from each other. Nor have we either Senſes or Inſtruments ſufficiently nice and accurate to find them out. /There are other Things in the World of Spirits
wherein

A page from Johnson's marked-up copy of Isaac Watts, *Logick* (8th edn, 1745) showing his working method

slips unfortunately allowed some of the illustrations to be lost.[2] We can see evidence of this occasionally in the finished *Dictionary*. Explaining one sense of the verb 'to cream', Johnson says it is 'used somewhere by Swift', while another word, 'dripple', is 'used somewhere by Fairfax'. Such lapses were frustrating, but a much deeper problem was exposed when Johnson decided to work the illustrative material up into a manuscript work-in-progress.

Johnson chose to do this in order to confirm that his chosen methodology was valid; he wanted to be sure that the materials he was collecting were sufficient. He also faced pressure from the booksellers, who, given their sizeable investment in his services, wanted tangible evidence of how he was getting on. Accordingly, the amanuenses copied the material on the slips into large notebooks, leaving space for Johnson to insert definitions and etymologies. There were eighty notebooks in all; the result was a skeleton dictionary. As this took shape, quite promisingly, the quotations were with increasing frequency transcribed straight into the notebooks, rather than on to individual copy slips.

The trouble with this system became apparent only slowly. Because the skeleton dictionary comprised entries ranging right through the alphabet, Johnson had to estimate in advance how much space he was going to need for his illustrative material. His expectations were informed by a rigid conception of how many shades of meaning a word could possess. In the *Plan* he had suggested that words would be shown to have, at most, seven different senses: a 'natural and primitive signification', a 'consequential meaning', a 'metaphorical sense', a 'poetical sense', 'familiar' and 'burlesque' senses, and finally 'the peculiar sense, in which a word is found in any great author'. In practice, as he read more books and reflected on the usage he found in them, Johnson discovered that many words had a wealth of meanings which required a more subtle and flexible approach; some words had ten, twenty or even fifty discrete senses. Initially he tried to squeeze new material into the notebooks, but there simply wasn't enough space to accommodate all his findings. First the manuscript became scruffy with addenda, then it became almost useless – impossible for Strahan's workers to follow.

Johnson was obliged to change his approach. This required him to admit that he had wasted a good part of the previous three years. It was not easy to accept this, but his decision was accelerated by his examining a copy of the *Lingua Britannica Reformata*, a dictionary recently published by Benjamin Martin, a self-taught former plough-boy and passionate disciple of Newtonianism. William Strahan was Martin's printer, and it may well have been that Strahan encouraged Johnson to examine Martin's new lexicon. Johnson cannot have failed to see that Martin's framework for discriminating between the different senses of words was similar to his own, and that Martin's dictionary showed the limitations of this system. Despite its zeal for lexicographical reform, it was too stiff and unempirical. Johnson grasped the implications of this, and – to the severe displeasure of the booksellers – decided to rethink his own methods of definition. While it was possible to reuse all the material he had collected, the notebooks had to be jettisoned. In order to do justice to the full spectrum of linguistic possibilities, he would have to start a fresh manuscript. It needed, in purely physical terms, to be a more open-ended document, capable of accommodating an unlimited number of senses and supporting quotations.

Fundamentally, Johnson was less interested in language than in its use by writers. Reading prevailed over philology: to paraphrase Sir James Murray, the editor of the first *Oxford English Dictionary*, he thought of lexicography as a department of literature. His decision to extract the word-list from books, and his generous deployment of illustrative material, meant that his conception of the *Dictionary* was rooted in the experience of reading and interpreting texts. In particular, it was the naturally critical tendency of his reading that shaped the work. Even when he read quickly, he read thoughtfully, sometimes stopping to argue with the author, or to add an explanatory marginalium. So for instance in his copy of the jurist Matthew Hale's *Primitive Origination of Mankind* (1677) he marks a passage in which Hale describes the usual forms of inter-action between natives and settlers in a newly colonized country. Hale writes that

> where the accessions are but thin and sparing, and scattered among
> the natives of the country . . . and are driven to conform themselves
> unto their customs for their very subsistence, safety and entertain-

ment, it falls out that the very first planters do soon degenerate in their habits, customs and religion; as a little wine poured into a great vessel of water loseth itself.

Johnson notes in the margin that 'This happened to the English in Ireland, they made court to the natives by imitating them.'[3] In his copy of John Norris's *A Collection of Miscellanies* (1699) he marks the following passage:

It is supposed by the Ancient Fathers, that the Sufferings which our Blessed Saviour underwent in his body were more afflictive to him than the same would have been to another man, upon the account of the excellency and quickness of his sense of Feeling.

In the margin Johnson writes 'my brother' – meaning either that Nathaniel, now dead more than ten years, was an example of those less excellent and quick of feeling or that Nathaniel was hypersensitive, or indeed that Johnson associated himself closely with Christ's sensitivity.[4]

Furthermore, it was not enough to find passages that merely showed words in use. Where possible, the passages had to be tutelary, since the *Dictionary* was intended for use by students. There was a longstanding tradition, especially within Islamic culture, of infusing dictionaries with moral teaching. In the *Plan*, Johnson proposed 'selecting, when it can be conveniently done, such sentences, as, besides their immediate use, may give pleasure or instruction, by conveying some elegance of language, or some precept of prudence, or piety'.[5]

This emphasis on moral education, and on the moral underpinnings of education, is suggested again and again. A few examples should suffice. For instance, there is this definition of the noun 'cross-row': 'Alphabet: so named because a cross is placed at the beginning, to shew that the end of learning is piety'. Or there are Johnson's two illustrations of 'education'; both emphasize the role of education in informing moral judgement, and the second, from Swift, states that the essence of education is 'the observance of moral duties'. Look under 'to teach' and the very first quotation comes from the Book of Isaiah: 'The Lord will *teach* us of his ways, and we will walk in his paths.' The first seven illustrations of 'to instruct' all come from the Bible; the first four are explicitly concerned with divine instruction.

This is a recurrent theme of the work as a whole: piety and learning are simultaneous. The moralistic flavour of the *Dictionary* is illuminated, too, when Johnson wants to illustrate the names of two typefaces, 'brevier' and 'burgeois'. In order to show what they look like, he provides quotations set in these fonts. The first is from *Paradise Lost*: 'Nor love thy life, nor hate, but what thou liv'st, / Live well, how long or short, permit to heav'n.' The second comes from Alexander Pope: 'Laugh where we must, be candid where we can, / But vindicate the ways of God to man.' Johnson could have set any sentences in these two typefaces; it is striking that he chose two snippets of verse replete with such pious sentiments.

From time to time Johnson edited the passages. For the most part he did no more than amend the spelling and punctuation – doing away, for instance, with what he thought to be gimmicky dashes and hyphens[6] – but sometimes he compressed sentences to save space, sometimes he improved their syntax, and occasionally he changed the words themselves. When quoting from memory he was susceptible to the odd lapse, and his amanuenses were not always accurate in their transcriptions, but it looks as though he amended some extracts to make them more pointed or mould them to his preferred ends. An instance of this can be seen in a quotation from *The Tempest*. Johnson has Caliban say, 'You taught me language, and my profit on't / Is, I know not how to curse: the red plague rid you / For *learning* me your language.' The 'not' is Johnson's addition; Caliban actually says he *does* know how to swear.[7] Perhaps the interpolation was an accident, but it feels deliberate. The *Dictionary* is in part an anthology of literature or at least of literary extracts, and it is, arrestingly, Johnson's anthology, a testament to his critical mode of reading as well as to the range of his erudition.

In his entry under the verb 'to antedate', Johnson quotes the essayist Jeremy Collier: 'By reading, a man does, as it were, *antedate* his life, and makes himself contemporary with the ages past.' It is Johnson's engagement with the past and his revival of a diffuse pot-pourri of materials that make the *Dictionary* such an unexpectedly vibrant work. At the same time, it was his wide and attentive reading that caused him to abandon his initial working methods: it alerted him to what he would come to call 'the exuberance of signification', and led him to practise a more descriptive style of lexicography. His decision to renounce a predetermined system and adopt a more empirical approach, though it caused confusion and resentment at the time, has had a lasting influence.

As Johnson grappled with these problems of method, he was beset by difficulties on every other side. His wife was sick, and spent a good deal of time in lodgings at Hampstead, which was then a tranquil village retreat, popular among exhausted city-dwellers on account of its therapeutic spring waters.★ A maid waited on her, and so did Elizabeth Swynfen, the daughter of Johnson's godfather Samuel. But though his visits were frequent, and would last for several days at a time, he could not relocate to Hampstead. In effect, he was running two households, and shuttling between them – a gentleman's lifestyle he could ill afford.

Meanwhile, the house in Gough Square seemed to be doubling as a convalescence ward for literary London's most indigent specimens. Johnson's capacity for acquiring needy friends was extraordinary. During the years in which he worked on the *Dictionary* his home became a menagerie of eccentrics. His natural charity made him susceptible to the pleas of even the most unworthy supplicants. Sir John Hawkins, with whom Johnson frequently associated at this time, explains how 'The visits of idle, and some of them very worthless persons, were never unwelcome to him; and though they interrupted him in his studies and meditations, yet, as they gave him opportunities of discourse, and furnished him with intelligence, he strove rather to protract than shorten or discountenance them.'[8] The truth, of course, was that these visitors were seldom rewarding company, and in time their presence had the effect of making Johnson uncomfortable under his own roof. Hester Thrale would later suggest that he 'was oftentimes afraid of going home, because he was so sure to be met at the door with numberless complaints'.[9] Increasingly, the temper of his domestic life was jangling and factious, his role in it tiringly remedial.

★ Curiously, under 'esurine' ('corroding; eating') Johnson quotes the following from one of Richard Wiseman's medical tracts: 'Overmuch piercing is the air of Hampstead, in which sort of air there is always something *esurine* and acid.'

No one benefited more from Johnson's charity than the scruffy physician Robert Levet. Hawkins describes him as 'one of the lowest practitioners in the art of healing that ever sought a livelihood by it', and records Johnson's observation that his 'appearance and behaviour . . . disgusted the rich, and terrified the poor'.[10] Boswell, more economically, styles him 'an obscure practiser in physick amongst the lower people'. Levet attended the patients no other doctor would examine; often they could not pay him and offered drink instead – a circumstance that caused Johnson to reflect that Levet was 'perhaps the only man who ever became intoxicated through motives of prudence'. Preternaturally ugly, he had the corrugated features of a man who has repeatedly been trampled by misfortune. But Johnson thought him solid and reliable. When Levet died, more than thirty years later, Johnson memorialized him in verse. 'Obscurely wise, and coarsely kind', he brimmed with 'merit unrefin'd': 'In misery's darkest caverns known, / His useful care was ever nigh.'[11] In these lines Johnson is evidently thinking of Levet's services to the dispossessed, but he too received this coarse kindness and care. However, the price he paid for them was high: as Johnson took in other petitioners, Levet's malodorous presence became increasingly awkward, and even though Levet was able to work he was in no position to contribute to the household finances.

Soon enough, money was a problem. Johnson was no expert in financial management, and his generosity meant that funds slipped through his fingers at an alarming rate. 'I am . . . awkward at counting money,' he would confess, 'but . . . the reason is plain; I have had very little money to count.' There is a romantic image, implicit in the *Life of Savage* and amplified by many of his biographers, of Johnson as a shoeless wretch, dining on other people's leftovers. This is inaccurate. Johnson was not poor, certainly not by the standard he defined in the *Dictionary*, in which 'the poor' are 'those who are in the lowest rank of the community . . . [and] cannot subsist but by the charity of others'. Yet he was never rich. At best, his financial circumstances were sufficient for him to be comfortable, and during the years he spent compiling the *Dictionary* he had enough only to discomfort himself by helping others become less uncomfortable.[12]

Lexicographer

A writer of dictionaries; a harmless drudge, that busies himself in tracing the original and detailing the signification of words

The verb I have most often used of Johnson's work is 'to compile', but he was in a real sense a 'writer of dictionaries'. Much of his time did have to be spent piecing together the fragments he collected in the course of his reading: the garret at Gough Square was not so much a counting house as an assembly line. But Johnson's spirit is imprinted on each page of the finished volumes, and we continually see him straining to impose himself on his materials, to sustain the logic of his choices, to marshal his findings and augment them with his judgement.

For the 'writer of dictionaries', simplicity of definition is paramount. A definition will often be more comprehensive for being made longer, but any gain in precision tends to be offset by the reader's resulting muddlement. From the dictionary-user's point of view, concision equals clarity. The art of definition is the art of balance, of abbreviating without impoverishing. At the same time, a definer has to be sensitive to the multiple meanings of words. Like any good lexicographer, Johnson had to find ways of being succinct without being slight, and of presenting subtle differences in meaning without letting his entries assume monstrous dimensions. Every word posed a new challenge.

Johnson's concept of definition stemmed from three sources. One was Aristotle, who reasoned that definitions should state what words meant, rather than what they didn't mean – a goal easier in principle than practice – and insisted that no definition should contain a word that was not to be found elsewhere in the lexicon. A more recent authority who argued along broadly similar lines was Isaac Watts, a dissenting minister who died not long after Johnson began collecting quotations for the *Dictionary*. One of the books from which Johnson drew many quotations was Watts's *Logick*, first published in 1725. Watts is now best known for his hymns ('O God, our help in ages past', 'Jesus shall reign where'er the sun'), but in the eighteenth century *Logick* was his seminal work, widely used as a primer in schools. Watts proposed that a definition should be 'reciprocal with the thing defined', that it 'must be universal, . . . proper and peculiar to the thing defined, . . . clear and plain . . . [and] short', that 'it must have no tautology in it, nor any words superfluous', and that 'neither the thing defined, nor a mere synonymous name, should make any part of the definition'.[1] Johnson effectively paraphrases this in the Preface, and throughout the *Dictionary* there are quotations from Watts on this very subject.

However, for a sense of language as a human construct – fallible, mutable – Johnson turned to another expert on general principles, John Locke. He consciously echoes Locke when he writes in the Preface that 'I am not yet so lost in lexicography as to forget that words are the daughters of earth, and that things are the sons of heaven.' Locke's *Essay Concerning Human Understanding* (1690) explored the origins and extent of knowledge, the scope of human intelligence, and, importantly for Johnson, the uses and workings of language. Locke's thesis was that words are the names of ideas, not of things, and that there are no innate ideas, but only ones picked up through sensory experience. In Roy Porter's neat summary, 'the mind is not like a furnished flat, prestocked before occupation . . . but like a home put together piecemeal from . . . acquisitions picked up bit by bit'.[2] What was more, Locke argued that dictionary definitions were often confusing, and that some words could not be adequately defined unless a context was provided.

Johnson cites Locke frequently, and many of the quotations deal with problems of a specifically linguistic turn. So for instance Locke is quoted to the effect that 'There is no such way to give defence to absurd doctrines, as to guard them round with legions of obscure and *undefined* words.' 'Now that languages are made, and *abound* with words,' he observes, 'an usual way of getting . . . complex ideas, is by the explication of those terms that stand for them.' Again, 'If the idea be not agreed on betwixt the speaker and hearer, the *argument* is not about things, but names.' Johnson shares Locke's insistence that experience is the basis of reason, as well as his fine insight into the slipperiness of language.[3]

Thanks to the influence of Locke, Johnson's definitions are 'genetic': he maps the evolution of words and their meanings. Around half the words in the *Dictionary* are adjudged to have a single meaning, but those that are not are traced with patient care. Johnson notes in his Preface that 'kindred senses· may be so interwoven, that the perplexity cannot be disentangled'. He invested deeply in the business of disentanglement, and this was why the *Dictionary* became a more laborious undertaking than either he or his backers originally anticipated. 'I like that *muddling* work,' he would say, when asked in old age about the pleasure he appeared to take in some of the more monotonous aspects of lexicography. The muddle, of course, was what he began with: what he left behind was a model of organization.

We can see the basic shape of a Johnsonian definition if we look at the entry for 'derivation'. The first sense Johnson discriminates is 'a draining of water; a turning of its course; letting out'. This can be traced to the Latin *de* ('down from') and *rivus* ('a stream'). Before the word 'derivation' was used in the context of language, it was employed by physicians to talk about the process of draining blood or pus – literally, the 'drawing' of a stream of fluid 'down from' a wound or a cyst. However, despite supplying a medical quotation to illustrate this sense, Johnson deliberately avoids mentioning the word's use in medicine; at this point he is concerned with isolating its root meaning. Only once he has done this does he go on to suggest how the word's range has expanded. The second sense he identifies is '(In grammar.) The tracing of a word from its original'; the words in parentheses locate a particular domain in which the sense applies. The third sense is broader: 'the tracing of any thing from its source'. Finally he identifies the word's meaning among medical practitioners: 'the drawing of a humour from one part of the body to another'. This is slightly different from the first sense, in that it refers to the doctrine of humours – a belief, originating with the Greek theorist Hippocrates, that the body was permeated by four essential substances (blood, phlegm, yellow bile and black bile) which determined its health. Although this sense of the word is very close to its literal meaning, it is understood by Johnson as a piece of specialized termin-ology: esoteric, obscure, and specific to a single profession.

The same pattern can be seen in Johnson's entry for 'flower'. In Nathan Bailey's dictionary there is no definition of the word in the singular, and 'flowers' is defined simply as 'the offspring of plants'. In Johnson, by contrast, the word is considered to have six distinct senses. The first of these is 'the part of a plant which contains the seeds'; this is followed by more than fifty lines of specifically botan-ical information. The senses that follow are: 'an ornament, an embellishment', 'the prime; the flourishing part', 'the edible part of corn; the meal', 'the most excellent or valuable part of any thing; quintessence', and 'that which is most distinguished for any thing valuable'. As in the case of 'derivation', Johnson's method is to move from the most tangible and literal sense of the word to the most abstract, metaphoric or specialized. What we end up with is a geneal-ogy of meaning. This is his customary approach. It suggests that he thought all figurative use of language could be traced back to the literal origins of words. His definitions, structured in this way, chart the role of human needs, enthusiasms and observations in expanding words' semantic range. More generally, they illustrate the way a changing world changes language. Meanings ramify. This logical and historical approach to mapping them has had huge implications for the way we think about language.

Johnson's *Dictionary* differs from its predecessors in the precisely technical nature of many of its definitions. Where necessary, he allows a quotation from a specialist work – such as the *Builder's Dictionary* (1734) or John Harris's *Lexicon Technicum* (1704) – to take the place of a definition of his own contriving. So, for instance, his definition of the noun 'gallop' comes straight from the *Farrier's Dictionary* (1726), and his definition of 'mushroom' is an informative paragraph from the *Gardener's Dictionary* of Philip Miller (1731).

In the past, dictionaries had been less scientific, and definitions often crudely brief. One example historians like to cite is the definition of 'mucus' in John Kersey's *Dictionarium Anglo-Britannicum* (1708) as 'snot or snivel'. Johnson, by contrast, defers to the author-ity of the medic John Quincy, and defines 'mucus' as 'that which flows from the papillary processes through the os cribriforme into the nostrils'. Kersey exemplifies the simplicity of the older dictionaries. He defines 'coffin' as 'a case for a dead body', 'penis' as 'a man's yard', 'eye' as 'the wonderful instrument of sight', 'heart' as 'a most noble part of the body', and 'man' as 'a creature endued with reason'. Johnson does not always improve on these, but consider his opening definition of 'heart': 'The muscle which by its contraction and dilation propels the blood through the course of circulation, and is therefore considered as the source of vital motion. It is supposed in popular language to be the seat sometimes of courage, sometimes of affection.' That's pretty good. And where a writer such as Kersey steers clear of difficult words like 'god', 'health', 'good' and 'soul', Johnson engages eloquently with these intangibles.

In the *Plan*, Johnson shows he is alive to the difficulties and dangers of writing definitions. He observes that 'there is often only one word for one idea; and though it be easy to translate the words *bright*, *sweet*, *salt*, *bitter* into another language, it is not easy to explain them'. He follows Locke in grasping that a handy way of defining certain simple ideas is to identify an object in which the relevant property can be seen. So, for instance, 'red' is 'of the colour of blood', while the adjective 'salt' means 'having the taste of salt: as *salt* fish'. He relies here on his readers' experience: their having seen blood, their having tasted salt fish (or some other salted food). In the same way, the first sense of 'bitter' is 'having a hot, acrid, biting taste, like wormwood', while the first of 'sour' is 'acid; austere; pungent on the palate with astringency, as vinegar, or unripe fruit'. The definition of 'rancid' is 'strong scented', which is supported with a quotation that refers to the rancid smell of fish oil. In each case Johnson invokes his readers' experience.

On the whole, the words it is hardest to define are common, everyday ones. According to the *Guinness Book of Records*, the most succinct word and the hardest to define succinctly is 'mamihlapinatapai', a term in the Fuegian language spoken in southern Argentina. It means, 'Two people looking at one another without speaking; each hoping that the other will offer to do something which both parties desire but neither is willing to do.' However, for all its length, this definition is straightforward; it is much harder to provide a satisfactory definition of 'time' or 'table' or 'identity'. When Henry Watson

Fowler and his brother Frank first edited the *Concise Oxford Dictionary* they noted in their preface that

> One of . . . [its] peculiarities is the large amount of space given to the common words that no one goes through the day without using scores or hundreds of times, often disposed of in a line or two on the ground that they are plain and simple and that everyone knows all about them by the light of nature, but in fact entangled with other words in so many alliances and antipathies during their perpetual knocking about the world that the idiomatic use of them is far from easy.

Verbs are especially difficult. They behave unpredictably. 'Set off' can mean the same thing as 'set out', while 'give up', 'give in' and 'give over' may also be synonyms. For a more extended example, take an everyday verb like 'to put'. In my *COD* its definition occupies almost an entire page, and twenty-two different senses are discriminated. Instinctively, you may think that the essence of *putting* something *somewhere* can be captured in a definition as simple as 'to move, to place'. Yet one has to distinguish precisely between putting something down (suppression) and putting it back (replacement, restoration), putting it over (conveying its significance), and putting it on – you can put on a manner, or a garment, or a light, or value, or weight, or a play. To put something out means to extinguish (a fire) or dislocate (a shoulder joint): to put *someone* out means to irritate or inconvenience, but also to eliminate your opponent from a tournament or render a patient unconscious. Someone who 'puts out' is relaxing his or her virtue. And this is just the beginning. It is the most quotidian words that have the most diverse applications.

Unlike his predecessors, Johnson devoted a great deal of energy to defining these words. He offers sixteen definitions for 'in', and twenty for 'up'; fifteen for the noun 'turn', and fourteen for 'time'. When we look these over, in all their detail, we can momentarily visualize the author hunched at his desk, his shadow pinned against the wall; this is the deep midnight of lexicography, bleared with the dark sweat of drudgework. As Johnson dolefully notes, the combination of verbs with prepositions can have troublesome consequences: some examples 'appear wildly irregular, being so far distant from the sense of the simple words, that no sagacity will be able to trace the steps by which they arrived at the present use'. 'These,' he informs us, 'I have noted with great care' – the sentence masks a huge and exhausting effort on his part. His definition of 'to put' runs to more than three pages in the first edition, and comprises over 5,500 words. The entry for 'to take' occupies five pages and amounts to 8,000 words, with Johnson discriminating 134 different senses of the verb.★ These entries called for a microscopic attention to the subtleties of usage, and for a painfully minute classification of the findings. Fittingly, Johnson supplies sixty-four senses of the verb 'to fall', before conceding, by way of a sixty-fifth, that 'This is one of those general words of which it is very difficult to ascertain or detail the full signification.'

We should not be surprised by this touch of humour, for defining words is a process rich in comic potential. Samuel Butler, author of the satirical novel *Erewhon*, described it as being like cutting steps in a slope made of ice: it is difficult to do, and even once it's done your chances of falling on your behind are approximately 100 per cent. While we are in the realm of comedy, it is worth recalling that one of the best and best-known episodes of the historical sitcom *Blackadder*, entitled 'Ink and Incapability', confronts this very subject. Its fidelity to history is limited (Jane Austen is Johnson's contemporary, and apparently has 'a beard like a rhododendron'), but its representation of the perils of lexicography is just.

The episode begins with Blackadder's master, Prince George, a young man 'as thick as a whale omelette', considering the merits of becoming Johnson's patron. He invites the great lexicographer to show him his handiwork. Unfortunately, Blackadder's dogsbody, Baldrick, uses Johnson's sole manuscript of the *Dictionary* to stoke a fire. Blackadder decides that the only reasonable course of action is to compile a new dictionary himself and hope Johnson doesn't notice. He struggles, however, to get past 'aardvark' – 'Medium-sized insectivore with protruding nasal implement'. A repentant Baldrick is on hand with some characteristically hopeless suggestions. 'C', he suggests, is a 'big blue wobbly thing that mermaids live in'. Blackadder is unamused. Baldrick tries out another of his efforts: 'I'm

---

★ In the first edition of the *OED* there were 341 separate senses.

quite pleased with "dog",' he says, pausing before supplying his definition – 'Not a cat'.

Droll this may be, but it points up two salient truths: it is hard to define complex phenomena without resorting to unhelpfully complicated terminology, and it is customary, because of the inherently differential nature of language, to phrase definitions in oppositional terms. When we want to tell our friends what something is like, we often tell them what it isn't. As Aristotle implied, capturing the essence of what something *is* proves altogether more difficult. So, for instance, among the ten senses Johnson gives of 'sweet' are 'not salt', 'not sour' and 'not stale; not stinking'. 'Cold' means 'not hot', 'low' means 'not high', and 'poor' means 'not rich'. All these words are more fully explained, but it is interesting to note Johnson's recourse to such methods.

As we have seen, however, Johnson's method of definition begins with etymology, and the title page announces that in what follows 'the words are deduced from their originals'. Long before Ralph Waldo Emerson noted that language is fossil poetry, Johnson saw that the etymology of every word, however commonplace the word itself, contains the gleam of a more lustrous past. Etymology is perennially fascinating because it revives the forgotten poetry of the everyday. While Johnson's modified approach to compiling the *Dictionary* meant that for many words he gave details of senses that diverged sharply from their etymological roots, he never abjured his use of what he understood to be the origins of words – their 'radical primitives' – as starting points in tracing their evolving meanings.

In the *Plan* Johnson reflects that 'our language . . . now stands in our dictionaries a confused heap of words . . . without relation'. Etymology is the key to remedying this. He wonders 'who . . . can forbear to wish, that these fundamental atoms of our speech might obtain the firmness and immutability of the primogenial and constituent particles of matter . . . ?' The question is playful: Johnson knows that 'this is a privilege which words are scarcely to expect', since 'language is the work of man, a being from whom permanence and stability cannot be derived'. He hopes to locate the etymologies of words in order to identify their root meanings, and to endow his readers with a full awareness of these roots, but he knows that he is a surveyor of language, not a physicist co-ordinating its microscopic particles. He concedes that 'This search [for etymologies] will give occasion to many curious disquisitions, and sometimes, perhaps, to conjectures, which to readers unacquainted with this kind of study, cannot but appear improbable and capricious.' The range of English borrowings from other languages means that his task is hard. He portrays the labours of the etymologist in whimsical terms: 'in search of the progenitors of our speech, we may wander from the tropick to the frozen zone, and find some in the valleys of Palestine, and some upon the rocks of Norway'.

Johnson's rather misty talk of wandering and conjecture reminds us that in the first half of the eighteenth century etymology was not an established science. The first English lexicon to contain etymologies was Sir Thomas Blount's *Glossographia* (1656), but etymology was not systematized until the nineteenth century, when it was transfigured by the work of scholars such as August Fick and Friedrich Kluge, and even in the first edition of the *OED* many of the etymologies were wayward and old-fashioned. Johnson's efforts in the field have often been disparaged – Macaulay pronounced him a 'wretched' etymologist, and even Boswell conceded that they were 'not . . . entitled to the first praise' – but he had limited resources at his disposal, and the only direct help he had was from an Anglican bishop, Zachary Pearce, who sent him twenty suggestions in the post.

The first thing we notice about the *Dictionary*'s etymologies is that they tend to be brief. This squares with Johnson's observation in the *Plan* that 'our etymologists seem to have been too lavish of their learning'. He believed that this part of a lexicographer's work should be lucid and pithy. 'When the word is easily deduced from a Saxon original,' he says, 'I shall not often enquire further.' It is a principle to which he sticks. He is brisk to acknowledge the Teutonic roots of English, and where his etymologies are not straightforward it is because a word's origins have been smothered in controversy.[4]

When William Adams asked him how he planned to trace the roots of words, Johnson's answer was disarmingly brief: 'Why, Sir, here is a shelf with Junius, and Skinner, and others; and there is a Welsh gentleman who has published a collection of Welsh proverbs who will help me with the Welsh.' True to this, his main sources are Stephen

Skinner, a Lincolnshire doctor whose etymological dictionary was published posthumously in 1671, and Francis Junius, a Franco-Dutch philologist whose life's research was published – also posthumously – in 1743. The Welsh gentleman seems to have played his part too: Johnson readily identifies such words as 'bastard', 'flannel' and 'skirmish' as having Welsh roots, though it is not clear on whose authority he does so. As he hinted to Adams, he also invokes a good number of other authorities – an assortment of now murky figures including John Minshew, Thomas Henshaw, Gilles Menage, and the wonderfully named Meric Casaubon and Richard Rowlands Verstegan.★ He is also not above nabbing a small number of etymologies from Nathan Bailey's rival dictionary, and on one occasion even states that 'curmudgeon' is a corruption of the French *cœur méchant*, on the strength of a letter from 'an unknown correspondent' – a statement which caused a later lexicographer, John Ash, to claim the word came from *cœur* ('unknown') and *méchant* ('correspondent').

Although Johnson readily cites these authorities, and compacts their often extensive findings into manageable parcels of information, he is not content to regurgitate them uncritically, and there are times when he presents a version of an etymology while making it clear that he does not endorse it. For instance, Skinner offers several hundred words on the etymologies of 'brawn' and 'admiral'; Johnson casually says they are 'of uncertain etymology'. Skinner derives 'to award' from the Saxon *weard* ('towards'), but Johnson feels he does so 'somewhat improbably'. He even criticizes Skinner's classical etymology of 'ferry', explaining a little theatrically – and not quite truthfully – that 'I do not love Latin originals.' Junius is accorded similarly sceptical treatment. A measure of Johnson's modest opinion of Junius's abilities is the assessment that his etymology of 'peevish' has 'more reason than he commonly discovers'. In the Preface Johnson disparages both men. Skinner is 'often ignorant, but never ridiculous', while Junius is 'full of knowledge', though 'his variety distracts his judgement, and his learning is very frequently disgraced by his absurdities'.

★ Richard Rowlands took the name Verstegan in order to make himself sound more Teutonic, and his philology displays a taste for all things German.

At least Johnson has a modicum of respect for these two. The prolific Casaubon is routinely trashed. Dismissed as a 'dreamer' for his Greek etymology of the verb 'to prowl', he either 'trifles . . . contemptibly' (in the case of 'spruce') or theorizes 'with more ingenuity than truth' (in the case of 'dream'). It comes as no surprise when Johnson assures us that 'to scamble' – a word 'scarcely in use' – has 'much exercised the sagacity of Meric Casaubon; but, as is usual, to no purpose'. Robert DeMaria and Gwin Kolb suggest it may well have been Johnson who inspired George Eliot to give the name Casaubon to the dry, pedantic clergyman in *Middlemarch*.[5] This looks plausible: at one point Eliot writes that Casaubon's scientific theories 'floated among flexible conjectures no more solid than those etymologies which seemed strong because of likeness in sound until it was shown that likeness in sound made them impossible'.

It seems odd that Johnson should bother to cite a source he holds in so little esteem, but his method of definition means that a suspect etymology is better than none at all. Sometimes he pays excessive homage to the roots of words. Under 'etymology' he quotes Jeremy Collier: 'When words are restrained, by common usage, to a particular sense, to run up to *etymology* . . . is wretchedly ridiculous.' Yet there are moments when Johnson does exactly that. He tells us that 'to thrash' is better than 'to thresh' – in the sense of beating corn from the chaff – because it is 'agreeable to etymology'. A 'journal' is 'any paper published daily', despite his own experience of journals that weren't daily. Occasionally he insists on a meaning that barely exists simply so as to enforce a strict sense of etymological correctness. For example, a 'terrier' is 'a dog that follows his game under ground', because it comes from the Latin word for 'ground', *terra*. The first sense of 'candid' is 'white', because this accords with its Latin root *candidus*, even though, as Johnson admits, 'This sense is very rare.' For the same reason an 'insult' is 'the act of jumping upon any thing' before it is an 'act or speech of insolence or contempt': *insultare* is the Latin for 'to leap on' or 'to trample'.

As if to license these fussy spurts of Latinism, the *Dictionary* frequently reminds its readers that etymology is no easy business. Johnson shows that even the best authorities can come up with wildly differing explanations, and more than once he quotes Isaac Watts's comment that 'the original derivation of words is oftentimes very dark'. Sometimes no one is convincing. Under 'gun' Johnson says that 'of this word there is no satisfactory etymology', while 'to smell' has a 'very obscure' etymology, and of 'pish' and 'pshaw' (each 'a contemptuous exclamation', and the sort of thing Johnson might have come across while dipping into the *Spectator*) he admits, 'I know not their etymology, and imagine them formed by chance.' Sometimes he is quietly sceptical about received opinion. For example, we can hear a note of doubt in his report that the word 'porcelain' is 'said to be derived from *pour cent années*; because it was believed by Europeans, that the materials of *porcelain* was matured under ground one hundred years'. In fact it comes from the Italian word *porcellana*, meaning 'cowrie shell' – a diminutive derived from the Latin *porcus* ('pig'), as the cowrie has commonly been thought to resemble a pig's back.

When the experts disappoint, Johnson shows himself perfectly capable of independent judgement.★ Thus his remarks on the adjective 'wicked': 'Of this common word the etymology is very obscure: *wicca*, is *an enchanter*; *waeccan*, is *to oppress*; *wirian*, *to curse*; *wiccd*, is *crooked*: all these however Skinner rejects for *vitiatus*, Latin. Perhaps it is a compound of *wic, vile, bad*, and *head, malum caput.*'

He is briefer in most other cases, but we can find plenty of evidence of his faith in his own skills. 'Bombast', he explains, is derived from 'Bombastius', which was one of the names of the sixteenth-century alchemist Paracelsus, whom he describes as 'a man remarkable for . . . unintelligible language'. In similar mood he informs us that 'gibberish' is 'probably derived from the chymical cant, and originally implied the jargon of *Geber* and his tribe' – a reference to

---

★ Crucial here was Johnson's knowledge of languages. This was strong rather than formidable. He understood Latin and Greek, French and Italian, a modest amount of Dutch and Spanish, and a rather smaller amount of Hebrew. He wrote Latin and French fluently. This is impressive, but a modest stock of learning compared to the twenty languages spoken by James Murray, or to the achievements of Johnson's friend Sir William Jones, who is reckoned in the *Dictionary of National Biography* 'to have known thirteen languages thoroughly and twenty-eight fairly well'. Johnson would have admired such accomplishments. He was perennially keen to learn foreign tongues, in order to get to grips with their literatures, and his knowledge was enough to qualify him to etymologize independently.

another alchemist, this time eighth-century, who was notorious for his enigmatic jargon. He believes 'sillabub' comes from the Old English *esil a bouc*, meaning 'vinegar for the mouth'. 'Caterpillar' seems 'easily deducible' from 'cates' (meaning 'food') and the French verb *piller* ('to rob'). As it happens, all four explanations now look doubtful: 'bombast' comes from the Greek *bombyx* ('silkworm') and from the association between puffed-up language and fluffed-up fabric; 'gibberish' is onomatopoeic; 'sillabub' is probably an English rendering of an Arabic list of the dish's contents; and 'caterpillar' derives from the Old French *chatepelose* ('hairy cat'). But our reservations take wing only when we read his etymology of 'spider': 'May not *spider* be *spy dor*, the insect that watches the *dor*?' To this hopeful question we may very comfortably answer no.[6]

Sometimes etymologies that sound risible turn out to be accurate. 'Avocado' comes from the Aztec *ahuacatl* (meaning 'testicle'); the strange-looking word 'teetotal' has its origins in the 't-t-total' abstinence of a stammering Lancashire temperance activist in the 1830s; and Johnson's beloved punch takes its name not from its punitive effect on the brain, but from the Sanskrit *panca*, meaning 'five' (the drink's standard number of ingredients). Unsurprisingly, none of these explanations appears in the *Dictionary*, but some of Johnson's etymologies are, after much the same fashion, both improbable and legitimate. For instance, he suggests that 'muckender', a slang term for a handkerchief, is a corruption of the French *mouchoir*. A more obvious explanation comes to mind; dextrous use of a handkerchief ends nasal muckiness. But the existence of the Spanish word *mocador* indicates that there may be something in Johnson's claim. He also believes that 'tennis' comes from the French *tenez* ('take it'). This dubious explanation turns out, on closer investigation, to be well founded, since early players – of 'real' tennis, not modern lawn tennis – apparently called out this word to alert the receiver that they were about to serve.

Reading over these etymologies, we have to imagine Johnson caught in a web of conflicting conjectures, struggling to break free. As he would ruefully observe in the Preface to his finished volumes, 'a whole life cannot be spent upon syntax and etymology, and . . . even a whole life would not be sufficient'. We have here a glancing hint at exactly what kind of occupation Johnson had in mind when he pictured the archetypal maker of dictionaries as a 'harmless drudge'.[7] In the Preface he reveals that 'When I had . . . enquired into the original of words, I resolved to show likewise my attention to things; to pierce deep into every science, to enquire after the nature of every substance of which I inserted the name, to limit every idea by a definition strictly logical.' Such ambitions were thwarted by the difficulties of executing even the most pedestrian parts of the task. His early aspirations were, he would ultimately reflect, 'the dreams of a poet doomed at last to wake a lexicographer'. A decade of toil and half a lifetime of disappointments are compressed in those dozen words.

Library

A large collection of books, public or private

> Then as they 'gan his *library* to view,
> And antique registers for to avise,
> There chanced to the prince's hand to rise
> An ancient book, hight Britain's monuments
> – Spenser, *The Faerie Queene* (1590–96)

A vital part of Johnson's enterprise, and his most important innovation as a lexicographer, was his decision to include quotations to illustrate the words he defined.* The self-imposed requirement that recorded usage support his definitions suggests a lawyer's voracity for precedent. At the same time, the quotations eloquently convey the complex feelings associated with words, and supplement the information contained in his own explanations of their meaning.

Johnson was not in fact the first to use quotations for this purpose. The practice had originated with a group of sixteenth-century Continental lexicographers – most notably the Lutheran schoolmaster Basilius Faber – whose works he had encountered while cataloguing the Harleian library. It had already been adopted by several authors of English legal texts. Nevertheless, Johnson was the first English lexicographer to provide illustrations of this kind, and the illustrative material is one of the *Dictionary*'s great strengths. Instead of stating dogmatically what words meant, he adduced evidence of their meaning. An incidental effect of this empirical method was that it hinted at both Johnson's tastes and those of his age. The *Dictionary* creates a canon of treasurable English authors, and anthologizes their writings in a giant commonplace book.

---

* There are no pictorial illustrations in the *Dictionary*. The first English dictionary to contain pictures was Blount's *Glossographia*, and the first lexicographer to make extensive use of them was Nathan Bailey. Although this type of illustration was recommended by Locke, Johnson deliberately avoided it.

The selection of authors was a delicate business. Modern readers will consider many of the authors from whom Johnson quotes extensively to be unsurprising choices, and few of Johnson's contemporaries can have been startled by the copious citations of Shakespeare, Milton, Dryden or Pope. In the Preface he states his conviction that

> From the authors which rose in the time of Elizabeth, a speech might be formed adequate to all the purposes of use and elegance. If the language of theology were extracted from Hooker and the translation of the Bible; the terms of natural knowledge from Bacon; the phrases of policy, war, and navigation from Raleigh; the dialect of poetry and fiction from Spenser and Sidney; and the diction of common life from Shakespeare, few ideas would be lost to mankind for want of English words in which they might be expressed.

The first sentence is arresting: it indicates Johnson's belief – which we are less certain to share today – that English enjoyed a sort of Golden Age.★ The second does not on the whole strike the modern reader as strange, though it is a little curious that Johnson should profess to find in Shakespeare what he calls 'the diction of common life'. There were, after all, more obvious reasons for using Shakespeare: the attractiveness of his artistry, the force and originality of his imagery. However, a decade later, in his *Preface to Shakespeare*, Johnson maintained that one of the dramatist's virtues was his representation of a kind of speech 'above grossness and below refinement', used 'among those who speak only to be understood, without ambition or elegance'. This was the language of 'the common intercourse of life'. To the busy lexicographer, Shakespeare was a valuable source of the ordinary, at least as much as of the ornate.

While the passage I have quoted identifies some of Johnson's preferred sources, it also suggests why he had to look beyond these favoured authors in order to find what he needed. Theology, 'natural knowledge', policy, war, navigation, poetry, fiction and everyday speech may be important and sizeable lexical fields, but a dictionary worth the name needs to embrace the lexis of many other spheres.

★ It is worth comparing this with the opening sentence of Johnson's 1756 *Introduction to the Political State of Great Britain*, which reads, 'The present system of English politics may properly be said to have taken rise in the reign of Queen Elizabeth.'

The fact that the *Dictionary* quotes not just these few authors, but also some 500 others, reflects the essential inclusiveness of Johnson's work. He selected illustrations from poetry, drama and novels, from the Bible and the literature of divinity, from lawyers and antiquarians, from historians and politicians, from philosophy and physics, from educational primers and medical works.

Partly for reasons of personal taste, partly to keep his research from becoming unmanageably diffuse, and partly to save himself having to purchase or borrow too many expensive volumes, Johnson imposed historical limits on his reading. 'I set myself Sidney's work for the boundary, beyond which I make few excursions': Sir Philip Sidney's major work, the *Arcadia*, was published in 1581. Johnson also states that 'My purpose was to admit no testimony of living authors, that I might not be misled by partiality, and that none of my contemporaries might have reason to complain.' 'Nor have I departed from this resolution,' he continues, 'but when some performance of uncommon excellence excited my veneration' – or when recent literature could supply an 'example that was wanting', or when 'my heart, in the tenderness of friendship, solicited admission for a favourite name'. We infer, then, that there will be no *Piers Plowman* or *Morte d'Arthur*, no *Beowulf* or Venerable Bede, because all pre-date Sidney, and that there will be very little from popular contemporary works like *Tom Jones* or the poems of Thomas Gray.

Johnson fosters an image of English as a self-sufficient resource. 'I have studiously endeavoured', he writes, 'to collect examples and authorities from the writers before the Restoration, whose works I regard as *the wells of English undefiled*.' He borrows this phrase from Spenser, who esteemed Chaucer as a source of purity and spoke of him in just such terms. In his reference to these repositories of 'undefiled' language, Johnson is implicitly criticizing the recent, modish assimilation of foreign words, while his emphasis on the need for purity is inherited from his favourite Renaissance humanists. By invoking these authorities, he legitimizes what is unmistakably a form of nationalism.

These were Johnson's principles, but he was not afraid to deviate from them. In the *Dictionary* there is a small but noticeable contingent of quotations from sources earlier than Sidney: Chaucer, Sir

Thomas More, the poet Thomas Tusser, the educationalist Roger Ascham, who had been tutor to Queen Elizabeth, and even, once, a thirteenth-century bishop and commentator on Aristotle, Robert Grosseteste. There is also a smattering of material from living authors, or authors who were alive at the point when Johnson chose to include samples of their work.

For technical detail Johnson draws, quite reasonably, on several up-to-date contemporary authorities, such as the botanist Philip Miller and the philologist Edward Lye. At the same time, it is clear that the 'tenderness of friendship' played its part. Among the cited living authors we find Robert Dodsley, Johnson's sometime doctor Richard Mead, and another friend, the 'little spitfire' Hester Mulso. He plundered material from an indexed concordance to the 'moral and instructive sentiments' in *Clarissa*, the masterpiece of his friend and occasional benefactor Samuel Richardson, and used the novel as a kind of conduct book, extracting for instance the axiom that 'A man who is gross in a woman's company, ought to be *knocked down* with a club.' Elsewhere, we can detect loyalty to his home town in his decision to cite Richard Gifford, a minor poet who had Lichfield associations, and Thomas Newton, a native of Lichfield who edited and annotated *Paradise Lost*.★

Johnson's decision to quote these authors enlivens the *Dictionary*, lending it a warm air of sociability. Another he quotes in this vein is Charlotte Lennox, to whom he served as an informal patron. Mrs Lennox was a colourful figure, the daughter of an army officer from New York State, married to one of Strahan's penurious employees, and a self-professed expert on the art of coquetry. When her first book was published, while the *Dictionary* was in progress, Johnson insisted on a lavish celebration at the Devil Tavern (a hostelry known for its bold sign depicting St Dunstan grabbing the Devil by the nose with a pair of tongs). He, Mrs Lennox and a party of friends com-

---

★ Johnson's veneration of the city where he was born has already been evidenced, and there are several references to his birthplace in the illustrative material. Furthermore, he explains that the word 'minster' is 'yet retained at York and Lichfield', while the word 'shaw' can mean 'a thicket; a small wood' and a 'tuft of trees near Lichfield is called Gentle *shaw*'.

memorated the event by staying up eating hot apple pie – although presumably it was cold apple pie by the time they finished, at eight o'clock in the morning. In the *Dictionary* his tribute consists of eight quotations, all for words in the second half of the alphabet, from *The Female Quixote* (1752), a novel to which he contributed not only the dedication but also, very probably, the ending.

As if this were not enough, he even directly quotes himself. Extracts from his writings appear thirty-three times in the *Dictionary*. Some are labelled; others are attributed to 'Anonymous'; and one of the quotations he labels as his own is actually from Pope's *Essay on Man*. Finally, in a few instances the 'anonymous' quotations are simply sentences Johnson made up on the spur of the moment.[1]

Johnson's quoting from living sources reflects the extempore nature of his work. The inclusion of Richardson was premeditated, but the use of snippets from *The Female Quixote* or Jane Collier's *Art of Ingeniously Tormenting* (a spoof conduct book published in 1753) seems likely to have been prompted simply by his day-to-day reading. He broke off from his labours on the *Dictionary* to peruse some curious new publication, chanced on a necessary word well used, and chose to add the relevant passage to his cache of quotations. Moreover, there were times when he simply quoted from memory. The inaccuracy of some of the quotations from Shakespeare, the Bible and even his own writings suggests that he did not have the relevant texts in front of him as he added the passages to his stock.

The selection of authorities is, however, largely consistent with the principle that they should give 'pleasure or instruction, by conveying some elegance of language, or some precept of prudence, or piety'. The writers chosen as authorities for the *Dictionary* were to be looked on not merely as convenient sources of illustration. They were, in addition, to be exemplars in matters of morality, scholarship, everyday wisdom, and literary value. The emphasis on prudence and piety is evident in Johnson's heavy use of educational and religious texts. For instance, nearly a fiftieth of the quotations are taken from Robert South, a cleric known for his powerful and sometimes gruff sermons (Johnson would eventually regret their 'violence' and 'coarseness'). A similar number come from Richard Hooker's seminal defence of Anglicanism, *Of the Laws of Ecclesiastical Polity*. There are many illustrations, too, from the Book of Common Prayer, and many from a group of writers usually referred to as the 'physico-theologians'. These latter were seventeenth-century natural philosophers whose scientific interests were calculated not to discredit the existence of God, but to exalt and magnify his works. Johnson's favourite among them is John Ray, who is chiefly represented by his resplendently titled *The Wisdom of God Manifested in the Works of Creation*.

Many of the educational works were the standard texts of the day – the sort of books Johnson had encountered in the schoolroom, both as pupil and as pedagogue, or items like Ascham's *Scholemaster* (1570), a volume 'specially prepared for the private bringing up of youth'. One educationalist he cites generously is George Cheyne, the contemporary diet guru whose successful reduction of his thirty-four-stone bulk encouraged him to talk up the merits of ritual vomiting. Here he appears in his capacity as a moralist: Johnson quotes his *Philosophical Principles of Religion*, a manual for 'younger students of philosophy'.

Yet the pious and educative thoughts of Cheyne, Ray and Hooker share space with a good deal of less weighty material. For instance, Johnson quotes dozens of times from *The Memoirs of Martinus Scriblerus* (1741), a scurrilous burlesque, written mostly by John Arbuthnot, that poked fun at Grub Street twittishness. He chose this indelicate item because it was a source of interesting words like 'chicanery', 'confidant', 'troglodyte' and 'piazza', and even the distinctly modern-sounding 'skylight'. Another lightweight source from which Johnson quotes liberally is the poet Matthew Prior, a fluent documentarist of human failings. Prior's predominantly comic verse furnishes Johnson with illustrations of many kinds of language, and is his sole source of examples for words such as 'bagatelle', 'go-cart', 'slapdash' and 'vermicelli'('a paste rolled and broken in the form of worms').

For all the usefulness of these authors, however, it is to the more exalted names that Johnson turns most frequently. In the *Plan* he stated his preference for 'writers of the first reputation'. True to this, he cites Shakespeare profusely, quoting from all the plays that were at that time considered to be his, with *As You Like It* the one most heavily quoted in relation to its size. He used William Warburton's recently published edition, although very occasionally he preferred the earlier edition of Lewis Theobald where its text seemed to make better sense.[2] Among the other authors he cites most freely are Dryden, Milton and Pope, along with Addison, Bacon, Swift, Locke and Sidney. There are an imposing 4,617 quotations from the Authorized Version of the Bible; about two-thirds of these are from the Old Testament, but there is a generous sprinkling from the New Testament and the Apocrypha.[3]

Still, it is the range of the *Dictionary*'s quotations that strikes anyone who examines it. Plenty of the authors Johnson cites copiously are scarcely known today. How many readers of this book could claim to be familiar with Richard Carew's *Survey of Cornwall*, Richard Knolles's *History of the Turks* (the style of which Johnson considered 'pure, nervous, elevated, and clear') or Samuel Daniel's poetic account of the war between the English houses of Lancaster and York? What about the 'water poet' John Taylor, who earned his living ferrying travellers along the Thames, or the clerics George Smalridge and Jeremiah Seed, or John Graunt, a London haberdasher who wrote a series of reflections on the bills of mortality during an outbreak of bubonic plague? Or, for that matter, the *Discourse of Tangiers under the Government of Earl Tiviot* that was written by Joseph Addison's father, Lancelot, sometime dean of Lichfield? Or Thomas Coryate, whom Johnson refers to by his nickname Furcifer, on account of his having alleged he was the first Englishman to eat using a fork?

Johnson includes all these and many others equally obscure. Yet he was not beyond omitting certain authors whose writings would have been favoured by others. There are not many women writers, for instance, and several popular Elizabethans are left out – notably Christopher Marlowe, who was then little known. He omitted the politician and philosopher Henry St John, Viscount Bolingbroke, on the grounds that his philosophy was impious and his English tainted with terms borrowed from French.[4] Nor do we find Thomas Hobbes, the latitudinarian divines Samuel Clarke and Isaac Barrow, Bernard Mandeville, social theorist and advocate of egoism or Anthony Ashley Cooper, third earl of Shaftesbury. All had published important books: all were in some way obnoxious to Johnson's taste. Clarke was a writer whom he admired, but was probably left out because his views on the Holy Trinity were controversial. The same was true of Barrow. Hobbes, Mandeville and Shaftesbury were denied space because Johnson was reluctant to ascribe any kind of authority to them. He later told Hester Thrale that he would never cite 'any wicked writer's authority for a word, lest it should send people to look in a book that might injure them for ever'.[5] In his eyes Hobbes, who had savaged the Church in *Leviathan* (1651), was unambiguously wicked, and excluding him was a pleasure. He told his friend Thomas Tyers that he had 'scorned' to quote Hobbes 'because I did not like his principles'.[6] Among the texts he did cite, however, was John Bramhall's 1658 *Castigations of Mr Hobbes*, a book now known, if at all, for having been praised by T. S. Eliot.

For all his studied omissions, Johnson was felt to have been too catholic in his tastes. When the *Dictionary* was published, he enquired of Garrick what people thought of it. His one-time pupil told him, censoriously, that they were shocked by the inclusion of authors 'beneath the dignity of such a work'. One of those who apparently fell into this category was Samuel Richardson – a mere novelist! Johnson could not help but be amused by Garrick's rather pompous complaint, observing: 'Nay, I have done worse than that: I have cited *thee*, David.'

The wide range of quoted authors and the breadth of material they provide combine, as I have suggested, to make the *Dictionary* more than just a lexicon. The semiotician Umberto Eco has argued, with his customary brio, that dictionaries are 'impoverished encyclopaedias', and that every dictionary is an encyclopedia in disguise.[7] His claim is suggestive: dictionaries are fraught with submerged ideas, narratives and histories. Johnson's is no exception. It offers no overarching system of knowledge, but it is a literary anthology, a compendium of quotable nuggets, and a mine of information – some trivial, some considerable – on subjects as diverse as heraldry and hunting, rhetoric and pharmacy, oracles and literary style, the zodiac and magic, law and mathematics, ignorance and politics, the art of conversation and the benefits of reading. Capitalizing on Eco's position, Robert DeMaria has argued persuasively that 'playing postman or note-taking student with [it] . . . is a way of recovering the encyclopedic tendency . . . that the alphabetical arrangement of the material obscures'.[8]

Clearly, the quotations that appear in the *Dictionary* are presented out of context, and it is in the nature of a dictionary that it cannot offer thematic consistency. While there are themes that appear to run through the entire work, Johnson almost always tries to record the diversity of experience and opinion. Though there are authors he refuses to accommodate, there are few kinds of thinking that do not find a space somewhere within its pages. A dictionary is a collection of fragments, and one should recognize that the quotations are unlikely to embody Johnson's views, because their multifariousness ensures that just about any reading of the *Dictionary*'s overall orientation can be undercut by a reading that is diametrically opposed to it. Equally, as Johnson acknowledges, 'it may sometimes happen, by hasty detruncation, that the general tendency of the sentence may be changed: the divine may desert his tenets, or the philosopher his system'. Yet, having conceded all of this, it is still possible to see patterns in his deployment of particular authors and particular works, as well as in the kinds of learning and information he seems to privilege.

In the Preface he mentions that he has occasionally exhibited 'a genealogy of sentiments, by showing how one author copied the thoughts and diction of another'. The result of this is 'a kind of intellectual history'. The phrase is a remarkable one, for the discipline that academics now label 'intellectual history' was then unknown. Although Johnson means rather less by it than a modern intellectual historian might, it is significant that he imagines his work having this dimension. There are also, he suggests, 'innumerable passages selected with propriety' – 'some shining with sparks of imagination, and some replete with treasures of wisdom'. In making such a claim, he asserts the encyclopedic qualities of his work. The appeal of his *Dictionary* lies to no small degree in this transcendence of a merely mechanical kind of lexicography.

Melancholy

1. 'A disease, supposed to proceed from a redundance of black bile; but it is better known to arise from too heavy and too viscid a blood: its cure is in evacuation, nervous medicines, and powerful stimuli' – John Quincy

2. A kind of madness, in which the mind is always fixed on one object

3. A gloomy, pensive, discontented temper

> This *melancholy* flatters, but unmans you;
> What is it else but penury of soul,
> A lazy frost, a numbness of the mind? – Dryden

At the same time as he was collecting his store of illustrations, Johnson was busy with other projects. His published writings of the period share the moral gravity so important to the *Dictionary*. In 1748 he composed a preface for Dodsley's *Preceptor*, a new educational textbook aimed at adolescents. He also contributed an allegorical essay, entitled 'The Vision of Theodore, the Hermit of Tenerife'. This dream vision was calculated, like the *Dictionary*, to instil in readers the understanding that education can achieve real inspiration only when it is bolstered by religion. Johnson reportedly thought it the best thing he ever wrote, although at this remove it is hard to agree. If this is partly because we no longer equate Tenerife – as Johnson did – with Homer's Elysian Fields, it is also because the tone of the work, despite occasional flickers of irony, seems thuddingly prosaic. Much the most distinctive feature is its fascination with mankind's insidious habits; the author advises students not to lapse into indolence, lest they become slaves to melancholy.

A deeper *Weltschmerz* runs through his poem *The Vanity of Human Wishes*, which Dodsley printed in January of the following year. It was the first substantial published work of Johnson's to have his name on the title page. Anticipation of the *Dictionary* had made his name more familiar to the book-buying public, and Dodsley wished to raise his profile further. Deliberately aimed at a broader readership than Johnson's previous writings, *The Vanity of Human Wishes* is none the less a testament both to his classical influences and to his personal distress. Garrick justly commented that it was 'as hard as Greek'. Now and then in the poem there are clear notes of autobiography. Johnson speaks of 'anxious toil' and 'buried merit', the 'opiate fumes' of sloth, and 'lacerated friendship'. In an explicit reference to his work on the *Dictionary* he identifies 'what ills the scholar's life assail': 'Toil, envy, want, the garret, and the jail'. The last of these was always a genuine possibility: it was common for people owing even modest debts to be incarcerated, and several writers known to Johnson had suffered this fate – the most memorable example being his dissolute friend Savage.

But in February 1749 Johnson was liberated from toil and want, at least briefly, when his play *Irene* was performed for the first time, at the Drury Lane Theatre. This was accomplished through the influence of Garrick, who had recently become the theatre's manager. Johnson attended rehearsals, and enjoyed the 'sprightly chit-chat' of the Green Room, but eventually told Garrick that he would have to stay away, since 'the white bubbies and the silk stockings of your actresses excite my genitals' – words that were toned down by Boswell, who didn't like the idea of Johnson having anything more palpable than 'amorous propensities'. In due course, the production opened, and ran for nine nights; the cheapest seats were a shilling, the dearest were five. The cast included not just Garrick – lively and naturalistic – but several of the most distinguished actresses of the day; the title role was taken by Hannah Pritchard, a brilliantly versatile performer later famous for her Lady Macbeth. Nevertheless, *Irene* met with only limited public enthusiasm. Asked how he felt about this, Johnson replied, 'Like the Monument': presumably he meant he was unmoved.

In truth, it is easy to see why the play was not a triumph. Set in Constantinople in the fifteenth century, it deals with the turbulent relationship between Sultan Mahomet II and his mistress, a young Greek woman. The subject matter, adapted from Knolles's *History of the Turks*, is not devoid of promise, but to London audiences its treatment seemed hopelessly old-fashioned. It strikes the modern reader as neither atmospheric nor engaging – perhaps one should expect this, given Johnson's *Dictionary* definition of 'drama' as 'a poem accommodated to action'. The didactic moral flavour of the play is cloying; the language is costive – feelings are described, not conveyed – and as theatre it seems exorbitant yet flimsy. Matters were not improved on the first night by Garrick's suggestion that Mrs Pritchard, as Irene, speak her last two lines while being (fatally) strangled with a bowstring. When the crucial moment came, Mrs Pritchard was unable to choke out her lines, and the audience heckled her with cries of 'Murder! Murder!'

Such embarrassments notwithstanding, the production afforded Johnson a break from his labours. He attended the opening, without the ailing Tetty, in an uncharacteristically bold outfit that included a scarlet waistcoat and a gold-braided hat. The extravagance was feasible: the play's receipts were not spectacular, but Johnson took as his share £195. 17s., and in September he was paid a further £100 by Dodsley for the right to publish the text.

After the play's run had ended, however, he had to return to the closet routines of lexicography. The regression was painful. His days were heavy, his nights restless. He associated the house at Gough Square with his exertions on the *Dictionary*, and found it hard to sleep there. He was often lonely. In April we find him writing to James Elphinston, a Scottish educationalist who happened also to be the brother-in-law of William Strahan, and referring to his 'recluse kind of life'. On 12 July he writes to Lucy Porter, owning that he has been ill and 'often out of order of late, and have very much neglected my affairs'. Tetty, too, is 'very weak'.[1]

He made a point of engineering pleasurable distractions. That winter he formed a club (he would define the word as 'an assembly of good fellows, meeting under certain conditions'). It convened every Tuesday at the King's Head, a steakhouse in Ivy Lane, near St Paul's. Besides Sir John Hawkins, its members included Edmond Barker and Richard Bathurst, both physicians, an amiable Scottish doctor called William McGhie, the bookseller John Payne, Samuel Salter, an antique clergyman notable chiefly for being very tall, a writer called Samuel Dyer, whom Hawkins describes as 'a sober sensualist',[2] John Hawkesworth, a jobbing author who would soon found the *Adventurer*, and John Ryland, a merchant who was Hawkesworth's brother-in-law and had business interests in the West Indies. This is far less grand a coterie than the cast of the later, famous, club that met at the Turk's Head on Gerrard Street, in what is now London's Chinatown. The Turk's Head Club initially included Goldsmith, Sir Joshua Reynolds and Edmund Burke, and later numbered Sheridan, Gibbon and Charles James Fox among its members. Yet if its prototype, the King's Head Club, was less august, it was certainly more relaxed. Meetings were easily convivial, except when Johnson clashed with the other members on doctrinal matters. Hawkins records Johnson's saying that 'As soon as I enter the door of a tavern, I experience an oblivion of care, and a freedom from solicitude.' With 'no other incentive to hilarity than lemonade', writes Hawkins, 'Johnson was . . . transformed into a new creature . . . his mind was made to expand, and his wit to sparkle'.[3]

Johnson had further opportunity to expand and aerate his thoughts in his periodical writings. Throughout the time he was at work on the *Dictionary* he turned out essays. He needed an income, and journalism was an easy way of earning one. His second *Dictionary* definition of 'essay' ('a loose sally of the mind; an irregular indigested piece; not a regular and orderly composition') gives an indication of how he viewed this kind of writing. But his essays are a good deal more than this. They range from ethical polemics to practical criticism, and from character studies to authoritative dissections of the novel and of the art of biography.

Johnson's most masterly essays appeared in the *Rambler*, a magazine underwritten by Cave, John Payne and another bookseller, Joseph Bouquet. The first issue appeared on 20 March 1750. Little more than a pamphlet, it consisted of six pages held together with a pin. It continued in this form for two years at a rate of two a week, published on Tuesdays and Saturdays, priced twopence. In all, 208 numbers appeared, and, as I have mentioned, Johnson was wholly responsible for the content of all but a handful of them. His authorship was not disclosed, and at first the magazine was not successful; its reputation was cemented only after the run had finished, when its articles were frequently reprinted in other magazines.

The *Rambler* is, more than anything, a work of moral instruction.

One of the most salient features is Johnson's language. Rich in technical vocabulary, it tends to be Latinate and polysyllabic. This is now and then offset by a rather more homely idiom, but when Johnson wishes to be scrupulous about moral and ethical distinctions he turns to the forensic exactitude of Latinism. His frame of reference is equally saturated with classicism. The editors of the standard edition of Johnson's works note that, of the 669 quotations or literary allusions in the *Rambler*, 60 per cent come from Greek or Latin authors. Horace, a particular favourite, accounts for 103 of them. By contrast, the Bible is cited a mere seven times.[4]

Johnson's invocation of classical authorities is, in part, the reflex behaviour of a man of his age and education. But it also has ideological significance: the classical world is dead and therefore immutable, and its language is resistant to the vagaries of fashion. Johnson enlists the authority of Latin and Greek authors because their names add prestige to his writing, yet also because the terms they employ sound – even after they have been transplanted into English – rigorous and persuasive. He chooses an exaggeratedly Latinate form of diction in the *Rambler* because he considers it to be forcefully rhetorical.

The *Rambler* gave Johnson an opportunity to try out words he had encountered during his reading for the *Dictionary*: words like 'adscititious', 'efflorescence', 'equiponderant', 'quadrature', 'to superinduce' and 'terraqueous'.[5] While his taste for these difficult terms can look like a form of intellectual self-display, it is symptomatic of the widespread eighteenth-century conflation of what we would now call 'science' with the language of power and argument.[6] Although the particular character of Johnson's rhetoric is inherited from seventeenth-century natural philosophy, rather than empowered by the latest mid-eighteenth-century developments, he remains an influential figure in giving the specialized terms of natural philosophy a real public currency.

In private he was much less confident. The *Dictionary* was advancing slowly. In the *Rambler* he could write that 'As any action or posture long continued, will distort and disfigure the limbs; so the mind likewise is crippled and contracted by perpetual application to the same set of ideas.'[7] Nobody reading this would have seen it as self-critique, but it was. The more he pushed himself, the more his mind bumped and jolted. While other kinds of work made him feel vigorous, his enthusiasm for lexicography was flagging.

No one was better placed to see this than Strahan, whose ledgers, written up with scrupulous neatness, reveal the fitful evolution of the *Dictionary*. His accounts show that by Christmas 1750 he had set the entries from 'A' to the twenty-first sense of 'to carry' – a total of 70 sheets, or 280 pages, as there were four folio pages to a sheet. He charged the partners £133. More than three years on from the *Plan*, and four and a half years after the auspicious breakfast at the Golden Anchor, this hardly seemed adequate progress.

Guided by Strahan, Johnson reviewed his work. He realized, disconcertingly, that the scope of entries would have to be narrowed, for if he continued in his present expansive manner the resulting book would run to at least three folio volumes, forcing its price up prohibitively. He saw he would have to learn to be more concise, even if it meant sacrificing a good many of the quotations he had collected. It is because he acted on this realization that, in the finished *Dictionary*, the entries for the letters *A* to *C* are more detailed than those that follow.

In his New Year prayer for 1751 a worried Johnson beseeched God to 'look upon my wants, my miseries, and my sins'.[8] His sins were no graver than those of any man, but his miseries were acute, and his wants – both spiritual and material – now pinched repeatedly. At least he could turn to others for financial assistance. On 15 April 1751 he wrote to John Newbery, who later published the *Idler*, requesting £2 to help him settle a bill. Newbery was a soft touch, a charitable type who, having pepped up his career by marrying his employer's widow, now indulged enthusiasms which included children's books and circulating libraries. In *The Vicar of Wakefield* he is memorialized by Goldsmith as 'a red-faced, good-natured man, always in a hurry', while Johnson would later give him the nickname Jack Whirler and depict him as one 'whose business keeps him in perpetual motion, and whose motion always eludes his business'.[9] Newbery was happy to lend the money, and on 29 July Johnson wrote to him again, requesting a guinea. Another such request was made less than a month later, on 24 August. These sums were, in effect, advances on future work, but Johnson's need to borrow in this way confirms the impression that he was a poor accountant; he was earning four guineas a week for his *Rambler* essays, yet was often surprised by some sudden necessity for which he had not allowed. That said, these sums were to be paid to one Thomas Lucy, a merchant, and it is likely that Tetty was the one who owed the money.

Johnson's correspondence confirms that his snail-like progress on the *Dictionary* was enervating. A letter of November 1751 sees him remonstrating with Strahan over a demand for copy. Evidently the project's financial backers were frustrated by Johnson's failure to make good on his promise that he would be done in three years. They were concerned that his dilatoriness would damage his reputation, and that rival lexicographers might steal a march on him. But Johnson was more troubled by his tardiness than they were. Some people feel, even as the hours are draining away, that time is on their side. Johnson was the very opposite: even when he was at his most productive, he felt he was moving too slowly.

Between December 1750 and May 1752, when fifty sheets were printed at a cost to the partners of £95, Johnson groped his way. He was chivvied by Strahan during his most fallow period in 1751, and it appears that the partners threatened to deny him essential supplies. In riposte, Johnson wrote to Strahan on 1 November, warning he might go on strike. It was a situation that called for diplomacy, but it seems that Johnson seized the advantage, for it was agreed that henceforth he would receive a guinea for every sheet of copy he provided. One of the amanuenses – most likely the financially desperate Peyton – attempted the feeble trick of slipping extra sheets into the parcels of manuscript that were sent to Strahan's printing house. Strahan's workers were not impressed: their master's patience was tested once again, and Johnson's credibility was tarnished, at least for a time.

Sickness compounded his distaste for the more mechanical parts of his work. In the early part of 1752 he wrote again to Elphinston, regretfully noting 'the failures of my correspondence'. 'I am often, very often, ill,' he explains, 'and when I am well am obliged to work.'[10] We may reasonably wonder what kind of illness he is talking about. In later years he was afflicted with almost every ailment imaginable. He had trouble with his eyes and his lungs, and with insomnia and asthma; suffered from gout and rheumatoid arthritis;

experienced dropsy, emphysema and at least one fainting fit; and in his seventies developed a malignant tumour on his left testicle. To combat these problems, he consumed a vast quantity of medicines: opium, oil of terebinth, valerian, ipecacuanha, dried orange peel in hot red port, salts of hartshorn, musk, dried squills, and Spanish fly. He was frequently bled, for complaints as disparate as flatulence and an eye infection. Yet Johnson's most enduring malady was mental. Throughout his life he suffered from a profound melancholy which periodically surged towards madness. It was this, much more than any other ailment, that blighted his middle years.

No one captures Johnson's psychological condition better than Boswell. He describes the morbid spirits 'lurking in his constitution', suggesting that 'all his labours, all his enjoyments, were but temporary interruptions of its baleful influence'. He writes poignantly of his friend's 'diseased imagination':

> To Johnson, whose supreme enjoyment was the exercise of his reason, the disturbance or obscuration of that faculty was the evil most to be dreaded. Insanity, therefore, was the object of his most dismal apprehension; and he fancied himself seized by it, or approaching to it, at the very time when he was giving proofs of a more than ordinary soundness and vigour of judgement.

This is Boswell at his most compassionate and thoughtful; his greatest contribution to the art of biography is his careful attention to the manners and language of the psyche, and here we sense very clearly his skill in charting the dark runnels of Johnson's mind. Another of his portraits of Johnson warrants quotation in its entirety:

> His figure was large and well formed, and his countenance of the cast of an ancient statue; yet his appearance was rendered strange and somewhat uncouth, by convulsive cramps, by the scars of that distemper which it was once imagined the royal touch could cure, and by a slovenly mode of dress. He had the use only of one eye; yet so much does mind govern, and even supply the deficiency of organs, that his visual perceptions, as far as they extended, were uncommonly quick and accurate. So morbid was his temperament, that he never knew the natural joy of a free and vigorous use of his limbs; when he walked, it was like the struggling gait of one in fetters; when he rode, he had no command or direction of his horse, but was carried as if in

a balloon. That with his constitution and habits of life he should have lived seventy-five years, is a proof that an inherent *vivida vis* is a powerful preservative of the human frame.

Boswell limns Johnson's personality by describing his appearance; physical characteristics are, implicitly, the tokens of mental traits. The creation of the *Dictionary* tested Johnson's body and psyche to the full, straining his consumptive temperament to breaking point.

Johnson in middle age by Sir Joshua Reynolds, 1756–7

Johnson suffered from a crazed imagination. The word 'imagination', which today has largely positive connotations, meant something very different to the lexicographer and his contemporaries. In the *Rambler* he described it as 'a licentious and vagrant faculty . . . impatient of restraint', and in *Rasselas* he wrote of 'The Dangerous Prevalence of the Imagination'.[11] He thought of it as one might think of a predatory animal, and studied its means of attack. A favourite source of information was Robert Burton's *Anatomy of Melancholy* (1621), which he told Boswell was 'the only book that ever took him out of bed two hours sooner than he wished to rise'. Burton famously cautioned, 'Be not solitary, be not idle'; the *Dictionary* contains plenty of comparable injunctions, as well as encouragements like Addison's promise that 'Labour casts the humours into their proper channels, *throws* off redundancies, and helps nature.' This was Johnson's concern. There were times when his work obliged him to be solitary, but at least he could follow the second half of Burton's counsel. He lived in fear of indolence, which contained the germ of madness, and fretted about his powers of attention, which were constantly in need of 'regulation'. In the *Dictionary* he defines 'attention', somewhat idiosyncratically, as 'the act of bending the mind upon any thing'. The definition implies an active, physical, supplicant mode of thought, made necessary by the all too real possibility of derangement. He habitually writes of the mind as if it is a chamber, needing to be filled. In the *Rambler* he stresses the need to 'relieve the vacuities of our being', 'fill up the vacuities of action', and supply what he variously calls 'the vacuities of life' and its 'vacancies'.[12]

Anyone who became Johnson's friend got to know a good deal about his fears, and most developed an understanding of their effect on him. Sir Joshua Reynolds, a thoughtful but not always sensitive observer, supposed that 'The great business of his life was to escape from himself; this disposition he considered as the disease of his mind.' Boswell goes into greater detail: 'His mind resembled the vast amphitheatre, the Coliseum of Rome. In the centre stood his judgement, which like a mighty gladiator, combated those apprehensions that, like the wild beasts of the arena, were all around in cells, ready to be let out upon him.' The force of the image comes from its graphic materiality. At the same time, Boswell is perceptive in seeing the heroism at the heart of Johnson's unquiet mind. It is an intrinsic fact of certain mental illnesses (manic depression, for example) that the pains they induce are counterbalanced by special gifts; sufferers may often rue the indignities and traumas they undergo, but they are endowed with energies, aptitudes or intuitions unavailable to others, and they would only with the greatest reluctance exchange these capabilities for a more stable, structured existence. As Dryden quip-pingly says in his comedy *The Spanish Friar*, 'There is a pleasure sure / In being mad, which none but madmen know.' The throw-away lines contain an important truth. Johnson would not have been Johnson without the fat white arms of melancholy hanging round his neck. His sickness is, inextricably, a part of his greatness.

When Johnson tells Boswell that 'Happiness consists in the multi-plicity of agreeable consciousness', we infer that his knowledge of happiness was limited, especially as he continues, 'A peasant has not the capacity for having equal happiness with a philosopher.' He was thinking of the backgammon-playing David Hume when he said this, but the history of philosophy is not exactly littered with stories of radiant *joie de vivre*. He comes a little closer to the truth in claim-ing that 'The happiest part of a man's life is what he passes lying awake in bed in the morning.' Closer still in pronouncing that 'There is nothing which has yet been contrived by man, by which so much happiness is produced as a good tavern or inn.' But these aphorisms are later, public offerings: the Johnson of the *Dictionary* is to a much greater degree a private, melancholy man.

Indeed, the *Dictionary* betrays Johnson's gloomy cast of mind. Many of his chosen texts are morbid, many of the quotations bleak or disturbing. More than 1 per cent of the *Dictionary*'s illustrative quotations refer explicitly to death, around 300 mention disease, and 'melancholy' and its cognates appear more than 150 times. We expect to find woebegone passages under headwords like 'sadness' and 'despair', 'miserable' and 'morbidness', but there are hundreds of others. 'From hour to hour we *ripe* and *ripe*, / And then from hour to hour we rot and rot,' says Shakespeare's Jacques, while Sir Walter Ralegh opines that 'The devil is now more laborious than ever, the long day of mankind drawing fast towards an *evening*, and the world's tragedy and time near at an end.' Johnson quotes his play *Irene*, im-agining the state of being 'immur'd and busied in perpetual sloth, / That gloomy slumber of the *stagnant* soul', and invokes the poet Sir John Denham to suggest paranoia in all its toxicity – 'Alas! My fears are *causeless* and ungrounded, / Fantastick dreams, and melancholy fumes.' When he cites the pamphleteer Sir Roger L'Estrange we can hear what sounds like self-reproach: 'We *snap* at the bait without ever dreaming of the hook that goes along with it.' In another possible self-reference, there is Swift's letter to his friend John Gay complaining that 'I have a large house, yet I should hardly prevail to find one *visiter* [sic], if I were not able to hire him with a bottle of wine', and from the *Spectator* he borrows this: 'The *gloominess* in which sometimes the minds of the best men are involved, very often stands in need of such little incitements to mirth and laughter as are apt to disperse melancholy.'

Several of the books Johnson read for the *Dictionary* were unambiguously Stygian. One he cites liberally is Jeremy Taylor's *The Rule and Exercises of Holy Dying* (1651), a work which contains extended meditations on such subjects as 'the vanity and shortness of Man's life' and the 'advantages of sickness'. Two other books he quotes which address similar subjects are William Wake's *Preparation for Death* (1687) and John Graunt's *Natural and Political Observations Mentioned in a Following Index, and Made upon the Bills of Mortality* (1662). He includes more than 150 quotations from the poet Samuel Garth, an old favourite of his cousin Cornelius Ford. Most of these come from Garth's malarial burlesque *The Dispensary* (1699). It is probably enough to list a few of the headwords under which quotations from Garth are to be found: 'bilious', 'devastation', 'flagellation', 'galley-slave', 'haggard', 'maggot', 'nauseously', 'puker', 'tornado', 'unneighbourly', 'to waste'. Garth is the laureate of sickness, and Johnson turned to him, as to Robert Burton, for an anatomy of his infirmity.*

---

* There are surprisingly few quotations from Burton in the *Dictionary*. Johnson marked a mere fifty-five passages for his amanuenses to transcribe, and only sixteen of these made it into the finished work.

Microscope

An optick instrument, contrived various ways to give to the eye a large appearance of many objects which could not otherwise be seen

Johnson's melancholia was exacerbated by his obsessive self-scrutiny. He was forever examining his motives and desires, his urges and beliefs. The habit stayed with him throughout his adult life. 'Will *any* body's mind', asked Hester Thrale, 'bear this eternal microscope that you place upon your own so?'[1] This corrosive introspection was dangerous, but for Johnson it was obligatory to try to understand the workings of the psyche. He abjured secondhand information about the human mind. In a trenchant *Rambler* essay, he argues that 'the great fault of men of learning is still, that they . . . appear willing to study any thing rather than themselves'. He suggests that the speculative thinker 'may be very properly recalled from his excursions . . . [and] reminded that there is a nearer being with which it is his duty to be more acquainted'.[2]

That Johnson's self-inspection went too far is hardly in doubt, but what is striking is its relationship to his scientific interests. Johnson's was an age in which natural philosophy was an object of public contemplation. Sir Isaac Newton's revolutionary work, though unintelligible to most readers, was enthusiastically popularized in the form of coffee-house lectures, public experiments, and expositions by his self-appointed apostles.* Equally influential were simplified versions

---

* I have used the terms 'science' and 'natural philosophy' interchangeably. In fact, during the seventeenth century and for at least a part of the eighteenth, 'science' meant something approximating to 'the state or fact of knowing' or 'knowledge acquired by study'. According to the *OED*, it was only in the second quarter of the eighteenth century that it began to acquire a new sense: 'A branch of study which is concerned either with a connected body of demonstrated truths or with observed facts systematically classified and more or less colligated by being brought under

of Newton's philosophy, such as that offered in Francesco Algarotti's *Sir Isaac Newton's Philosophy Explain'd for the Use of the Ladies* – a work published in 1739 by Edward Cave, in an English version by Elizabeth Carter, a woman Johnson commended because she 'could make a pudding, as well as translate Epictetus'.

More generally, ideas from science were likely to find their way into literature and popular culture. This was a period, more than any other before or since, when poets, essayists and impresarios celebrated the excitement of natural philosophy. Johnson was a keen scientific amateur, and like many of his contemporaries he was not content merely to read about science, but insisted on dabbling in botany and chemistry. According to Hester Thrale, when the Irish actor and dramatist Arthur Murphy first met Johnson at his lodgings he was surprised to find him 'all covered with soot like a chimney-sweeper, in a little room, with an intolerable heat and strange smell, as if he had been . . . making *aether*'.[3] Murphy should not have been surprised, for Johnson frequently attempted ventures of this kind. Even as an old man, he was not above commandeering the Thrales' garden for use as an outdoor laboratory. He carefully documented shaving his arms to see how quickly the hairs would grow back, and drying laurel leaves in order to prove to himself that their weight would be decreased by desiccation.

Advanced experiments were beyond Johnson's means, but he enjoyed reading about them. One area of particular interest was microscopy. The development of the microscope, initiated by Galileo and accelerated by Marcello Malpighi in the early 1660s, changed the frame of human perceptions. It coincided with the Great Plague of 1665, and one of the first practical uses of the microscope in England was for examining plague-bearing insects. In his *Journal of the Plague Year* (1722) Defoe describes the belief that a sufferer's breath, condensed on a piece of glass, might be magnified to reveal a troupe of dancing devils – but 'we had not

---

general laws, and which includes trustworthy methods for the discovery of new truths within its own domain.' Isaac Watts is the first cited user of the word in this more modern sense, in 1725. However, the sense did not become common until the nineteenth century, and Johnson does not record it in the *Dictionary*.

microscopes at that time, as I remember, to make the experiment with'. It is relevant, therefore, that one of the scientific words Johnson defines in the *Dictionary* is 'animalcule', the term that was then most often used of the organisms observed under the microscope. It was the Dutch linen-draper Anton van Leeuwenhoek's observation of the 'animalcules' in water that precipitated a popular fascination with microbiology.

One of the corollaries of this was an awareness that the human body contained foreign organisms that were often injurious to its health. Robert Hooke's *Micrographia* (1665), with its famous engraving of a magnified flea, left readers in no doubt that the body harboured some disgusting secrets. The horrors of the human form seen at close quarters are vividly imagined by Swift in *Gulliver's Travels* (1726), a book which mocks the grotesque misadventures of science. Gulliver is nauseated by the imperfect fleshliness of the Brobdingnagians' bodies, much as the inhabitants of Lilliput are shocked by his 'disagreeable' complexion and the 'great holes' in his skin. Microscopy meant that educated eighteenth-century citizens were suddenly aware of the multitude of previously unseen creatures swarming among them. Naturally, this engendered a new kind of self-consciousness (it is worth noting that the word is first used in its modern sense by John Locke in 1690), and Johnson subscribed to the burgeoning study of the mind's intimate functions.

When Hester Thrale speaks of Johnson's subjecting his mind to the microscope, the image is apposite. Introspection was something he carried out with scientific exactness. But the tiny traits he discovered inside himself looked freakish once magnified. It is telling that in the *Dictionary* he offers under 'bristly' this heavily edited quotation from the brilliant but erratic classicist Richard Bentley: 'If the eye were so acute as to rival the finest microscope, the sight of our own selves would affright us; the smoothest skin would be beset with rugged scales and *bristly* hairs.' The quotation reappears in unedited form under 'microscope' itself. Three times, too, Johnson quotes a passage from Isaac Watts in which Watts reports that observers are 'disgusted' by the things they are able to see under the microscope. And so they were, although sometimes their imagination got the better of them: when the Dutchman Nicolas Hartsoeker examined a sample of human sperm, for instance, he was convinced that he could see little men tucked up inside the cells.

As all this suggests, contemporary scientific advances inspired wonder and horror at the same time. Johnson experienced both reactions, and the *Dictionary* incorporates new ideas from science while also preserving some pretty medieval notions. Even well-informed members of eighteenth-century society continued to make use of almanacs, deferred to the advice of herbalists, and believed in the spurious doctrines of physiognomy. The *Dictionary*, even as it embodies certain obvious Enlightenment values, preserves vestiges of a pre-Enlightenment world. For example, we know that Johnson was not unreceptive to alchemy, and in the *Dictionary* he defines it as 'the more sublime and occult part of chymistry, which proposes, for its object, the transmutation of metals, and other important operations'. The fact that Johnson writes 'proposes' rather than 'professes' suggests he does not regard alchemy as something merely frivolous.

More commonly, however, the *Dictionary* testifies to the growth of scientific thought. Johnson mined scientific terms from Bacon and Newton, from Robert Boyle and from Thomas Burnet's influential *Sacred Theory of the Earth*, as well as from a host of other sources that included the pious botanist Nehemiah Grew, the geologist John Woodward and the infamous quack herbalist 'Sir' John Hill. As this choice of authors suggests, the *Dictionary*'s science is not always the most vibrantly contemporary, but modernity does jostle for space. We find definitions of words like 'atom', 'fossil', 'gravity', 'parallax' and 'telescope', and of altogether more rarefied terms – 'aphelion', 'colliquation', 'gymnospermous', 'zoophyte'. Some of the definitions provided are tantalizingly brief. For instance, 'ophiophagous' means 'serpenteating' and is 'not used', while 'brontology' is simply 'a dissertation upon thunder'. But under 'airpump' – a word that reminds any art-lover of Joseph Wright of Derby's beautiful painting in London's National Gallery – he proffers an astonishingly lengthy explanation from Chambers. It informs us, *inter alia*, that 'the invention of this curious instrument is ascribed to Otto de Guerick, consul of Magdeburg, . . . in 1654', and then narrates the improvements that have been made in airpump technology in more recent years. The 'orrery', meanwhile, 'was first made by Mr Rowley, a mathematician born at Lichfield' – but of course! – and took its name from Rowley's patron, Charles Boyle, fourth earl of Orrery, 'by one or other of . . . [whose] family almost every art has been encouraged or improved'.

Johnson captures the contemporary distaste for astrology when he defines it as 'the practice of foretelling things by the knowledge of the stars; an art now generally exploded, as without reason'. In the revised fourth edition he comes down on it rather harder: 'without reason' is amended to 'irrational and false'. Another topical entry appears under 'phlogiston'. Eighteenth-century scientists believed that the reason burning caused materials to change – from wood to ash, for instance – was that they gave off phlogiston, an undetectable substance which had 'negative mass'. The theory, originally advanced by Johann Becher and Georg Stahl, may sound bizarre, but it was generally accepted until Antoine Lavoisier debunked it in the 1770s. This is why the *Dictionary* does not include the word 'oxygen': it was discovered – by a Swede, Carl Scheele, who rarely gets credit for the discovery – only in 1772.

On the other hand, there is an entry for 'electricity', even though Faraday did not discover electromagnetic induction until 1831. While Johnson's understanding of the word differs from ours, he was conversant with fresh developments in physics, and had kept up with the latest findings – such as those of the correspondent who had lately informed readers of the *Gentleman's Magazine* that cats' hair was 'surprizingly electrical'.[4] 'The industry of the present age', Johnson notes in the *Dictionary*, 'has discovered in electricity a multitude of philosophical wonders'. For 'philosophical' we can read 'scientific'; and when he adds that 'The philosophers are now endeavouring to intercept the strokes of lightning' he is referring to the recent work of Benjamin Franklin, who famously flew his kite under a thundercloud to prove that lightning was a form of electricity. Johnson later encountered Franklin at a meeting of a charity called the Associates for Founding Classical Libraries and Supporting Negro Schools. What passed between them we sadly do not know, but the entry for 'electricity' sees the lexicographer straining to capture the immediacy of a vitally exciting moment in the history of science.

Network

Any thing reticulated or decussated, at equal distances, with interstices between the intersections

Johnson's zeal for science can be detected not only in his inclusion of technical terms and in the fields of knowledge he registers, but also in the language of his definitions. The *Dictionary* contains many definitions that are 'philosophical' in character. 'To rattle' is 'to make a quick sharp noise with frequent repetitions and collisions of bodies not very sonorous: when bodies are sonorous, it is called *jingling*'. A 'cough' is 'a convulsion of the lungs, vellicated by some sharp serosity'.[*] 'To graft' is 'to impregnate with an adscititious branch'. A 'blister' is 'a pustule formed by raising the cuticle from the cutis, and filled with serous blood'. 'To roll' is 'to move any thing by volutation, or successive application of the different parts of the surface, to the ground'. 'Drossy' means 'full of scorious or recrementitious parts'. These definitions are a deliberate attempt to avoid a mass of synonyms of the kind that clog – just to give one example – Johnson's second definition of 'to plague', which reads 'to trouble; to teaze; to vex; to harrass; to torment; to afflict; to distress; to torture; to embarrass; to excruciate; to make uneasy; to disturb'. This is impressionistic: as we read a definition of this type we can see Johnson floundering in search of the word's quintessence, ransacking his mind's thesaurus for the best likeness, and ensnaring himself in a thicket of equivalent terms. But the alternative is a scientifically punctilious style of definition, and the great danger of this is that the 'philosophical' can slide pretty quickly into a sesquipedalian avalanche.

---

[*] This is actually a compression of a definition that appeared in Chambers's *Cyclopaedia*: 'a disease affecting the lungs, occasioned by a sharp serous humour, vellicating the fibrous coat thereof, and urging it to a discharge by spitting'.

Occasionally the definition of an everyday word causes real problems. Johnson recognizes in the Preface that 'the easiest word, whatever it be, can never be translated into one more easy'. Yet sometimes an easy word is translated into a bafflingly polysyllabic alternative. 'Rust', we are assured, is 'the red desquamation of old iron' or 'the tarnished or corroded surface of any metal', while a 'scale' is 'any thing exfoliated or desquamated'. Confusingly, when we turn to the entry for 'desquamation' we are told that it is 'the act of scaling foul bones'. Sometimes there is a failure to capitalize on the quality of one definition in defining its alleged synonym. 'To peel' is said to mean 'to decorticate; to flay'. But 'to decorticate' is defined as 'to divest of the bark or husk', which would have been an altogether better definition of 'to peel'. The trouble with Johnson's difficult definitions is that they can leave us with husks, rather than kernels.

Johnson's definition of 'network', cited at the start of this chapter, is, of all his quirkier efforts, the one most often held up to ridicule. Obscurely polysyllabic, it would be of little use to someone ignorant of the word's meaning. If you are unfamiliar with the term 'network' – by which, incidentally, he appears to mean 'an arrangement of intersecting horizontal and vertical lines', not 'a group of interconnected people' – you are unlikely to understand the fabulously abstruse 'reticulated' and 'decussated'.* It scarcely helps that Johnson explains 'reticulated' as 'made of network; formed with interstitial vacuities'; this is circular definition at its most frustrating. Moreover, one might reasonably challenge the assumption that the intersections within a network must be 'at equal distances', and the phrase 'interstices between the intersections' sounds like a playful academic joke. Yet Johnson's definition is not as absurd as it initially seems.

At first blush, we might share the view of the compilers of the *Cambridge English Dictionary* that a network is simply 'a work formed like a net'. But what exactly is a 'net'? Johnson provides two

---

* The terms appear to have been borrowed by Johnson from one of his favourite writers, Sir Thomas Browne, who in a treatise entitled *The Garden of Cyrus* (1658) – largely concerned with the number five and its manifestations in the physical world – uses the words 'reticulate' and 'network' almost interchangeably, as well as repeatedly using the words 'decussated' and 'decussation'.

definitions: 'a texture woven with large interstices or meshes, used commonly as a snare for animals' and 'any thing made with interstitial vacuities'. The first of these is clear enough to anyone who has seen fishermen at work; the second a return to obscurity, which in any case fits several things that could hardly be described as forms of 'net' – a window frame, for instance, or an artificial sponge, or Swiss cheese. Nevertheless, Johnson is trying to produce a definition that has technical integrity, rather than one that uses analogy. These definitions, instead of being evidence of his inability to write transparently, are proof of his commitment to what we may call philosophical lexicography. It is not enough to say what something resembles: the lexicographer must try to capture the quintessence of what it *is*, however elusive this may be.

The art of definition, according to this model, is the art of revitalizing readers' perceptions. Johnson does this by estranging them. His definition of 'network' compels one's thoughts and powers of interpretation in a way that obliges one to think very carefully about the nature of a network. To put it another way, he grasps that many people turn to dictionaries in a mood somewhere between curiosity and complacency: a common reaction to looking a word up in a dictionary is to forget almost immediately the explanation that was offered. But by provoking or piquing the reader, and by forcing him or her to dwell for an unusually long time on a certain entry, he invites a more critical kind of readership.

For Johnson the pedagogue, this is a priority. It also explains why he felt able to be opinionated in some of his definitions. Rather than hoping that no one would notice his peculiar entries under 'grub-street' or 'oats', he intended them to spark controversy; instead of being a lexical morgue, his *Dictionary* could, for a moment, be a battleground. Naturally, this ambition could not be allowed to intrude too far on his orthodox lexicographical aims. Nevertheless, the reason why some of Johnson's definitions and illustrative quotations are piquant is that he hopes to awaken debate. Under 'contest' he quotes Locke's judgement that 'A definition is the only way whereby the meaning of words can be known, without leaving room for *contest* about it.' Yet the instability of language and its openness to question are frequently mentioned. He twice quotes the following from Milton: 'Though a linguist should pride himself to have all the tongues that Babel cleft the world into, yet if he had not studied the solid things in them as well as the words and *lexicons*, yet he were nothing so much to be esteemed a learned man.' Paradoxically, Johnson's entry for 'network' prompts us not to reach for further technical explanations, but to think about what a network really is, and also to consider for a moment the difficulties of definition – not just in this case, but in general.

When all this is said, however, one must concede that Johnson does have a small weakness for the word 'interstice' and its cognate forms. In the first edition it appears in fourteen definitions: a 'battlement' is 'a wall raised round the top of a building, with embrasures, or interstices, to look through, to annoy an enemy', one of the meanings of 'dense' is 'having small interstices between the constituent particles', and a hole is, among other things, 'a small interstitial vacuity'. When he came to revise the *Dictionary*, a quarter of a century later, he added one more instance, defining 'birdcage' as 'an enclosure with interstitial spaces made of wire or wicker in which birds are kept'. By then, however, he was able to laugh at his weakness for fiddly words. When he and Boswell were in the Highlands and passed through Glen Shiel, Boswell described a mountain as 'immense', but Johnson corrected him – 'No; it is no more than a considerable protuberance.'

Nicety

1. Minute accuracy of thought

2. Accurate performance

3. Fastidious delicacy; squeamishness

4. Minute observation; punctilious discrimination; subtilty

5. Delicate management; cautious treatment

6. Effeminate softness

7. Niceties, in the plural, is generally applied to dainties or delicacies in eating

Johnson's finest definitions remind us that he was a poet. They are succinct, accurate and elegant. He is especially skilled in explaining some of those abstract or intangible things that seem least amenable to definition. 'Conscience' is 'the knowledge or faculty by which we judge of the goodness or wickedness of ourselves'. A 'trance' is 'a temporary absence of the soul'. An 'imp' is a 'puny devil'. A 'rant' consists of 'high sounding language unsupported by dignity of thought'. Anything described as 'tawdry' is 'meanly showy; splendid without cost; fine without grace; showy without elegance'. An 'expletive' is 'something used only to take up room; something of which the use is only to prevent a vacancy'.

Sometimes Johnson's best definitions build on foundations laid down by his predecessors, yet when they are most richly expressive we have the sense of his having paused to examine his experience or to reach into the hive of his imagination. For instance, when he describes a 'nightmare' as 'a morbid oppression in the night, resembling the pressure of weight upon the breast', we may not necessarily agree with the image he creates, but we are clear that he writes from intimate knowledge of nightmares, and that he is intent on doing justice to what seems to him to be the exact somatic effect of a bad dream.★

Johnson the poet recognizes that there are times when a little scientific precision may be sacrificed in the interests of a memorable formula. Thus 'to hiccough' is 'to sob with convulsion of the stomach', while an 'embryo' is 'the offspring yet unfinished in the womb'. 'Thumb' is defined simply as 'the short strong finger answering to the other four'. A 'puppet' is 'a wooden tragedian'. A 'rainbow' is 'the semicircle of various colours which appears in showery weather' – he saves the technical details and allows Newton to explain them. When he states that a 'catheter' is 'a somewhat crooked instrument, thrust into the bladder, to assist in bringing away the urine', the choice of verb ('thrust') is suitably discomfiting. It recurs in the definition of 'pessary': 'an oblong form of medicine made to thrust up into the uterus upon some extraordinary occasions'. Here is a miniature of the world of eighteenth-century medicine, or at least of Johnson's experience of it: a theatre of thrustings and pokings, invasions and incisions, sometimes efficacious but invariably painful.

In describing types of people and their behaviour, Johnson often requires no more than a stroke or two of his brush. A 'grimace' is 'a distortion of the countenance from habit, affectation, or insolence'. A 'misdemeanour' is 'something less than an atrocious crime'. An 'uxorious' man is 'infected with connubial dotage'. A 'coquette' is 'a girl who endeavours to attract notice'; a 'cynic' is 'a philosopher of the snarling or currish sort' (which is precise, since the word in the strictest etymological sense means 'like a dog'); a 'backbiter' is 'a privy calumniator; a censurer of the absent'; and 'favourite' – as in 'Gaveston was King Edward's favourite' – is defined, among other things, as 'a mean wretch whose whole business is by any means to please'.†

Johnson neatly defines 'to strut' as 'to walk with affected dignity': the definition would come to mind when he wrote a life of Thomas

---

★ Johnson is fond of using the word 'morbid' in definitions. For example, an abscess is 'a morbid cavity in the body', gonorrhoea 'a morbid running of venereal hurts', diabetes 'a morbid copiousness of urine', indigestion 'a morbid weakness of the stomach', and lethargy 'a morbid drowsiness'.

† On the same theme, 'to curry favour' is 'to become a favourite by petty officiousness, slight kindnesses, or flattery'.

Gray, who in his verse 'has a kind of strutting dignity, and is tall by walking on tiptoe'.[1] To 'compliment' a person is 'to sooth with acts or expressions of respect'; that verb, 'sooth', suggests Johnson's feelings about the sort of people who need to be paid compliments. 'Obsession' is explained as 'the act of besieging' or 'the first attack of Satan, antecedent to possession' – a pair of definitions together more eloquent than the whole of *Fatal Attraction*. A 'hope' is, among other things, 'an expectation indulged with pleasure', while a 'junket', besides being a kind of creamy dessert consumed in *The Taming of the Shrew*, is 'a stolen entertainment'.

These definitions, in all their sharpness, are suggestive of Johnson's life beyond the *Dictionary*. He was a keen observer of human weakness and vanity, and it is easy to imagine where he might have found them – in his dealings with other writers, among his drinking companions, or in the oaths and promises of the hucksters and vagrants he encountered each time he stepped outdoors. When he creates his vignettes of uxoriousness or favouritism, it is as if he has particular examples in mind, and we are continually left wishing we knew more of his existence, for very few of his diaries and letters from the period survive, and we cannot tell which of his more pointed definitions were provoked by individuals.

Of his biographers, only Hawkins had close contact with him during the *Dictionary* years. He assures us that 'the great delight of . . . [Johnson's] life was conversation and mental intercourse', that his disposition was 'to please and be pleased', and that he was 'a great contributor to the mirth of conversation', but he offers little about Johnson's day-to-day activities, and can digress infuriatingly – to reproduce a Latin account of the constituents of breakfast, or to explain fourteen different ways in which a criminal can evade justice – when he ought to be writing about the Club or Gough Square.[2] Still, from Hawkins we get a picture of Johnson's relations with others: he was not slow to involve himself in controversies, both public and personal, and he was perceptive about manners and motives, the many shades of human conduct, and the cruel machinations of love and hope, ambition, avarice and pride.

As we have seen before, this finely tuned judgement also allows Johnson to discriminate deftly between the different senses of a particular word. Thus there are sixteen senses of 'world', ranging from 'the great collective idea of all bodies whatever' to 'the earth; the terraqueous globe', and from 'great multitude' (as in Shakespeare's 'You a *world* of curses undergo') to 'a collection of wonders'. 'Art' has six senses, 'pain' seven, 'thought' twelve, and 'spirit' nineteen. His definition of 'life', which a little surprisingly makes no mention of death, runs to fifteen senses. The first is 'union and co-operation of soul with body' (note the religious emphasis), and we then proceed, through 'enjoyment, or possession of terrestrial existence' and 'continuance of our present state' to 'animated existence; animal being'. The seven different senses of the word 'nicety' – displayed at the head of this chapter – show once more this scrupulous care over shades of meaning.

Johnson can sometimes amuse us with a definition which edges round the truth rather than getting straight at it. Thus a 'bagnio' is 'a house for bathing, sweating, and otherwise cleansing the body'. The word, like the modern 'bathhouse', in fact connotes nothing so much as the fever of sexual activity. Bagnios were brothels disguised as public baths, and it was in such an establishment that his cousin Ford had expired. Johnson's definition isn't naive so much as decorous; he leaves it to the reader to make the connection between the intended use of bagnios – as places to exercise and purge the body of toxins – and their actual use, as places for immersing oneself in luxury, sweating in the throes of sex, and venting one's various secretions. The same kind of archly humorous touch can be detected in his definition of 'bawd' as 'one that introduces men and women to each other, for the promotion of debauchery'. Johnson disapproves of pimps and panders; his elegant summary of their business mocks the real seediness of their activities, and suggests his distance from their ethics, if not from their common haunts.

Certain words were omitted from the *Dictionary* for reasons of propriety. For instance, 'buggery', which had appeared in more than one earlier dictionary, is excluded, and readers will not find 'shit', though the word was commonly used. Less remarkably, 'fuck' and 'cunt' are absent: neither found its way into a mainstream British or American dictionary until the 1960s, although the *OED* did include 'windfucker', a 'term of opprobrium', as early as 1926.

Occasionally Johnson's omissions seem coy. He feels able to define 'vaginopennous' ('sheath-winged'), but not 'vagina', although the word appears, oddly enough, in his definition of 'daffodowndilly'. There is no entry for 'penis'. And his definitions can be euphemistic. He defines both 'jakes' and 'boghouse' as a 'house of office'. 'Priapism' is a 'preternatural tension', even though the supplied quotations give the impression that it's specifically sexual. 'To lie with' means 'to converse in bed'.* 'Retromingency' is defined as 'the quality of staling backwards', although in the supporting quotation it is glossed as 'pissing backwards' – something that hares do, apparently.

For all this, Johnson was not a prude, and did not refrain from including words that might offend his more delicate readers' sensibilities. 'Bum' and 'arse' are in, along with 'fart' ('wind from behind') and 'turd'. 'Piss' is also included; it could, after all, be found in the Authorized Version of the Bible, in the books of Kings and Isaiah. 'Sodomy' is omitted, but there are ten references to Sodom in the illustrative quotations, as well as one in the definition of 'asphaltos'. 'To hang an arse', we learn, is 'a vulgar phrase, signifying to be tardy, sluggish, or dilatory'. There are entries for a plant called an 'arse-smart' and a water fowl known as an 'arse foot'.† 'Pissburnt' means 'stained with urine', and Johnson includes the old colloquial name for the dandelion, 'pissabed', which it earned on account of its supposedly diuretic properties.

These last two words belong to a special class in which the *Dictionary* is rich: the deliciously evocative. Many are forms of invective, be it old or new. A 'bedpresser' is 'a heavy lazy fellow' (such as Falstaff – or Johnson on his slower days). A 'giglet' is 'a lascivious girl', an 'abbey-lubber' is someone who loiters in religious places 'under pretence of retirement and austerity', and 'pricklouse' is 'a word of contempt for a tailor'. A 'fopdoodle' is 'a fool; an insignificant wretch'. Johnson accommodates such Shakespearean insults as 'jolthead' and

---

* The fifth sense of 'to converse' is 'to have commerce with a different sex', which is what Johnson has in mind here, but he could certainly have been more straight-forward.

† These appear to be, respectively, the diuretic plant now usually called smartweed and a type of grebe.

'garlickeater', along with 'linseywoolsey' (a term used of anything considered to be 'vile'), 'pickthank' ('a whispering parasite'), 'seek-sorrow' ('one who contrives to give himself vexation') and 'witworm' ('one that feeds on wit'). We find, too, more durable terms of abuse: 'bitch', 'half-wit', 'minx', 'oaf', 'trollop'. Such straightforward cusses were, he felt, preferable to sophisticated ones: 'Abuse is not so dangerous when there is no vehicle of wit or delicacy, no subtle conveyance. The difference between coarse and refined abuse is as the difference between being bruised by a club, and wounded by a poisoned arrow.'

Johnson has no aversion, then, to including slang. Slang is language with its sleeves rolled up or its necktie loosened. Ephemeral it may be, but the vigour of slang is part of language's vitality, and Johnson commemorates slang at its most vigorous. Part of the appeal of the *Dictionary* for a modern reader lies in its stock of lost words, many of them terms of abuse like 'dandiprat', 'jobbernowl' and 'looby'. For some of Johnson's contemporaries it was just as droll a source of unlikely slurs. But not all the *Dictionary*'s early users were happy with his coverage of low and profane language. According to Sir Herbert Croft, who knew Johnson in the 1770s, a mature lady once congratulated him on the omission of 'naughty words'. Johnson answered her, 'No, Madam, I hope I have not daubed my fingers. I find, however, that you have been looking for them.'[*]

---

[*] In a somewhat different version of the story, there were two ladies, a Mrs Digby and a Mrs Brooke, and Johnson, quick as ever with a dart of humour, exclaimed, 'What, my dears! Then you have been looking for them.'[3]

To note

1. To observe; to remark; to heed; to attend; to take notice of

3. To charge with a crime

There would always be quarrels over what was in and what was out, over proper and improper usage, over the need to regulate language and the need to indulge it. Johnson helpfully provides us with a term for this – 'logomachy', meaning 'a contention in words; a contention about words'.* In the *Plan* he suggests he will refrain from such contests, claiming that he was drawn to the idea of putting together a dictionary because 'though it could not make my life envied, [it] would keep it innocent'. His work would 'awaken no passion, engage me in no contention, nor throw in my way any temptation to disturb the quiet of others by censure'. But making a dictionary is a politically sensitive task. Words are weapons, freighted with ideology. Because language is so important to social identity, debates about language tend to be incendiary: in Britain, concern for the state of the language is usually a covert expression of concern for the state of the nation. Even a map is a means of exercising control: colonists map their new territories in order to personalize them, and Johnson – who likens himself to 'the soldiers of Caesar' – proves, in his own country, a colonist as well as a cartographer.

One of the best modern accounts of the development of English offers a helpful summary of Johnson's colonial instincts:

> The rise of dictionaries is associated with the rise of the English middle class, keen to ape their betters and anxious to define and

---

* In his *Devil's Dictionary* (1911) the American satirist Ambrose Bierce defines 'logomachy' as 'a war in which the weapons are words and the wounds punctures in the swim-bladder of self-esteem'. In the 1870s a card game of this name was produced by an Ohio firm called F. A. Wright, and won the prize for Best New Parlour Game at the Cincinnati Industrial Exposition in 1874.

> circumscribe the various worlds to conquer – lexical as well as social
> and commercial. It is highly appropriate that Dr Samuel Johnson . . .
> should have published his *Dictionary* at the very beginning of the
> heyday of the middle class. Johnson . . . raised common sense to the
> heights of genius.[1]

Lexicography was an instrument of Empire, and one of Johnson's
guiding principles was 'common sense', that most blunt of intellectual instruments. His *Dictionary* postulates standards and ideals that are
middle-class (although the term would have been meaningless to
him). Proper English is equated with moral rectitude, and 'otherness'
is usually given brisk, dismissive treatment. In one of his essays of the
period Johnson explains that 'I have laboured to refine our language
to grammatical purity, and to clear it from colloquial barbarisms,
licentious idioms, and irregular combinations.'[2] Here, and in his
definition of 'chaste' as 'not mixed with barbarous phrases', we can
see his protectionist instincts and moral conservatism.

Johnson stigmatizes words of which he disapproves. He does this
by applying denigratory labels to them. 'To ponder on' is 'improper',
'ambassadress' is 'ludicrous', 'bouncer' (meaning 'an empty threat-
ener') is 'colloquial', 'overwhelmingly' is 'inelegant', the alarming-
sounding 'to powder' ('to come tumultuously and violently') is
'corrupt', 'coxcomical' is 'unworthy of use', 'from hence' is 'vitious',
and 'uncircumstantial' is simply 'bad'. Other Johnsonian tags include
'vile', 'affected', 'erroneous' and 'wanton', while in one of his more
acerbic moments he tells us that the noun 'opiniatry' is 'not yet
received, nor is it wanted'.[3] But his key label is 'cant'. He defines the
word as follows:

1. A corrupt dialect used by beggars and vagabonds
2. A particular form of speaking peculiar to some certain class or
   body of men
3. A whining pretension to goodness, in formal and affected terms
4. Barbarous jargon
5. Auction

When a word is given the tag 'cant', Johnson is generally using the
term in the first, second and fourth of these senses, but the other two
apply. People who employ cant are guilty both of affectation and of

selling the language short. He would later expand on this in conversation with Boswell, counselling 'Clear your *mind* of cant.' For, while it was acceptable, he believed, to use in casual conversation the everyday formulae of cant (like saying 'I am sorry you had such bad weather' to a man without caring sixpence whether he has been wet or dry), it was not acceptable to allow such foolish prattle to find its way into one's thoughts.

A few examples will suggest the scope of Johnson's distaste. 'To bamboozle' is 'a cant word not used in pure or in grave writings'. 'To cabbage' ('to steal in cutting clothes') is 'a cant word among tailors'; 'nervous' ('having weak or diseased nerves') is 'medical cant'; 'plum' is 'in the cant of the city' a term for £100,000. Other words are identified as the cant of artificers, soldiers, gamesters, maltsters, workmen and thieves. 'Bishop' is 'a cant word for a mixture of wine, oranges, and sugar' – according to Edmund Hector, it was a favourite drink of Johnson's, and he liked to take it with a whole roasted orange. 'Brogue' is 'a cant word for a corrupt dialect, or manner of pronunciation', 'stout' 'a cant name for strong beer', and 'pigwidgeon' 'a kind of cant word for any thing petty or small' (it is the name of Ron Weasley's tiny owl in the Harry Potter novels).

'Flirtation', which Johnson defines as 'a quick sprightly motion', is 'a cant word among women' – though Lord Chesterfield claimed to have 'assisted' at its birth. The only other word to be flagged in this way is 'frightful': the more fanciful reader may suspect that while Johnson was working on the letter *F* he suffered an especially strident feminine salvo ('I am sick of this frightful dictionary . . .') and chose to requite it.

The decision to stigmatize a word as 'cant' comes down in the end to personal opinion. However, Johnson usually targets words that have little or no etymological legitimacy. He may tolerate these words in the chatter of company, but he is troubled to find them in print. He directs particular criticism at words whose very existence hints at moral laxity – be it avarice, gluttony, lust or sloth. For similar reasons he is scathing about what he calls 'low' words. These are the terms of gutter life or indolence, the gossip of the street and the tavern: 'to dumbfound', 'ignoramus', 'shabby', 'simpleton', 'uppish' and 'mighty' (as in 'That was mighty close'). Some of the objects of

Johnson's contempt, like 'width' or 'latterly' ('a low word lately hatched'), will surprise the modern reader. His disapproval of 'lingo', which he considers both low and cant, probably won't.

Not all the labels he attaches are denigratory. Some, indeed, are positive. 'Ultimity', meaning 'the last stage', is 'a word very convenient'. 'Determent' is 'a good word'. 'Pictorial', the sole authority for which comes from Sir Thomas Browne, is 'a word not adopted by other writers, but elegant and useful'. Other items designated 'useful' include the nouns 'effumability' ('the quality of flying away, or vapouring in fumes') and 'indesert' ('want of merit'). 'To vade', which means 'to vanish; to pass away', is 'a word useful in poetry'. In the fourth edition 'to warray', meaning 'to make war upon', is deemed 'very elegant and expressive'.

Furthermore, one of Johnson's apparently denigratory labels is in fact nothing of the sort. Several hundred words are marked 'obsolete': they range from the plausibly outdated ('eftsoons', 'to swink') to the less clearly defunct ('to astound', 'deftly', 'henchman'). On the face of it, we may wonder why Johnson troubled to include them. The answer lies in the Preface, where he explains that 'Obsolete words are admitted, when they are found in authors not obsolete, or when they have any force or beauty that may deserve revival.'* Significantly, the epigraph to the finished *Dictionary* is a passage on this very theme from the second of Horace's *Epistles*; it celebrates the efforts of the prudent critic who weeds out undignified language and rehabilitates forgotten but elegant words. Johnson accommodates 'obsolete' terms to help his readers understand writers like Francis Bacon, Spenser and Shakespeare, and sometimes he suggests they should be salvaged from oblivion.†

Johnson is attentive to the question of who uses particular words, as well as to the situations in which words are appropriate. When a word belongs to a certain domain (poetry, for example, or

---

* Three times in the *Dictionary* he quotes Dryden's judgement that 'Obsolete words may be laudably revived, when either they are more sounding, or more significant than those in practice.'

† One example is 'manurance', a term he has found in Spenser, meaning 'agriculture' or 'cultivation'. It is 'an obsolete word, worthy of revival'.

hunting, or law), he marks this at the start of his definition. If a word is, in his opinion, the property of a certain social group, he says so. Thus the verb 'to doff' is 'in all its senses obsolete, and scarcely used except by rusticks', while 'to careen' is 'a term in the sea language'. 'Brother' is used 'in theological language, for man in general'. 'To walk' is employed as a synonym for 'to come' or 'to go', but only 'in the ceremonious language of invitation'. Other words are considered unique to trade, to the scriptures, to philosophy or to anatomists. 'Turtle' is a word 'used among sailors and gluttons for a tortoise'. And when a word or a sense appears to be unique to an author, Johnson names him; Shakespeare is the figure whose quirks of usage are most often noted in this way, but others include Milton and Dryden, as well as Bacon and Spenser. Thus the verb 'to compromise' 'in Shakespeare . . . means, unusually, to accord; to agree', while 'scull' means 'in Milton's style, a shoal or vast multitude of fish'.

In his capacity as a defender of good usage, Johnson is also on the lookout for barbarism. When he stigmatizes a word as 'barbarous', he implies that it is associated with barbarians – which is to say, foreigners.★ In the *Plan* he states that barbarisms are 'carefully to be eradicated wherever they are found', yet he concedes that they occur frequently 'even in the best writers'. In the *Dictionary* 'barbarism' is defined as being above all else 'a form of speech contrary to the purity and exactness of any language'.

Again, a few examples will give a sense of what Johnson dislikes. The use of 'extraordinary' to mean 'extraordinarily' seems 'only a colloquial barbarism'. 'Gules' is 'a barbarous term of heraldry'. 'Irresistless' is 'a barbarous ungrammatical conjunction of two negatives'. The word 'nowadays' is 'common and used by the best writers', but is still 'perhaps barbarous'. 'To have rather', which we might use in an expression such as 'I had rather be in Utah', is 'a barbarous expression of late intrusion into our language'. 'To shab', meaning 'to play mean tricks', is given a thorough dressing-down: it is 'a low barbarous cant word'. 'Slippy' is 'a barbarous provincial word', as is 'to tole' ('to train; to draw by degrees'), and the abbreviation of

---

★ In the 1750s, 'barbarous' and 'barbaric' were still synonyms.

'through' to 'thro" is a vice exclusive to 'barbarians'.★ 'Vastidity' and 'viz' are definitely barbarous, while 'to unloose' is 'perhaps barbarous and ungrammatical' since it should technically mean 'to bind', not 'to loose'. One of the best examples of a word stigmatized in this way is the verb 'to banter'. Johnson pronounces it 'a barbarous word, without etymology, unless it be derived from [the French verb] *badiner*'. The implication is that a French etymology isn't much of an etymology at all.

The *Dictionary*'s robust sense of national identity is clear in its dismissal of modish French imports. As I have suggested, Johnson's omission of Lord Bolingbroke had something to do with the latter's morals and something to do with his taste for Frenchified diction. The verb 'to Frenchify' is defined by Johnson as 'to infect with the manner of France; to make a coxcomb', and in his entry for 'Gallicism' he directs his feelings *ad hominem*, claiming that these imported foreign words are often used by Bolingbroke.† Johnson's hostility to French terms is obvious. There are no entries in the *Dictionary* for 'bourgeois', 'unique', 'champagne' or 'cutlet', though all were by then in use. 'Trait' he considers to be 'scarce English', while 'ruse' is 'a French word neither elegant nor necessary', and 'undefiled' is 'a French word which with many more is now happily disused'. Given this aversion to terms imported from French, it seems

---

★ By the middle of the eighteenth century there was an impressive consensus about English spelling, but Johnson has a few grievances to ventilate. 'Grocer', we are told, should be written 'grosser', because a grocer was originally a wholesaler – someone who dealt in large ('gross') volumes. He prefers the antique spellings 'phrensy' and 'turkois' to 'frenzy' and 'turquoise'. 'Beggar' is 'more properly written *begger*', while the Saxon origins of 'burden' mean, he believes, that it should be written 'burthen'. He prefers 'cacao' to 'cocoa', and 'gray' to 'grey'. 'Currant' should, he alleges, be spelt 'corinth', and 'devil' perhaps ought to be 'divel'. 'Phiz' is formed 'by a ridiculous contraction from *physiognomy*, and should therefore, if it be written at all, be written *phyz*'.

† The hostility to Bolingbroke is well illustrated in Johnson's example of 'irony', which consists of the sentence 'Bolingbroke was a holy man.' He is not the only author to be derided in this way. In the abridged *Dictionary* (1756), Johnson provides an example of the use of word 'alias': 'Mallet alias Malloch; that is, *otherwise* Malloch'. This is a reference to the poet David Mallet, born Malloch, of whom Johnson was no admirer. Mallet changed his name to dissociate himself from his somewhat disreputable roots, possibly in response to a satirical attack by the critic John Dennis.

odd that Johnson should include without comment 'escargatoire' ('a nursery of snails'). Generally, when he does acknowledge an imported French term, his manner is condescending. 'Fumette', for instance, is 'a word introduced by cooks'. 'Finesse' is 'an unnecessary word which is creeping into the language'. 'Fraischeur' is 'a word foolishly innovated by Dryden'. He even manages a two-pronged dig in his entry under 'scelerat', a word meaning 'villain' which he considers to have been 'introduced unnecessarily from the French by a Scottish author'. Pointedly, he does not tell us who this author is, but the illustrative quotation comes from his sometime physician and native of Aberdeenshire, George Cheyne.

One of the main things to notice here is that the language Johnson explicitly decries is often that of the fashionable and the affluent. Linguistic corruption is most common at the extremes of the social spectrum, and the rich are at least as guilty of solecisms as the poor. At the same time we should be clear that Johnson was not the first lexicographer to stigmatize terms in this way, and that he was less aggressive in his dislikes than many of his contemporaries. What is more, for all his unhappiness about words such as 'nowadays' and 'lingo', he includes them. It would have been possible to discard them – to pretend they did not exist – but Johnson's characteristic approach is to censure, rather than to censor.

Nevertheless, the *Dictionary* is a key moment in the establishing of a national standard English. When Johnson applies one of his denigratory labels to a word, he is evidently hoping to curb its use. He is trying to repress what he considers illegitimate. Furthermore, his emphasis on the written word necessarily excluded the language of illiterates and groups whose chief mode of communication was oral.[4] Later, when he visited Scotland, he would remark the high level of rural illiteracy, and would suggest that those who knew nothing of written language were doomed to live only in the present tense – for 'what is once out of sight is lost for ever'. The restriction of the *Dictionary*'s illustrative material to written texts, and to British authors (most of them English), excludes Britain's colonial subjects and a whole tranche of British society. Clearly, this was done for practical reasons, as Johnson explains in the Preface: 'I could not visit caverns to learn the miner's language, nor take a voyage to perfect my skill in the dialect of navigation, nor visit the warehouses of merchants, and shops of artificers, to gain the names of wares, tools and operations.' By the same token, he could not travel the country – or the world – looking for variant forms of English.

When the *Dictionary* includes words that are conspicuously foreign, they are most often terms of luxury or the fruits of curious observations made by leisured scholars and travellers: 'aborigines', 'barbecue', 'caliph', 'czar', 'felucca', 'ginseng', 'Hegira', 'palanquin', 'sanhedrim', 'savanna', 'Talmud', 'vizier'. Closer to home, although Johnson finds room for a good many 'country' terms, there is a very modest recognition of regional variations.[5] The only regional variants to receive much notice are those used in Scotland. The identification of these may be a Johnsonian dig at the predominantly Scottish booksellers and amanuenses, or, conversely, it may be the work of the amanuenses, in compensation for their master's Sassenach proclivities.[6] On the whole, however, regionalism is unheard. When Johnson allows 'low' language into the *Dictionary*, it is because he has heard it from the mouth of a Shakespearean rogue, not because he has come across it on the streets of London. This is limiting, and it has not failed to provoke criticism.

We should be wary of thinking that Johnson's was a peculiarly narrow, imperialistic view. Few of his contemporaries would have conceived of their language as a collection of different Englishes, and, as someone trying to amplify the intelligibility of English, he was hardly likely to celebrate its kaleidoscopic variety. All the same, in its emphasis on purity and on eradicating barbarisms, its deference to the language (and thus the wider cultural affinities) of the sixteenth and seventeenth centuries, its particular celebration of Elizabethan language, and its professions of linguistic uniformity, the *Dictionary* transmits an image of English and Englishness which is not just predominantly middle-class, but also backward-looking, Anglocentric and male. Two hundred and fifty years later, debates about 'proper' English are still permeated by these values.

Opinionist

One fond of his own notions

'Every conceited *opinionist* sets up an infallible chair in his own brain' – Joseph Glanvill

As we reflect on the business of legislating language, we perceive that the meanings of words are not in the words themselves, but in us, their users. 'When I use a word,' said Humpty Dumpty, 'it means just what I choose it to mean.' Johnson could be Humptyish. His definitions are usually dispassionate, but there are times when the bright colours of subjectivity burst in, and some entries are tinged with prejudice, or even tainted by it. (In his definition of 'prejudice' Johnson says it is 'commonly *a bad thing*'.) He chooses to define the word 'lexicon' as 'a dictionary; a book teaching the signification of words', and that reference to 'teaching' reminds us of his pedagogic aims.

While it would be wrong to say that a large percentage of Johnson's definitions are quirky, partisan or dictatorial, those that are tell us something about him and about his age. They also tell us about the very nature of lexicography, for in truth there is scarcely such a thing as a totally colourless definition.★ To register language is to form it: definition is rarely untouched by ideology. Ephraim Chambers argued in the preface to his *Cyclopaedia* that 'The

---

★ Modern dictionaries are more objective, but some quirks survive. The 1972 edition of the *Chambers Twentieth Century Dictionary* defines 'jaywalker' as 'a careless pedestrian whom motorists are expected to avoid running down' and 'middle-aged' as 'between youth and old age, variously reckoned to suit the reckoner'. I have borrowed these examples from Henri Béjoint, *Tradition and Innovation in Modern English Dictionaries* (Oxford: Clarendon Press, 1994). Béjoint also cites the old *OED* definition of 'canoe' as 'a kind of boat in use among uncivilized nations', as well as an example from a Dutch dictionary of the 1970s, in which 'cosmonaut' is defined as 'a somewhat hyperbolic designation for persons who make a tiny jump in cosmic space'. One further example, from the 1988 edition of *Chambers*, is the definition of 'éclair' as 'a cake, long in shape but short in duration'.

Dictionarist is not supposed to have any hand in the things he relates': 'like an Historian, [he] comes after the affair, and gives a description of what has passed'. But lexicographers perpetually experience the tension between observation and regulation, between passivity and activity, between the duty to record and the wish to civilize.

In the opening chapter of this book I quoted Johnson's definition of 'oats'. It is appropriate to quote it again: 'a grain, which in England is generally given to horses, but in Scotland supports the people'. This is barely a definition at all: it tells one nothing about the distinctive characteristics of oats, for even if English horses and Scottish people stopped consuming them, oats would still be oats. Johnson's definition is, rather, an opinionated jibe. In fact it is a secondhand jibe, derived either from Burton's *Anatomy of Melancholy* or from Philip Miller, author of the *Gardener's Dictionary* which Johnson used for many definitions.[1] But, in a dictionary compiled by a single individual, flashes of opinion, together with the odd indulgent flourish, are inevitable. The real surprise of Johnson's *Dictionary* is that, despite its author's reputation as a man of rather cramped sympathies, its entries are as clinical and unprejudiced as they are.

Many of Johnson's opinions are localized: they do not betray any large-scale passions or commitments. For instance, there are scattered snippets of covert literary criticism. The sonnet, he declares, 'is not very suitable to the English language'. While admirers of Donne or Shakespeare will find this startling, it is fair to say that the form was not in wide use in Johnson's age, and recent practitioners had done little to inspire its revival. Johnson states as much, in noting that it 'has not been used by any man of eminence since Milton'. A quarter of a century later, in his *Life of Milton*, he would assert that 'the fabric of a sonnet, however adapted to the Italian language, has never succeeded in ours'. The essential problem, as he saw it, was that fewer words rhyme in English than in Italian.[2] Johnson's antipathy to the form was long-lived, and the *Dictionary* reflects this antipathy, perhaps gratuitously. By much the same token, his dislike of brackets is evident in his definition of 'parenthesis' – 'a sentence so included in another sentence, as that it may be taken out, without injuring the sense of that which incloses it'. Again he is consistent: Boswell would later note that 'he disapproved of a parenthesis; and I believe in all his voluminous writings, not half a dozen of them will be found'. Elsewhere a 'history' is 'a narration of events and facts delivered with dignity'. Are histories intrinsically dignified? No, but Johnson suggests that they ought to be, and implies that sometimes they are not.

These are matters of critical taste, albeit charged with a certain conscious rectitude, and it is when Johnson comes to moral considerations that his judgemental tone becomes most clear. We can hear it, at high volume, in that previously mentioned definition of 'suicide' – 'the horrid crime of destroying one's self' – or in his dismissal of a 'stockjobber' (in modern parlance, a broker-dealer or a stockbroker) as 'a low wretch who gets money by buying and selling shares in the funds'. So too a 'poetaster' is 'a vile petty poet' (because he debases poetry), and a 'fortuneteller' is 'one who cheats common people by pretending to the knowledge of futurity'. A 'foxhunter' is 'a man whose chief ambition is to shew his bravery in hunting foxes', while a 'gambler' is 'a knave whose practice it is to invite the unwary to game and cheat them'. An 'absentee' is someone 'absent from his station or employment, or country', and the word is 'used commonly with regard to Irishmen living out of their country' – a caustic reference to Ireland's many absentee landlords, whose residence in England meant that most of Ireland's wealth was exported. He defines 'crime' as 'an act contrary to right' or 'an act of wickedness': the implication, with which few modern readers will concur, is that law and morality are one and the same. Intriguingly, too, 'luggage' is 'any thing cumbrous and unwieldy that is to be carried away; any thing of more bulk than value': Johnson dismisses the human tendency to encumber oneself with material things that are impressive yet ultimately worthless.

In some definitions it is one word in particular that gives the reader pause for thought. For example, a 'pressgang' is 'a crew that strolls about the streets to force men into naval service'. We need hardly be told that Johnson disapproved, but it is the verb 'strolls' that most shockingly portrays the pressgang's casual brutality. More obviously provocative is his definition of 'distiller': 'one who makes and sells pernicious and inflammatory spirits'. 'Pernicious' is not a word to use lightly, and the condemnation recalls the contemporary distrust of all who made their living by lubricating poverty, violence and sickness. A comparably scathing judgement is contained in the definition of a 'skeptick' as 'one who doubts, or pretends to doubt of every thing': the word 'pretends' is the key, for Johnson, secure in his own religious faith, saw scepticism less as a school of thought than as a posture.

Some of Johnson's most pungent opinions are drawn out by the animal kingdom. His familiar national pride is in evidence when he announces that bulldogs are 'so peculiar to Britain, that they are said to degenerate when they are carried to other countries'. He notes that a canary is 'an excellent singing bird', while the sheep is 'remarkable for its usefulness and innocence', and the spaniel is 'remarkable' too, on account of its 'sagacity and obedience'. The word 'swine', on the other hand, denotes 'a hog; a pig. A creature remarkable for stupidity and nastiness', and when he defines 'seal' his description is borrowed from a text which informs readers that the seal is 'in make and growth not unlike a pig, ugly faced, and footed like a moldwarp'. In later life he changed his mind. Having heard about a 'learned pig' in Nottingham, he admitted that 'the pigs are a race unjustly calumniated'. At least he refrains from condemning pigs as sweaty and foul-smelling: there are several other occasions when feral odours, real or imagined, goad his sensibilities. A 'bug' is 'a stinking insect bred in old household stuff', a 'fitchew' (polecat) is a 'stinking little beast, that robs the henroost and warren', and a 'fulimart' is apparently 'a kind of stinking ferret', while a 'stoat' is simply 'a small stinking animal'.

These are the opinions of someone whose fragmentary knowledge of the natural world is coloured by received opinion and folklore. Johnson had almost certainly never smelt a polecat or a stoat, and his opinion of pigs probably came from literature, not from direct experience. 'Stinking' seems to have been a stock eighteenth-century word for dealing with anything considered unpleasant: in Swift's 'Description of a City Shower' the streets are flooded with 'dung, guts, and blood, / Drowned puppies, stinking sprats', and the word was frequently used in vilifying Jews and homosexuals. All the same, Johnson's language is emphatic. Polecats are still noted for their fetid smell, but Johnson leaves us in no doubt that this is their principal trait.★

★ When Johnson defines 'ortolan' as 'a small bird accounted very delicious', we infer that he has never eaten ortolan and is relying on someone else's opinion. But when he explains that 'rasp' is short for 'raspberry' and is 'a delicious berry that grows on

We can see a more sustained and personal outlook in his treatment of politics and religion. Johnson may be a pragmatist and an advocate of common sense, but he also has High Anglican and royalist tendencies. The *Dictionary*'s definitions of 'Whig' and 'Tory' are well known. 'Whig' is 'the name of a faction', whereas 'Tory' is 'one who adheres to the ancient constitution of the state, and the apostolical hierarchy of the Church of England, opposed to a Whig'. This leaves one in little doubt of Johnson's political allegiances.[3] However, Johnson's Toryism was rather different from contemporary Conservative politics. In his commitment to social welfare and opposition to the still common practice of slavery, he was a progressive liberal.[4] He disliked Whig politics because of their inherent republicanism and religious unorthodoxy, though his definition of 'republican' – 'one who thinks a commonwealth without monarchy the best government' – shows sober self-control. Compare, if you will, his remark to Boswell that 'the first Whig was the Devil'!

Johnson's hostility to Whig politics is plain for all to see. The fourth sense of 'leader' is 'One at the head of any party or faction: as the detestable Wharton was the *leader* of the Whigs.'[5] His distaste for Whig taxes is apparent in his definition of 'excise': 'a hateful tax levied upon commodities, and adjudged not by the common judges of property, but wretches hired by those to whom excise is paid'. This incensed the Commissioners of Excise, who called on the Attorney General, William Murray, to determine whether it was libellous. Murray decided that it was, but Johnson, despite being counselled to change it, never did. We may note too this quotation, under 'royalist': 'The old church of England *royalists*, another name for a man who prefers his conscience before his interests, are the most meritorious subjects in the world, having passed all those terrible tests, which domineering malice could put them to, and carried their credit and their conscience clear.' Although we should be wary of taking the *Dictionary*'s illustrations as indicative of Johnson's own views, this quotation, taken from Robert South, does chime with

---

a species of the bramble', we learn that he likes raspberries. Similarly, 'usquebaugh' is 'a compounded distilled spirit', and 'the Irish sort is particularly distinguished for its pleasant and mild flavour': Johnson has tasted this spirit and enjoyed it.

Johnson's monarchist inclinations.[6] These are richly manifest too in the 350-odd quotations from *Eikon Basilike*, a meditative book of instruction which he believed to have been written by the martyred King Charles I.

South is one of a number of High Church bishops whom Johnson favours, and the religious values of the *Dictionary* are unambiguous. A 'Protestant' is 'one of those who adhere to them, who, at the beginning of the reformation, protested against the errors of the church of Rome'. This is the classic eighteenth-century image of Protestantism – embattled and anti-Catholic – and, predictably, the *Dictionary* strafes Catholicism. Under 'popery', Swift speaks for the Protestant majority in asserting that it is 'for corruptions in doctrine and discipline . . . the most absurd system of christianity'. The sixteenth-century archbishop John Whitgift testifies, emotively, that 'a great number of parishes in England consist of rude and ignorant men, drowned in *papistry*'. 'When a Papist uses the word *hereticks*,' writes Isaac Watts, 'he generally means Protestants; when a Protestant uses the word, he means any persons wilfully and contentiously obstinate in fundamental errors.'

Watts's quotation implies not only that Catholicism is fundamentally erroneous, but also that good Protestants have other enemies besides Catholics. True to this, the *Dictionary* attacks Protestant nonconformism. The second definition of 'disciplinarian' is 'a follower of the Presbyterian sect, so called from their perpetual clamour about discipline', and the Presbyterian himself is 'an abettor of . . . calvinistical discipline', while 'prig' ('a pert, conceited, saucy, pragmatical, little fellow') may derive from '*prickeared*, a term of reproach bestowed upon the presbyterian teachers'. Johnson objected to the Presbyterians' noisy Unitarianism and their rejection of ecclesiastical hierarchy; he argued against them concertedly in his life of the seventeenth-century minister Francis Cheynell, which was published in a magazine called the *Student* in 1751. He was thoroughly mistrustful of Puritanism too. The word 'Puritan' is defined as 'a sectary pretending to eminent purity of religion', and there are slighting references to Puritans in the illustrative material. His suspicion of Quakers and Methodists ('a new kind of puritans lately arisen') can be seen in his definition of 'enthusiasm', the mystical fervour that enabled them to speak in tongues. Locke had argued that it rose 'from the conceits of a warmed or overweening brain'. Johnson quotes this, adding that it is 'a vain belief of private revelation; a vain confidence of divine favour or communication'. The crucial word here is 'vain'. Anything that deviates from Johnson's own perceived orthodoxy is impugned, and at the heart of this orthodoxy is the conviction that there should be a single, authoritative national Church, cementing not just the religious practices of its members, but the very idea of Britishness.

These are Johnson's public values – views to which he felt able to put his name. Throughout the time he was writing the *Dictionary* he was engaged in public business. Sometimes it was parochial: standing bail for Peyton's rackety wife Mary after she had got into a ruck with a woman called Humphreys, helping his friend Bathurst try to find a publisher, advising Giuseppe Baretti when he was accused of stealing a forty-guinea watch. But at other times he made himself conspicuous: promoting the talents of Charlotte Lennox, writing satirical verse, and, regrettably, supporting with some vigour the claims of William Lauder, a Scotsman with a wooden leg who wrote a series of articles claiming that Milton had stolen large parts of *Paradise Lost* from other, lesser-known, authors. Johnson's judgement and values were continually and visibly called into service. As in the *Dictionary*, he displayed his opinions in all their colour.

Yet anyone who looks for long into the *Dictionary* will discern someone very different from the public Johnson. As we have seen, there appears to be a streak of autobiography embedded in the illustrative quotations. This is especially true with regard to his marriage. As his work on the *Dictionary* intensified, his relationship with the increasingly valetudinarian Tetty was foundering, and occasionally – only occasionally, but still quite palpably – his illustrative material seems to afford us a poignant commentary on this. Here, for instance, is John Dryden, illustrating one of the senses of 'world': 'Marriage draws a *world* of business on our hands, subjects us to law-suits, and loads us with domestick cares.' There were no lawsuits in the literal sense, but Johnson's marriage was frayed by dispute. In later years he would recall this with a touch of humour. He could tell against himself the story of preparing to say grace when his wife interrupted him, saying, 'Do not make a farce of thanking God for a dinner which you will presently protest not eatable.'[7] But his laughter at the wranglings of the sexes was seldom tender. Often it played up to stereotype. 'The man', he would reflect, 'calls his wife to walk with him in the shade, and she feels a strange desire just at that moment to sit in the sun.'[8]

The *Dictionary* contains numerous snapshots of marital dishar-mony. One of the most stinging comes from Robert South: 'When a man thinks himself *matched* to one who should be a comfort to him, instead thereof he finds in his bosom a beast.' There is plenty more in this vein. Francis Bacon harks back to pre-Socratic philosophy, recalling that 'Thales being asked when a man should marry, said, young men not *yet*; old men, not at all.' Elsewhere the same author observes that '*unmarried* men are best friends, best masters, best ser-vants, but not always best subjects, for they are light to run away'. He claims, too, that 'Women to govern men, slaves freemen, are much in the same degree; all being total violations and *perversions* of the laws of nature and nations.' And for an illustration of 'stocks' ('prison for the legs'), Johnson turns to Henry Peacham's instructional volume *The Complete Gentleman* (1622): 'Matrimony is expressed by a young man standing, his legs being fast in a pair of *stocks*.' This quotation, like the others, is not a direct expression of Johnson's view, but if it is really to be of any help in suggesting what stocks are it calls for a sour conception of marriage.

There can be no doubt that the trials of compilation distracted Johnson from his marital responsibilities. Tetty had long since made it plain that his sexual attentions were unwelcome, and he, for his part, had taken to sharing his ambitions, fears and everyday concerns with friends rather than with her. Communication between them had slowed to a trickle. Although Johnson knew that his wife was ill, it was hard to tell the difference between real suffering and the mut-terings of hypochondria, and the sheer volume of his work blocked out worries about her health. But when she died, on 17 March 1752, just three days after he had published the final *Rambler*, his grief was incapacitating. He could not even rouse himself to attend her funeral in the parish church at Bromley, and was racked with guilt, since he felt responsible for her decline. Their marriage had never been sweetly harmonious, but it had throbbed with feeling. Now he wished he had expressed his love more tenderly.

For the benefit of those who had known her, Johnson recalled his wife's powerful literary intuitions and her excellent manner of declaiming comic speeches, yet he also remembered their arguments. He found some relief in the company of his friends, and some in prayer and meditation. But the memory of neglected duties festered. He took Tetty's wedding ring and stowed it in a little wooden box, which from time to time he would piously consult. For the rest of his days he would honour Tetty's memory with a mixture of prayerful unction and self-reproach.*

Within a fortnight of her death, however, Johnson's gloomy household was animated by the arrival of a new member. This was Francis Barber, a ten-year-old Jamaican boy entrusted to Johnson's care by Richard Bathurst. Dr Bathurst's family owned plantations in Jamaica, and Francis, freed from slavery by Bathurst's father, had come to London in 1750. Quite what use Johnson found for Francis is unclear – Hawkins suggests that 'Diogenes himself never wanted a servant less than he seemed to do'[9] – but it appears that the dusty atmosphere of Gough Square was not to the young man's taste, for he twice ran away, the first time to become a servant to an apothecary, and the second time to go to sea. Later Francis was reconciled with Johnson, and he would in due course be the principal beneficiary of his will. He not only named his first son Samuel after his former employer, but settled in Lichfield, where young Samuel would later achieve some note as a Methodist preacher.

As the weeks crept by, Johnson's spirits lifted slowly. According to Hawkins, his depression was 'of the blackest and deepest kind'.[10] However, the responsibility of looking after Francis, who was nominally a servant but really a surrogate child, forced him to be active. Francis would recall that in the first months he spent at Gough Square his master received a good number of visitors, including Garrick and Cave, Strahan and Dodsley, as well as a druggist called Diamond, who

---

* Moreover, although misgivings about matrimony proliferate in the *Dictionary*, there are plangent notes of tenderness. Under 'marriage' Johnson chose to quote, from Richard Crashaw's 'An Epitaph Upon Husband and Wife', the lines 'For though the hand of fate could force / 'Twixt soul and body a divorce, / It could not sever man and wife, / Because they both liv'd but one life.'

tried to interest Johnson in a trip to Iceland. Moreover, even as Johnson grieved for his wife, he began to wrestle with the idea of remarrying. Several diary entries excluded by Boswell from his account of Johnson's activities in 1753 mention this, and, although entries for later years emphasize the remembrance of his first wife rather than the intention of taking a second, it is clear that he did give the matter serious consideration. On 22 April 1753 – Easter Sunday – he wrote in his diary, 'As I purpose to try on Monday to seek a new wife without any derogation from dear Tetty's memory I purpose at sacrament in the morning to take my leave of Tetty in a solemn commendation of her soul to God.' The next day he did take the sacrament at the church where she was buried: 'During the whole service I was never once distracted by any thoughts of any other woman or with my design of a new wife.'[11] To record one's resistance to distraction is to acknowledge the very real possibility of succumbing to distraction; Johnson was not congratulating himself so much as agonizing about the legitimacy of his 'design'.

Perhaps the most obvious candidate for his affections at this time was Hill Boothby, a cultured, pious, well-born spinster of his own age, whom he had met a dozen years before on a trip to Derbyshire. But at the very time when Johnson was thinking of paying court to her she was distracted by the death of a friend, Mary Fitzherbert (née Meynell). She was named Mrs Fitzherbert's sole executor and residual legatee, and immediately took charge of her six children. This put her out of reach, and in any case Johnson would have felt awkward about courting a woman who was set to acquire some wealth. Yet he wrote to her several times a week, addressing her as 'My Sweet Angel', and when she died, three years later, he felt the loss deeply. He was to become contemptuous of second marriages ('a triumph of hope over experience'), but there can be little doubt that marriage, for all its inconveniences, seemed at this time a plausible means of arresting his melancholy. Without company, he was all too likely to fall prey to the depravities of his imagination.

Yet Johnson was sturdy, and, as he stemmed the tide of his grief, his work on the *Dictionary* began to accelerate. In the *Rambler* he had written that 'The uncertainty of our duration ought at once to set bounds to our designs, and add incitements to our industry; and when we find ourselves inclined either to immensity in our schemes, or sluggishness in our endeavours, we may either check or animate ourselves, by recollecting . . . that *art is long, and life is short*.'[12] Tetty's death drove this adage home. He had written too that whoever has 'trifled away those months and years, in which he should have laboured, must remember that he has now only a part of that of which the whole is little; and that since the few moments remaining are to be considered the last days of Heaven, not one is to be lost'.[13] Now, reaching out for guidance in his unhappiness, he found solace in his own counsel.

Crucially, he rediscovered his appetite for the task of compilation. He began work on the second volume on 3 April 1753, and seemed newly energized. 'O God who hast hitherto supported me,' he could write in his diary, 'enable me to proceed in this labour & in the Whole task of my present state', so that 'when I shall render up at the last day an account of the talent committed to me I may receive pardon for the sake of Jesus Christ'.[14] His letters meanwhile suggest a healthy pragmatism: he is borrowing books, offering advice to Richardson about how to deal with Irish piracies of his new novel, and discussing the *Adventurer*, to which he first contributed in March of that year. He writes to Strahan to apologize, none too penitentially, for a problem with the manuscript; it appears that the ever-vigilant printer had complained about the poor layout of the pages he was receiving.[15]

In October 1753 Strahan was able to print a further 100 sheets, taking the work up to the word 'grate', and Johnson, who had been sluggish for so long, was now delivering copy faster than it could be printed. Conscious of this, he stopped providing manuscript as it was produced, waiting instead until he had completed the material for the second volume. He was racing towards its end. He had embraced afresh the drama of his task, learning again to enjoy its difficulty. In the *Rambler* he had written of how 'The traveller that resolutely follows a rough and winding path, will sooner reach the end of his journey, than he that is always changing his direction, and wastes the hours of daylight in looking for smoother ground, and shorter passages.'[16] This now stood as an ironic summary of his struggle to complete the *Dictionary*.

Opulence

Wealth; riches; affluence

> There in full *opulence* a banker dwelt,
> Who all the joys and pangs of riches felt;
> His sideboard glitter'd with imagin'd plate,
> And his proud fancy held a vast estate. – Swift

For all Johnson's darts of opinion and veiled self-revelations, the *Dictionary* is an important testament to the tastes and values of the age in which it was produced. It chronicles some of the innovations of chic metropolitan life, as well as suggesting larger preoccupations. In 1754 a commentator wrote in the *Gentleman's Magazine* that 'England is no more like to what England was than it resembles Borneo or Madagascar.' The reference to 'England' is misleading. Writers and politicians often used it as a synonym for 'Britain', and it did not automatically imply the exclusion of the Scottish or the Welsh. Nevertheless, the statement highlights the period's cultural and semantic flux. Had a typical citizen of 1720 been magically transported forward fifty years, he or she would have been struck dumb with disbelief. Even by the 1750s the changes were luminously clear. As one of the best historians of the period suggests, the earlier generation would have marvelled at the achievements of the commercial spirit. They would have been 'startled to find it threading the landscape with waterways, raising cities and suburbs where there had been only villages, revolutionizing farms and manufactures, dictating war against the American colonies, and promoting parliamentary legislation on an unprecedented scale'.[1] Without slavishly documenting the changes it effected, the *Dictionary* bears witness to the march of commercialism.

One development was the rise of commercial fashion. In the *Dictionary*, London fashions are the province of Addison, Johnson's favourite documentarist of urban pretentiousness. Addison is strong on modish contemporary slang ('fiddlefaddle', 'wiseacre', 'incog' as a short form of 'incognito') and on modish phenomena (the chop house, the sofa, the practice of eating snails). It is to the highly quotable essayist that Johnson owes his entries for 'whitewash', a kind of make-up used by women who wished to make their skin look fair; for 'mantuamaker', the producer of a popular style of lady's gown; and for 'modesty-piece', a word Addison coined to describe the lace which concealed the more exciting parts of women's breasts. If only Garrick's actresses had availed themselves of the last of these: his former teacher might have felt more at ease in the Green Room, and could have arrived at a better understanding of the theatre.

Johnson records plenty of other fashions and innovations: the toy-shop, mezzotints, spa towns, the tobacconist (where once the word had signified a tobacco addict, it now denoted a vendor), the newspaper advertisement, the shoeblack, spatterdashes (a forerunner of spats, worn by Robinson Crusoe), the popular hard, dark varnish known as 'japan', the mania for tulips, and the cosmetic 'beauty-spot', which he defines as 'a spot placed to direct the eye to something else, or to heighten some beauty'. Commenting obliquely on the contemporary rage for vases – such a boon to that other famous native of Staffordshire, Josiah Wedgwood – he defines 'vase' as 'generally a vessel rather for show than use'. He even has an entry for 'umbrella', which is a 'skreen [sic] used in hot countries to keep off the sun, and in others to bear off the rain'. He doesn't seem too sure of the spelling of the word: he offers 'umbrel' and, in his definition of 'parasol', the sadly unadopted 'umbrello'. Umbrellas were certainly something new. They are mentioned by Dryden, Swift and Defoe (as well as his spats, Robinson Crusoe has an umbrella made of goatskin), and are recognized in more than one dictionary before Johnson's, but they were rarely used as a form of protection against British rain until the late eighteenth century. The powerful philanthropist Jonas Hanway was supposedly the first Londoner to carry one for such a purpose, in the early 1750s, and he was ridiculed for doing so.★

There are hints, too, of wider social trends. The first edition of the *Dictionary* contains more than thirty references to coffee, and even

---

★ The first Americans to use them were in Windsor, Connecticut, around 1740.

more to tea. Johnson would vigorously defend the latter, not long after the *Dictionary* was published, in his review of an essay by the umbrella-toting Hanway, who believed it was 'pernicious to health, obstructing industry and impoverishing the nation'.[2] Johnson's love of tea was deep but not exceptional: the leaf had been available in England since the 1650s (Pepys records drinking it for the first time in September 1660), and by 1755 it was being imported to Britain at the rate of 2,000 tons a year. The fashion for tea-drinking, facilitated by Britain's imperial resources, drove demand for another fruit of the colonies, sugar ('the native salt of the sugar-cane, obtained by the expression and evaporation of its juice'). Tea also played a crucial role in the dissolution of the eighteenth-century British Empire, for it was of course Bostonian opponents of a British tax on tea who opened the final breach between Britain and colonial America.

All the same, it was coffee that proved the more remarkable phenomenon of the age. Johnson gives a clue to this when he defines 'coffeehouse' as 'a house of entertainment where coffee is sold, and the guests are supplied with newspapers'. It was this relationship between coffee and entertainment (by which Johnson meant 'conversation') that made it such a potent force. Coffee was first imported to Europe from Yemen in the early part of the seventeenth century, and the first coffee house opened in St Mark's Square in Venice in 1647. The first in England opened five years later – a fact to which Johnson refers in his entry for 'coffee' – but its proprietor, Daniel Edwards, could hardly have envisioned that by the middle of the following century there would be several thousand coffee houses in London alone, along with new coffee plantations, run by Europeans, in the East Indies and the Caribbean.

Then as now, coffee houses were meeting places, where customers (predominantly male) could convene to discuss politics and current affairs. By the time of the *Dictionary* they were not so much gentlemanly snuggeries as commercial exchanges. As the cultural historian John Brewer explains, 'the coffee house was the precursor of the modern office'; in later years Johnson would sign the contract for his *Lives of the English Poets* in a coffee house on Paternoster Row, and the London Stock Exchange and Lloyd's have their origins in the coffee-house culture of the period. 'Besides being meeting places', the coffee houses were '*postes restantes*, libraries, places of exhibition and sometimes even theatres'. They were centres, too, of political opposition, and, because they were open to all ranks and religions, they allowed a rare freedom of information and expression.[3]

The popularity of coffee houses was a symptom of the increasingly secular nature of urban society. It was a symptom, too, of the century's openness about pleasure. Eighteenth-century society, and particularly the London society with which Johnson was best acquainted, cultivated and fetishized luxuries. These were usually associated with foreignness and femininity, and were often subject to special taxes; typical indulgences were watches, fine linen, imported lace, satinwood and mahogany, Persian rugs, exotic spices, rare dyes such as indigo, Chinese silks and porcelain, and choice foodstuffs like pineapple and chocolate (the latter still a drink – the first chocolate bars were not marketed until the 1840s). Johnson is not up to date about all of these, and the most crazed excesses of consumerism did not present themselves until the two decades after the *Dictionary* was finished, but its pages often suggest the trappings of luxurious living. In defining 'luxury' as 'addictedness to pleasure', he touches upon the contemporary debate about the dangers of these fashionable accoutrements. It was a debate in which he, a little surprisingly, stood up for luxury, arguing that its abundance was the mark of a truly civilized society.[4]

One of the signs of luxury was a new fastidiousness about the minutiae of personal appearance. Besides beauty spots and 'whitewash', Johnson notices the vogue for 'dentifrice', 'a powder made to scour the teeth'. Extravagant claims were made about the efficacy of dental powders, which often had the opposite of the desired effect, causing irreparable damage to users' teeth. But dentifrice was popular among the upper classes. So were toothpicks, although they were abhorred by Lord Chesterfield, who was one of the great advocates of dental hygiene. Johnson defines 'picktooth' as 'an instrument by which the teeth are cleaned'. It is not a colourful definition, but the attendant quotation from Swift intimates the glittering politics of foppery: Swift suggests that if any of your dinner guests leaves behind a picktooth case when he goes home you should look on it as an unpurposed sort of thank-you. The practice of cleaning one's teeth might have had

entirely reasonable origins, but it allowed followers of fashion to accu-
mulate an extraordinary range of modish paraphernalia.

Health care was subject to the vagaries of fashion. Johnson, who
was interested in contemporary medicine for reasons both scholarly
and personal, offers pertinent information about the contemporary
use of ginseng, opium and hartshorn – ginseng, for example, is 'a
good medicine in convulsions, vertigoes, and all nervous complaints',
while opium 'removes melancholy' and 'dissipates the dread of
danger'. On the evidence of the *Spectator* he provides a definition of
'posturemaster': 'one who teaches or practises artificial contortions
of the body' – a sort of prankish eighteenth-century Pilates. The
English vogue for callisthenics and contortionism was initiated in the
late seventeenth century. It began with a visit to London by Tiberio
Fiorelli, a Neapolitan actor known for his interpretation of the *com-
media dell'arte* character Scaramouch. The fashion persisted, and
eventually metamorphosed into the Victorian equation of properly
regulated posture and moral rectitude.

More broadly, the *Dictionary* acknowledges changes in eighteenth-
century leisure. Alongside traditional activities such as falconry, deer-
hunting, hare-coursing and marbles, there were newer, codified
sports like cricket, real tennis, boxing and football. Johnson mentions
all of these, and, although cruel sports were falling into decline (this
was an age of pets and of an increasing sympathy for animals), he
notes the enthusiasm, chiefly plebeian, for cockfighting and bear-
baiting. 'No man is a hypocrite in his pleasures,' he told Reynolds,
towards the end of his life: what a man enjoys doing in his spare time
is a more accurate index of his tastes and values than what he professes to like.

The new public amusements reflected the increasing com-
mercialization of leisure. They were money-making spectacles,
generously advertised, and calculated to attract a paying audience,
many of whom would also gamble on the outcome. This was controversial. An item in the *Gentleman's Magazine* of September 1743
sums up the widespread anxiety about the abuse of recreation: 'The
diversion of Cricket . . . upon days when men ought to be busy, and
in the neighbourhood of a great city . . . is not only improper but
mischievous in a high degree'; it 'propagates a spirit of idleness'

and 'draws numbers of people from their employments, to the ruin of their families'.[5]

Competitive sports encouraged a sense of local identity. When the gentlemen of Sussex beat the gentlemen of Kent, they were as jubilant as if they had won a war. But other kinds of game tested the character of the individual. The popularity of gambling, and of games combining strategy and chance, is plain. The *Dictionary* contains the names of numerous card games: among them piquet, quadrille, ombre, basset, whist, landsquenet and loo. Johnson also mentions backgammon and billiards, although with these games, as with others, there is little sense that he has ever tried them. Chess is 'a nice and abstruse game', which suggests he may at least have seen it played.

There is evidence of a more sociable Johnson in his detailed explanation of 'snapdragon', which is 'a kind of play, in which brandy is set on fire, and raisins are thrown into it, which those who are unused to the sport are afraid to take out; but which may be safely snatched by a quick motion, and put blazing into the mouth, which being closed, the fire is at once extinguished'. This is leisure of a primitive, uncommercial, exhibitionist kind – a piece of macho theatre of a type almost as old and lasting as the practice of drinking is itself. Did he see this in Lichfield, as a young man, or in Birmingham while drinking his 'bishop', or when consorting with the likes of Levet and Savage? We cannot know. But brandy-drinkers he admired. 'There are . . . few who are able to drink brandy,' he would reflect in later years, over dinner with Sir Joshua Reynolds. 'Claret is the liquor for boys; port, for men; but he who aspires to be a hero . . . must drink brandy.'

With its sketches of falconry, cricket and snapdragon, the *Dictionary* is an invaluable record of the diversity of eighteenth-century pleasures, yet it also reminds us of what society lacked. Johnson defines 'police' as 'the regulation and government of a city or country', noting that the word is French in origin. The generality of the definition conveys the flimsiness of contemporary law and order; a professional police force was established by Sir Robert Peel only in 1829. At the time of the *Dictionary* the Bow Street Runners, a band of constables formed by the novelist Henry Fielding, had lately begun to patrol the streets of London, but elsewhere lawlessness went unchecked. Johnson reminds us of exactly why a police force was necessary in his entry for 'mohock', which is 'the name of a cruel nation of America given to ruffians who infested, or rather were imagined to infest, the streets of London'. The Mohocks were an obnoxious rabble of patrician rakes who terrorized innocent Londoners in the early part of the century.* Their favourite amusement was slashing people's faces; it was not unusual for them to slice off their victims' noses. Johnson is explicitly sceptical of their existence: as far as he is concerned, stories of their excesses owe more to the febrile imagination of city-dwellers than to palpable reality. But contemporary evidence suggests he was wrong, and urban pleasures were perpetually jeopardized by the threat of violence.

To the modern reader the definition of 'police' appears imprecise. So it should, for in the eighteenth century the word was imprecise: semantic breadth reflects social latitude. It is for the same reason that Johnson's definition of 'hieroglyph' seems lax. He explains it as a 'figure by which a word was implied'. Again, the definition records the limits of contemporary expertise. In the eighteenth century the significance of hieroglyphics had not been fathomed, although a good deal of energy had been expended on trying to discover the origins of language. Not until forty-four years after the first edition of the *Dictionary* did Napoleon's soldiers discover the Rosetta Stone during excavations near Alexandria, and it was then another twenty-three years before Jean-François Champollion began successfully to decipher the inscription engraved on it two millennia before. Champollion's pioneering work was a significant moment in the history of archaeology, which became in the nineteenth century a systematic discipline in its own right. But in the *Dictionary* 'archaiology' is merely 'a discourse on antiquity'. In Johnson's mind, and in the estimate of most of his peers, it was associated with the quaint antiquarianism of dilettanti, and was an amateur pursuit, not a science.

Finally, of course, there are the broad intellectual currents of the

---

* Johnson's definition of 'rake' shows his fondness for a *millefeuille* of adjectives: 'a loose, disorderly, vicious, wild, gay, thoughtless fellow'. A 'rakehel', meanwhile, is 'a wild, worthless, dissolute, debauched, sorry fellow'. That 'sorry' is a lovely touch, though the implied distinction between the rake and the rakehell is less than clear.

age, to which Johnson alludes in passing. So, for example, he glances at the 'freethinkers', whose dismissal of revealed religion, transmuted into republicanism, would inspirit both the French and the American revolutions. He has an entry for 'missionary'; although Catholic missions had been operative for a hundred years, Johnson would only have acknowledged Protestant missions, and these were a more recent development. He offers no entry for 'freemason' or 'freemasonry', but there is a reference to this increasingly popular, clandestine fraternity in an illustrative quotation from Swift. Furthermore, in noting that one of the meanings of 'taste' is 'intellectual relish or discernment', he indicates the word's centrality in the aesthetic debates of mid-century. The reign of taste gave individuals, regardless of their political status, an unprecedented stake in public affairs. No word evoked the new importance of personal feelings more keenly than 'sensibility'. Johnson glossed it as either 'quickness of sensation' or 'quickness of perception'. Only for the fourth edition did he add that it could mean 'delicacy', hinting at the growing cult of sensibility, the beatification of delicate feelings espoused by his friend Richardson and by most of polite society.

In general, Johnson avoids saying much about fashionable theories. So, for instance, he deals curtly with the 'sublime'. He defines it as 'the grand or lofty style', adding that it is 'a Gallicism, but now naturalized'. From Addison he quotes a passage which sums up what it is: 'The *sublime* rises from the nobleness of thoughts, the magnificence of the words, or the harmonious and lively turn of the phrase; the perfect *sublime* arises from all three together.' The doctrine of the Sublime originated in a first-century tract by Dionysius Longinus, and was promulgated in the 1670s by Nicolas Boileau. It had been popularized in Britain by Addison, and in a translation by Leonard Welsted (who is mocked by Pope in the illustration of 'beer' as 'thin, yet never clear; / So sweetly mawkish, and so smoothly dull; / Heady, not strong; and foaming, tho' not full'). Longinus's text had recently been the subject of a detailed commentary by William Smith, and it was soon to be further popularized in Britain by Burke. Yet Johnson was suspicious, and not just because he considered the word 'sublime' a barbarous import. The theory threatened to unite aesthetics and psychology. As Napoleon would remark, '*Du sublime au ridicule il n'y a qu'un pas.'* It had already resulted in a flood of mere-tricious poetry, and, post-Burke, it would inspire a flurry of alpine tourism. The doctrine of the Sublime, which appropriated the vocabulary of religion, was another chapter in the devaluation of religious language.[6] It was something to register, but not to celebrate.

Voguish philosophies did little for Johnson. He saw his contemporaries 'dazzled in a bazaar of facile systems' which promised to resolve their problems.[7] In his view, however, experience was a far more reliable guide than the tenets of artificial theories. In one of the earliest instalments of the *Rambler* he observed how many people's minds were 'not fixed by principles' and were therefore susceptible to 'the current of fancy', 'to every false suggestion and partial account'.[8] The *Dictionary* manifests his resistance to such newfangledness. Intended as a lasting, exemplary resource, it marks the eddies of fashionable thought, but evinces Johnson's belief that popular theories could debilitate or deprave moral standards, and that religious values were far more durable than the shiny bric-a-brac of topicality.

Pastern

The knee of an horse

Traditionally, Johnson's adversaries have fastened on the *Dictionary*'s more opinionated moments, using them to exaggerate his Toryism or his hostility to the Scots, and they have dwelt on its errors, employing the familiar technique of using one or two mistakes as evidence of wholesale incompetence. Johnson's faults and misconstructions are scarce, but some of them are undeniably flagrant.

Seven years after the *Dictionary* was published, Johnson made a six-week trip to Devon with Sir Joshua Reynolds. He stayed at Plymouth with his friend John Mudge, a likeably garrulous surgeon, to whose son he would be godfather. During his time with the Mudges he was at his most sociable, meeting many local people – including a number of nautical types, whose colourful language distressed him. But it was his own choice of words that caused most embarrassment. According to Frances Reynolds, who presumably heard the story from her brother, a lady happened to ask – 'before a large company at dinner', and 'in a very audible voice' – how he had come to proffer so inaccurate a definition of 'pastern'. Johnson confessed himself guilty of what could only be considered 'ignorance, Madam, ignorance'. His mood became grave, and when the lady tried to press more food on him he 'rose up with his knife in his hand, and loudly exclaimed, "I vow to God I cannot eat a bit more", to the great terror . . . of all'.[1]

When Johnson came to revise the *Dictionary*, he was mindful of this awkward episode, and amended the entry accordingly: 'That part of the leg of a horse between the joint next the foot and the hoof'. But the original mistake stands as a reminder of his fallibility. His definitions may often be excellent, but there are a few that prove almost useless or, as in this case, just plain wrong. Some of his contemporaries reacted with gripes and grumbles, others with laughter. Thomas Bagshaw, the Bromley curate who buried Tetty, played a game with his brother-in-law John Loveday, a rich philologist and collector, in which they exchanged by post examples of Johnson's more risible efforts, carefully scissored from their copies of the *Dictionary*.[2]

One trait which occasionally surfaces in Johnson's work is a capacity for dismissing things he does not understand or cannot be bothered to research. For example, he defines a 'sonata' merely as 'a tune' – a typical gesture from a man who admitted he was 'very insensible to the power of music' and once remarked, of a violin solo, 'Difficult, do you call it [?] . . . I wish it were impossible.'[3] He does rather better with 'bar' and 'tune', and borrows for a technical term like 'fugue'. But the vocabulary of music is for the most part quickly dispatched: an 'aria' is 'an air, song, or tune', the 'hautboy' (oboe) is 'a wind instrument', and the guitar and violin are each merely 'a stringed instrument of musick'. Deaf to the appeal of Handel and Bach, he would later suggest to his friend Charles Burney, an eminent musicologist, that he help him with a revision of the entries pertaining to music. Regrettably, this never happened.

Such shortcomings are dangerous in an educational work, but they are part of the *Dictionary*'s charm – proof that even Johnson, the Hercules of literature, could stumble. He defines the noun 'strappado' as 'chastisement by blows', though it seems in fact to have been a crudely medieval form of punishment involving hanging. 'Leeward' and 'windward' are both defined as 'towards the wind'. 'Archery' is unhelpfully explained as 'the use of a bow' (but not, one imagines, for playing the violin). This minimalism can be absurd; for instance, a 'runner' is simply 'one who runs'. A 'shoe' is 'the cover of the foot' – the vagueness of which is not completely transformed by the definition of 'sock' ('something put between the foot and the shoe'). 'Soup' is a 'strong decoction of flesh for the table' – but what about vegetable soup? 'Lunch' is 'as much food as one's hand can hold', but surely the relationship between appetite and hand size is not strictly proportional. 'Garret' is, as we know, 'a room on the highest floor of a house', but what then of the 'cockloft', which is 'the room over the garret'? Now and again material is duplicated confusingly. Thus a 'scate' is 'a kind of wooden shoe, with a steel plate underneath, on which they slide over the ice', while a 'skate' is 'a sort of shoe armed with iron, for sliding on the ice'. What, if anything, is the difference? And what is the difference between a 'herbalist' ('a man skilled in herbs') and a 'herbarist' ('one skilled in herbs')? We have to assume there is none.

Johnson glosses 'reptile' as 'an animal that creeps upon many feet', which is poetic but unhelpful. The leopard is apparently 'a spotted beast of prey'; other entries suggest he was unaware of the difference between the lynx, the leopard and the panther. A 'fish' is 'an animal that inhabits the water'. But seals and ribbon worms and sponges are not fish. Nor is a crab, although Johnson considered it 'a crustaceous fish'. Indeed, definitions of terms in nature, though commonly good, can find Johnson at his most quaintly imprecise. A 'vegetable' is 'any thing that has growth without sensation, as plants'. There is a good deal of information about individual vegetables – the cabbage, the lettuce, the leek – but much of it is expendable. For instance, 'parsnep' – a parsnip to us – is defined with a quotation from Philip Miller's *Gardener's Dictionary*: 'A plant with rose and umbellated flowers, consisting of many petals or leaves placed orbicularly, and resting on the empalement, which turns to a fruit composed of two seeds, which are oval, and generally casting off their cover; to which you may add, that the leaves are winged and large.' This is bafflingly redundant, and Johnson, perhaps baffled himself, later cut this definition down to two words: 'a plant'.[4]

If a similar vagueness clouds Johnson's definition of 'adder' ('a serpent, a viper, a poisonous reptile; perhaps of any species'), his definition of 'tarantula' is positively opaque. Johnson tells us that it is 'an insect whose bite is only cured by music'. This curious belief is recorded by Samuel Pepys among others, and had recently been confirmed by a Neapolitan violinist, who had described in the *Gentleman's Magazine* his success in curing a man who had been bitten under the lip of his ear.[5] Johnson, with a touch of self-mockery, quotes Locke: 'He that uses the word *tarantula*, without having any idea of what it stands for, means nothing at all by it.'

In his attempts to settle signification a little more resolutely, Johnson can fall victim to the easy vice of circularity. 'Commerce', for instance, has the meaning 'Intercourse; exchange of one thing for another'; 'intercourse' means 'commerce; exchange'. A 'poet' is in essence a 'writer of poems'; a 'poem' is before all else 'the work of a poet'. Johnson generally manages to avoid this pitfall, but there are occasions when his imagination seems to have deserted him, as in his entry for the noun 'defluxion', which he defines as 'defluxion'.

Then there are mistakes of a different stripe. Johnson asserts of the elephant that 'in copulation the female receives the male lying upon her back'. He accepted this on the strength of a claim made by the scholar William Stukeley, an eclectic eccentric whose many ambitious projects included an attempt to trace the Hebrew roots of Welsh. Together with Sir Hans Sloane, the president of the College of Physicians, Stukeley had in 1720 dissected the genitalia of a female elephant that had been brought back from Sumatra (and had died as a result of being given a great deal of ale). He concluded from his observations that elephants had recumbent sex. But he was wrong, and Johnson perpetuates his error.[6]

Furthermore, it was not just over definitions that Johnson erred. His spellings, for instance, are not consistent. 'Uphill' he spells with two *l*s, but he has only one *l* in 'downhil'. The verb 'to install' is spelled thus, but 'to reinstal' with a single *l*. Such anomalies were his to resolve. His failure to do so has proved lasting: it is thanks to Johnson that the opposite of 'moveable' is commonly written 'immovable', and thanks to him too that one person can 'deign' to do what another 'disdains' to.

Of the verb 'to hiss' Johnson observed, 'It is remarkable, that this word cannot be pronounced without making the noise which it signifies.' It was not remarkable: the voice of onomatopoeia whispers or sizzles in plenty of other words he included in the *Dictionary*. To his embarrassment, he allowed the verb 'to foupe' as a result of misreading the word 'soupe' in an old text of William Camden's *Britannia*, and he extravagantly claimed that the letter *H* 'seldom, perhaps never, begins any but the first syllable'. This last mistake drew a withering response from the politician John Wilkes, who wrote a piece for the *Public Advertiser* in which he illustrated the absurdity of the statement. Wilkes joked that 'The author of this observation must be a man of quick *appre-hension*, and of a most *compre-hensive* genius.' Perhaps Wilkes was incensed by Johnson's scathing definition of 'distiller' (his father Israel had practised this trade). Whatever his motives, he was right, and Johnson was bothersomely wrong. Even Boswell admits that 'the position is undoubtedly expressed with too much latitude'.[7]

One man's intelligence, negotiating so many minute considerations, was certain to lapse occasionally. Generalizations were necessary, albeit dangerous. A related problem was the impossibility of comprehensiveness. The *Dictionary* could not include every word in use. Johnson's decision to define only those words he could find in books had made his task a little easier, but even so there was no chance of catching every word in all its senses. The first edition contained 42,773 entries – a figure that increased only slightly for later editions – and this, to most modern English-speakers, will sound worryingly small.

It is worth pausing a moment to consider the size of an average adult English-speaker's vocabulary. Popular estimates are in the range of 10,000 words. We are told that Shakespeare's published works comprise 29,066 'different' words. Consequently, we are given to believe that Shakespeare's word power was three times that of modern man. This is a fallacy. On a minor point, Shakespeare's true lexicon, as evidenced in his writings, is closer to 20,000 words, but, more importantly, users have an active vocabulary and a passive one. I know what a 'pickle' is, and what it means to be 'picky', and I use these words in everyday life, but I am also familiar with terms like 'pickerel' and 'picklock', even though I am unlikely to use them, and I may even have a sense of what is meant by the words 'pickelhaube' (it's a type of helmet) and 'picong' (a taunt), although I shall never put them to use – except here. Which of these words form part of 'my' vocabulary, and which do not? The difficulty in determining the boundaries of vocabulary means that estimates like those given above tend to be spurious. However, it is perhaps reasonable to suggest that a well-educated adult (even though 'well-educated' is itself a vague, picayune sort of term) has an active vocabulary of around 50,000 words, and a further, passive, vocabulary of more than 10,000.[8]

We may note, by way of comparison with the scope of Johnson's *Dictionary*, that *Webster's Third New International Dictionary* (1961) contained almost half a million words, yet its editor conceded its incompleteness. The first edition of the *OED* comprised 15,490 pages, defined 414,825 words, and contained 1,827,306 illustrative quotations, selected from the 5 million collected by the work's 2,000 contributors. The type, laid out in a single straight line, would have stretched from London to Manchester (178 miles), and consisted of 227,779,589 characters. But the *OED* was still not exhaustive. Nor was the second edition that succeeded it, which runs to 21,730 pages and contains almost 2,500,000 quotations.[9] The history of lexicography is a history of deficits and delays. The brothers Grimm began their *Deutsches Wörterbuch* in the early 1840s, but the work was not finished until the 1960s. The first of the forty volumes that make up the *Woordenboek der Nederlandsche Taal* appeared in 1864, but the last came out only in 1998. Work on the definitive Welsh dictionary began in 1921, and was finished in 2002. Is any of these exhaustive? Again, the answer is no.

Clearly Johnson, who had no army of volunteers to support him, was not in a position to achieve what academies and consortia have since failed to accomplish. There were limits to his reading, and to his knowledge. But when we note, even briefly, his omissions, we refine our sense of the world in which he lived, and of his perception of it.

A large part of our modern vocabulary consists of words for things and ideas that were unknown or unnamed in eighteenth-century Britain: the telephone and television, the personal computer, bacteria, chromosomes, racism, shower gel, the unconscious. Other absentees – missing because they had not been coined, although in several cases this may take us by surprise – include 'funny', 'alcoholic', 'normal', 'diplomacy' (which was first used by Burke in the 1790s), 'autobiography', 'nostalgia', 'pessimism', 'speculation' (in the financial sense) and 'strike' (as in a workers' strike). Nor will readers find one of the familiar senses of 'balloon': the Montgolfier brothers did not orchestrate the first public balloon flight until 1783. But Johnson's harvest of 42,773 words still doesn't sound like very much, especially when we consider that English actually comprised between 250,000 and 300,000 words at that time. Moreover, the *Dictionary* abounds with words one would surely never use – words like 'deosculation' and 'extispicious'. Johnson's mind was extraordinarily compendious, but he was capable of oversights and omissions.[10]

What is more, Johnson left out headwords he should or at least could have included. Contrary to the belief popular among aficionados of *Blackadder*, the word 'sausage' can be found in the *Dictionary*, but readers will not find entries for 'ultimatum', 'nemesis', 'bank-note', 'blond', 'virus', 'irritable' (which he uses in four of his definitions), 'authoress' (used by Pope among others), 'zinc' (even though he defines 'tutty' as 'a sublimate of zinc'), 'inaugural', 'engineering' and 'anus' (which appears in two of his definitions). He omits 'to chirrup', 'athlete' (although 'athletic' is included), 'port' (the wine, that is, which was certainly known to him), 'euphemism' (which is in Blount's *Glossographia*), 'shibboleth' (which is in *Samson Agonistes* and in one of Johnson's illustrations from Dryden), 'malaria', 'zebra', 'annulment', and 'underdone'. 'Ambush' and 'orphan' are not recognized as verbs. 'Average' is not recognized as an adjective. He leaves out 'civilization' – he told Boswell it was not a proper word, but he was able all the same to pronounce that 'a decent provision for the poor is the true test of civilization'.

Finally, after all the inadvertent lapses, there are Johnson's glaringly candid admissions of ignorance. Commonly judged a dictator – a colossus of authority – he is here, we can see, a more tentative creature. 'To swelt' is 'to puff in sweat, if that be the meaning'. 'Cyprus', a type of fabric, takes its name 'I suppose from the place where it was made; or corruptly from *cypress*', while a particular sense of the verb 'to knuckle' derives 'I suppose from an odd custom of striking the under side of the table with the knuckles, in confession of an argumental defeat'. 'To clink', he informs us, 'seems in Spenser to have some unusual sense'; we are provided with the relevant passage so we can work it out for ourselves. Having included the unusual word 'urim', which occurs in Book VI of *Paradise Lost*, he defers to the authority of Milton's editor Thomas Newton: '*Urim* and thummim were something in Aaron's breastplate; but what, critics and commentators are by no means agreed.'* The verb 'to worm' means 'to deprive a dog of something, nobody knows what, under his tongue, which is said to prevent him, nobody knows why, from running mad'. Even more puzzling was 'trolmydames', a word which

---

* The *OED* hardly does better, with a definition that begins 'Certain objects, the nature of which is not known. . .'.

Shakespeare put in the mouth of the meddlesome pickpocket Autolycus in *The Winter's Tale*. The defeated lexicographer confesses simply that 'Of this word I know not the meaning.'

No work of reference can include everything, and in the case of the *Dictionary* it was better to publish an incomplete version than to hold back in the vain hope that it could one day be brought to perfection. The wisest word on the matter belongs to Johnson. 'Dictionaries are like watches,' he wrote shortly before his death. 'The worst is better than none, and the best cannot be expected to go quite true.'[11]

Patron

1. One who countenances, supports, or protects. Commonly a wretch who supports with insolence, and is paid with flattery

Johnson's mistakes may be amusing, and his elegant formulae may catch the eye, but it is his barbs that linger longest in the mind. They are, of course, faults of a sort – failures to be dispassionate – but they are integral to the *Dictionary's* appeal. Johnson was not gratuitously harsh: to be rude, he had to be provoked. Seven years before, he had dedicated the *Plan of an English Dictionary* to the Earl of Chesterfield. Now, as he neared the end of his labours, the Earl's attempt to claim some part in the achievement of the *Dictionary* licensed one of Johnson's most mischievous definitions.

When preparations for the *Dictionary* were beginning, the patronage of Chesterfield had seemed appropriate, for his profile was considerable. Since becoming a Member of Parliament at the age of twenty, he had enjoyed a stellar career, and had recently become Secretary of State. He was also keenly interested in the arts – and in adding the English language to the nation's portfolio of lucrative exports. Strongly encouraged by Dodsley, and perhaps by the memory that his cousin Ford had once been Chesterfield's chaplain, Johnson initially saluted the Earl as an 'authority in our language': 'the power which might have been denied to my own claim, will be readily allowed me as the delegate of your Lordship'. This was the familiar shape of the author–patron relationship: the talented author had to fawn before the inferior intellect of his sponsor. While the project was in its inception, Johnson played along: the Earl's involvement was the final, vital guarantee of credibility, which would persuade the booksellers to commission a gifted but obscure author.

Early on, Chesterfield imparted a few suggestions about how Johnson could improve the *Plan*. Yet, over the seven years that followed, his patronage was desultory. He made Johnson a single payment, and that a modest £10. He was a busy man, and susceptible to illness, but his inattention savoured of disdain. Only in 1754, when the *Dictionary* was nearing completion, did he venture any further contribution. On 28 November he published the first of two pieces in the *World*, a fashionable weekly owned by his 'worthy friend Mr Dodsley'. His ostensible purpose was to promote the *Dictionary*, but the tone of his article is at once calculated and smug, and it is clear that he aspired to have the finished volumes dedicated to him. 'I hope that none of my courteous readers will . . . suspect me of being a hired and interested puff of this work,' he insists, playfully protesting that 'neither Mr Johnson, nor any person employed by him, nor any bookseller or booksellers concerned in the success of . . . [the dictionary], have ever offered me the usual compliment of a pair of gloves or a bottle of wine.' 'Nor,' he continues, 'has even Mr Dodsley, though my publisher, and, as I am informed, deeply interested in the sale of this dictionary, so much as invited me to take a bit of mutton with him.'

Of course, Chesterfield was 'an interested puff' – at the time 'puff' was the word for the person doing the puffing, as well as for the sales pitch itself. The trouble was, he had to maintain his patrician dignity: in his promotional essays he appears too wrapped up in his own idea of politeness to be completely open in eulogy. 'Many people have imagined that so extensive a work would have been best performed by a number of persons,' he observes, but 'the public in general, and the republic of letters in particular, [are] greatly obliged to Mr Johnson, for having undertaken and executed so great and desirable a work'. Here his vagueness betrays his ignorance. He tells his readers that the *Plan* 'seems to me to be a proof' of the *Dictionary*'s excellence – 'Nothing can be more rationally imagined, or more accurately and elegantly expressed.'[1] This infuriated Johnson, who had long ago abandoned the design proposed in the *Plan*, and whose ambition was not to 'civilize' language, like Chesterfield, but to understand it. The Earl's inaccuracy was a reminder of his negligence. If he had bothered to monitor Johnson's progress, he would have known something of his methods: instead, he blithely misrepresented them. The second article, published a week later, did not improve matters. Chesterfield had already remarked on Johnson's inattention to 'the genteeler part of language', and now discoursed with embarrassing flippancy on 'the incontinence of female eloquence' and the various ways in which his 'fair countrywomen' had proved 'the enrichers, the patronesses, and the harmonizers of our language'.[2]

This was not helpful, but in truth Johnson's expectations of Chesterfield had been snuffed out several years before. Boswell tells the story of the lexicographer going to visit his patron in order to

Doctor Johnson in the Ante-Room of the Lord Chesterfield Waiting for an Audience, 1748, by Edward Matthew Ward

discuss the state of his work. To Johnson's annoyance, he was kept waiting in an ante-hall. On eventually being admitted, he was horrified to discover that he had been made to wait because Chesterfield was entertaining the louche poet Colley Cibber. Johnson later dismissed the episode, assuring Boswell that 'there was not the least foundation' for his story. In his own version, 'there never was any particular incident which produced a quarrel'; rather,

Chesterfield's 'continual neglect' was the reason why he 'resolved to have no connection with him'. But the episode, whether true or not, has been nicely memorialized by the genre painter Edward Ward. The artist depicts Johnson waiting for an audience with the Earl; he looks bored and grumpy, which is hardly surprising, as the ante-room is packed with a medley of fops and twits. This was Chesterfield's natural milieu – a world of highfalutin sycophants and courtly poseurs, fluttering their wares in the hope of finding favour. Johnson could not have been more out of place.

As early as 1751 he was renouncing patronage in print. In a *Rambler* essay of March that year he writes that 'To solicit patronage is . . . to set virtue on sale', for 'none can be servile without corruption'. In October another *Rambler* depicts a patron treating an author contemptuously. And in March the following year he writes, 'I must remain accountable for all my faults, and submit, without subterfuge, to the censures of criticism, which . . . I shall not endeavour to soften by a formal deprecation, or to overbear by the influence of a patron.'[3] His growing distaste for patronage was discernible elsewhere. In the 1749 edition of *The Vanity of Human Wishes* he describes the ills that assail the busy scholar: 'Toil, envy, want, the garret, and the jail'. For a revised edition, published in 1755, he makes a crucial amendment, changing the line to 'Toil, envy, want, the patron, and the jail'.[4]

When Chesterfield dared to revive his association with the *Dictionary*, Johnson was incensed. He expressed his disgust to Garrick: 'I have sailed a long and painful voyage round the world of the English language; and does he now send out two cock-boats to tow me into harbour?'[5] On 7 February 1755 he wrote to Chesterfield, as much to salve his own nausea as to admonish the impostor. His letter is a masterpiece of controlled anger, and of epistolary theatre, worth quoting at length:

> I have been lately informed by the Proprietor of The World that two Papers in which my Dictionary is recommended to the Public were written by your Lordship. To be so distinguished is an honour which, being very little accustomed to favours from the Great, I know not well how to receive, or in what terms to acknowledge.
>
> When upon some slight encouragement I first visited your

Lordship I was overpowered like the rest of Mankind by the enchant-ment of your address . . . but I found my attendance so little encour-aged, that neither pride nor modesty would suffer me to continue it . . . I had done all that I could, and no Man is well pleased to have his all neglected, be it ever so little.

Seven years, My Lord, are now past since I waited in your outward Rooms or was repulsed from your Door, during which time I have been pushing on my work through difficulties of which it is useless to complain, and have brought it at last to the verge of Publication without one Act of assistance, one word of encouragement, or one smile of favour. Such treatment I did not expect, for I never had a Patron before.

The shepherd in Virgil grew at last acquainted with Love, and found him a native of the rocks. Is not a Patron, My Lord, one who looks with unconcern on a Man struggling for Life in the water and when he has reached ground encumbers him with help? The notice which you have been pleased to take of my Labours, had it been early, had been kind; but it has been delayed till I am indifferent and cannot enjoy it, till I am solitary and cannot impart it, till I am known and do not want it.

I hope it is no very cynical asperity not to confess obligation where no benefit has been received, or to be unwilling that the Public should consider me as owing that to a Patron, which Providence has enabled me to do for myself . . .

I have been long wakened from that Dream of hope, in which I once boasted myself with so much exultation, My lord, your Lordship's Most humble, most obedient Servant, Samuel Johnson.[6]

Johnson's passing definition here of 'patron' ('one who looks with unconcern on a Man struggling for Life in the water and when he has reached ground encumbers him with help') is matched in the *Dictionary* by the delightfully acerbic entry quoted at the head of this chapter. Chesterfield's apathy had its reward: Johnson's fury was spent.*

The lexicographer's rejection of his patron's belated assistance has often been identified as a key moment in the history of publishing,

---

* The tone of Johnson's definition of 'patron' is unmistakable. Rather more ambigu-ous, but possibly calculated to serve the same end, is his first definition of 'grateful-ness', which reads: 'Gratitude; duty to benefactors. Now obsolete.' Is it the word that is obsolete, or the custom?

marking the end of the culture of patronage.[7] This is not strictly accurate. Patronage had been in decline for fifty years, yet would survive, in attenuated form, for another fifty. Indeed, Johnson was in the 1760s awarded a pension by the Crown – a subtle form of sponsorship, tantamount to state patronage. The letter's importance is not so much historical as emotional; it would become a touchstone for all who repudiated patrons, and for all who embraced the laws of the marketplace.

In the short term, however, Johnson's rejection of Chesterfield did not endear him to the booksellers who had underwritten the *Dictionary*. Dodsley pointed out that he 'had a property' in it 'to which his Lordship's patronage might have been of consequence'. For 'might' we can read 'would'; Dodsley is trying not to inflame Johnson any further, yet is also trying to palliate his own sense of commercial disadvantage, for Chesterfield's endorsement would certainly have helped the *Dictionary*, and Johnson's rebuff, though later famous, seemed at the time both naive and pig-headed.

When Chesterfield died, in 1773, Johnson had further opportunity to pass judgement. A selection of the Earl's letters was published, exciting a good deal of debate. These letters, addressed to his illegitimate son Philip, were a manual of male comportment, explaining the mechanics of etiquette and worldly success. They were cynical, glib and quotable: 'Style is the dress of thoughts', 'Despatch is the soul of business', 'Whatever is worth doing at all, is worth doing well.' Such maxims made him sound like a *philosophe* in pimp's clothing. Johnson was not impressed. He conceded that the letters might have made a 'very pretty' book (the faintest of faint praise), then commented, stingingly, that they 'teach the morals of a whore, and the manners of a dancing master'.[8] Here, as in the famous letter and the *Dictionary*'s entry under 'patron', Chesterfield's errors are more lastingly preserved than any of his achievements.

There is, however, a final twist in the tale. Johnson and Chesterfield were related. The link was not close, but, in one of those ramifications of kinship that delight the sort of people who like nothing more than to clamber around in a family tree, Parson Ford's wife, Judith, had a great-niece, Mary Crowley, who was married to the Earl's younger brother. Johnson was ignorant of this, though

Chesterfield may not have been. Yet even in his ignorance Johnson sensed the limits of the quarrel. Some years later, he encountered John Douglas, a churchman who would later be bishop of Salisbury, and whose taste for literary controversy had led him to seek out a copy of the notorious letter. Douglas wondered if he could show it to Lord Hardwicke, who was himself a literary man and a fellow of the Royal Society. Johnson might easily have enjoyed the opportunity to remind himself of a past triumph, but instead replied, 'No, Sir; I have hurt the dog too much already.'

Philology

Criticism; grammatical learning

'Temper all discourses of *philology* with interspersions of morality' – William Walker, *English Examples of the Latin Syntaxis* (1683)

Chesterfield's articles in the *World* alerted readers to the imminent appearance of the *Dictionary*. It was not the first time that its 'forwardness' or 'readiness' had been announced, but this time it really was approaching publication. In fact it might have come out sooner but for certain finishing touches that Johnson had to apply before his endeavours could be set before the public. After so many years of work, it was essential that the finished product be properly rigged out.

By the spring of 1754 the text was nearing completion. Johnson had finished writing his definitions, but there were three parts still to be composed: the Preface, the Grammar and the History. On 16 July Johnson wrote to the young literary historian Thomas Warton, praising his recent *Observations on the Faerie Queene of Spenser*, which had been published by Dodsley. He mentioned that he would shortly be making a trip to Oxford, in order to use the university's exceptionally well-stocked Bodleian Library, where he planned to gather materials for the introductory part of the *Dictionary*. Warton was a useful contact within the university. A fellow of Trinity College, he was a notoriously negligent tutor, a scruff and a tavern-goer, who belonged to the waggish Jelly-Bag Club and knew a thing or two about Oxford's seedier entertainments. But he was also an expert on the development of the language, and would later serve as the university's Professor of Poetry, as its Professor of History, and as Poet Laureate. He had already begun his monumental *History of English Poetry*, even though its first volume would not come out for twenty years. Aware of Warton's research, Johnson hoped to peruse his notes. Warton agreed, and during Johnson's visit to Oxford he put him up at Kettell

Hall, a fine stone house today flanked by Blackwell's famous book-shop. The two men evidently discussed the History, and it is hardly a surprise that this part of the *Dictionary* shares a good deal of its content with Warton's work in the field.[1]

While Johnson was in Oxford, nostalgia drew him back to his old college. He was pleased to find that many of the college servants remembered him, and he called on the Master, John Ratcliff, expecting hospitality. But Ratcliff was unwelcoming and showed no interest in the *Dictionary*, causing Johnson to remark that '*There* lives a man, who lives by the revenues of literature, and will not move a finger to support it.' Altogether more rewarding were his meetings with Francis Wise, the university's Radclivian librarian and keeper of its archives. Wise lived in the tiny village of Elsfield, three miles out of town, and Johnson walked out to see him there several times. Wise's home must have been an intriguing place to visit: it was known for its fine garden, which included a triumphal arch and a tiny model of the Tower of Babel, and Johnson described it in a letter to Warton as a 'nest . . . of Antiquities'.[2] Wise had amassed a valuable collection of books in Northern literature, and it was with these in particular that Johnson busied himself. In the finished *Dictionary* there is proof of the Oxford scholar's more personal contribution: in the entry for 'warlock', Johnson notes that his Icelandic etymology for the word 'was communicated by Mr Wise'.

Johnson enjoyed his stay in Oxford. Having originally told Strahan that 'I shall not be long here',[3] he remained in the city for a month. The reasons for this were social as much as scholarly. He and Warton shared an enthusiasm for Elizabethan literature which was at once scholarly and cordial. Both were poets, and both were historians of poetry. Dynamic as well as bookish, they enjoyed a rivalry that extended beyond intellectual pursuits. Returning from one of their visits to Elsfield, Johnson was outpaced by the younger man. Warton later recalled that Johnson cried out '*Sufflamina*' – 'a Latin word, which came from his mouth with peculiar grace, and was as much as to say, *Put on your drag chain*'.

Having at last completed the labours of compilation, Johnson felt able to unbend his intelligence. He was entertaining ideas of new and ambitious schemes, including the long-projected edition of

Shakespeare. For this reason he was eager to complete the History and Grammar quite briskly. Instead of subjecting himself to another odyssey of original research, he relied where possible on existing scholarship. We can glean an impression of his earnestly technical reading at this time from the title of one of the books he consulted: a three-volume grammar and dictionary of Old English, Gothic and Icelandic entitled *Linguarum Veterum Septentrionalum Thesaurus Grammatico-Criticus et Archaeologicus*.

Of the three essays he put together after finishing the main body of the *Dictionary*, the Preface is the only one that is at all well known – and will be considered in a separate chapter. It is followed by the History, which Johnson hoped would help readers understand the development of English. Its twenty-seven pages consist of specimens of texts, punctuated with brief comments. Johnson makes no extravagant claims, and has an eye to the work of his predecessors. There are fragments from *the Anglo-Saxon Chronicle*, the poetry of John Gower ('the first of our authors who can be properly said to have written *English*', says Johnson), Chaucer and Sir Thomas More, the fourteenth-century travel writer Sir John Mandeville, and King Alfred, among others. Johnson concludes that, a certain 'want of materials' notwithstanding, these extracts present the history of the language 'in such a manner that its progress may be easily traced, and the gradations observed, by which it advanced from its first rudeness to its present elegance'.

The intended effect is achieved, but the half-heartedness of Johnson's efforts is barely concealed. 'Of the Saxon poetry', he writes, 'some specimen is necessary'; the implication is that it is not something to which he would turn for pleasure. He quotes the poets Wyatt and Surrey from what he blithely describes as an 'edition that has fallen into my hands'. The prevailing mood is one of academic boredom; the underlying message is 'This isn't what I'm good at, and I'm not going to waste a lot of time polishing it.' On the opening page he uses the unusual word 'inconnection', which is not in the *Dictionary*, though it can be found in the fourth edition of Edward Phillips's *New World of Words* (1678). Does this suggest he was writing hastily? The History undeniably feels like a quick and dirty solution to a problem its author found numbingly dull.

All the same, it is innovative; Johnson was the first scientific historian of English. His predecessors had claimed that the essential identity of the language had not been altered by the influence of other tongues. This was untrue. No more than 5,000 or so Old English words have survived into modern usage, and, although I write this a quarter of a millennium after Johnson, the same was largely true in the middle of the eighteenth century: English is a ragout of regional dialects, rich in Norman and French, and thick with words imported directly from Latin and Greek.* The expansion of English vocabulary was especially diffuse during the reigns of Elizabeth I and James I. In documenting this, even crudely, Johnson breaks with tradition: he distinguishes sharply between contemporary English and the Saxon language, and, rather than suggesting the continuity of English, he displays its changes.

After the History comes a shorter section, thirteen pages long, on English Grammar. This too feels rushed. It opens with the suggestively bold statement that 'Grammar is the art of using words properly', yet the sense of purpose peters out. Johnson admits that he is interested not in the theory of grammar, but in its everyday practice. Space is given to the conjugations of verbs and their irregularities, to the principles of prosody, to the elementary rules of pronunciation, and to a section on the proper use of pronouns. He briefly considers spelling reform, but dismisses it: 'what advantage would a new orthography procure equivalent to the confusion and perplexity of such an alteration?' Pragmatism always has an answer for idealism – which is, in miniature, the story of this dictionary, as of any.

---

* Nor do the borrowings stop. Consider such widely adopted imports as 'cannibal' (Spanish), 'marmalade' (Portuguese), 'kiosk' and 'coffee' (Turkish), 'violin' and 'balcony' (Italian), 'anorak' and 'kayak' (Greenland Eskimo), 'tattoo' (Polynesian), 'algebra' (Arabic), 'robot' (Czech), 'schmuck' and 'ziggurat' (Yiddish), 'bungalow' and 'shampoo' (Hindi), 'ombudsman' (Swedish), 'safari' (Swahili), 'landscape' and 'cruise' (Dutch), 'boomerang' (Native Australian), 'horde' (Polish), 'paprika' (Hungarian), 'delicatessen', 'angst' and 'gimmick' (German), 'corgi' (Welsh), 'tycoon' (Japanese), 'typhoon' (Chinese), 'samizdat' and 'apparatchik' (Russian), 'caravan' and 'sofa' (Persian), 'voodoo' (Louisiana French), and 'sauna' (Finnish). Incidentally, the term 'borrowing', though standard, seems a nonsense: now that the words have been adopted, they're not going to be given back.

The scrappiness of the Grammar is best suggested in the section on the sounds and rhythms of verse. Here Johnson quotes ballads and songs, in addition to literary texts, and appears to quote from memory. He gives meagre details of his sources, but several of them are authors unrepresented in the main body of the *Dictionary*. Why does he quote balladeers here, though not elsewhere? The decision smacks not so much of inconsistency as of improvisation. He is reverting to the habits of the Grub Street quill-driver. Weary of his task, yet sensitive to the possibility of criticism, he finally protests that 'To have written a grammar for such as are not yet initiated in the schools, would have been tedious, and perhaps at last ineffectual.' Embedded in this sentence is an awareness that the Grammar he has written is incomplete and, in all likelihood, redundant.

The deficiencies of the History and Grammar, and their heavy borrowings from other works, are signs that Johnson was keen to complete the *Dictionary* as quickly as possible. He could have invested another year in researching these sections, but the booksellers were anxious to have their book, and he must have suspected that anyone wanting a detailed account of the history or grammar of English would be happy to look elsewhere. Indeed, had he surmised that most users of his volumes would never even look at these two parts of the front matter, he would surely have been correct. They were not integral to its success, might comfortably have been omitted, and seemed necessary mainly because earlier dictionaries had included in their front matter articles of this kind.[4]

There was still one more thing to be done before the *Dictionary* could be laid before the world. Johnson wished to appear as 'A.M.' (*Artium Magister*) on the title page, and this caused a delay. As we have seen, he had gone down from university without taking a degree; this had hampered him in his teaching career, and he did not want it to hamper him again. He thought, with some justification, that advertising his status as a Master of Arts would endow the title page with an appropriate air of scholarly seriousness. But an overwhelmingly strong case had to be made to warrant conferring a degree on anyone who had failed to meet Oxford's statutory requirements, and it took the combined efforts of Warton and Wise to secure Johnson his diploma. It was only on 20 February 1755 that he was finally awarded a degree. The certificate, which survives in the British Library, is a scruffily handwritten Latin document on a ruled sheet not unlike a leaf from a child's exercise book. From it there hangs a brick-red seal that resembles an oversized and well-licked lollipop. To Johnson, however, this document was magically significant.

Anticipating the award and the publication of the *Dictionary*, Johnson wrote on 1 February to Warton, his tone rich in a playful humour that can muffle neither his sense of the grandeur of his work nor his anxieties: 'I now begin to see land, after having wandered . . . in this vast sea of words. What reception I shall meet with upon the shore I know not, whether the sound of bells and acclamations of the people . . . or a general murmur of dislike.' He continues, 'I know not whether I shall find . . . a Calypso that will court or a Polypheme that will eat me. But if Polypheme comes to me have at his eyes.'[5] That plural is surprising – the Cyclops notoriously had just one eye – but more important is the way that Johnson likens himself to the hero of Homer's *Odyssey*. He has often been diverted from his course by storms and misadventures, and even now his journey goes on; he is vulnerable not just to assault by those who feel he has blundered into their territory, but also, he senses, to the sinister allure of praise.

This was not the first time Johnson had compared himself to the great Greek hero. His pointed definition of 'grubstreet' had ended with an equally pointed Homeric quotation, which translates as 'Hail Ithaca, after strife and bitter trials / Gladly do I approach thy threshold.' Here he casts himself as Odysseus returning to his homeland after years of wandering. The sentiment is ambiguous. Are we to understand that Johnson is saluting Grub Street, and that he half-jokingly, half-seriously considers it his natural habitat? Or that Ithaca represents the environment from which he has been removed ever since his arrival in London, a realm of enlightened scholarship, reminiscent not of journalistic drudgery, but of the rewards of learning intimated all those years before in his conversations with his mentors Ford and Walmesley? The latter seems more likely. The *Dictionary* had afforded a temporary release from financial insecurity, but had consigned him to years of 'wandering'. Its completion promised at last to remove him from Grub Street and enable him to renounce its sweated piecework. Triumph, it seemed, was at hand.

Pleasureful

Pleasant; delightful. Obsolete

'This country, for the fruitfulness of the land and the conveniency of the sea, hath been reputed a very commodious and *pleasureful* country' – George Abbot, *Geography, or a Brief Description of the Whole World* (1599)

The Greek quotation Johnson slipped into his entry for 'grubstreet' is one of the *Dictionary*'s more erudite jokes, but it is symptomatic of the work's rich texture. Embedded within its fabric are countless unexpected delights. Macaulay called it 'the first dictionary which could be read with pleasure'.[1] One's reaction to this may reasonably be '*Who* would *read* a dictionary?' We tend to think of dictionaries as repositories of verbal lumber, ossuaries of decayed distinctions and obsolete jargon, or just impenetrable forests of words.

Yet some people do read them. In July 2000 a court in Kalamazoo, Michigan, gave an unusually lenient sentence to José Rodriguez, a member of a street gang called the Latin Kings who had been found guilty of firebombing. According to a report in the *Holland Sentinel*, a local newspaper, the defendant's counsel 'noted that Rodriguez was a unique person because he reads the encyclopedia and dictionary for pleasure'. We are all unique, but Rodriguez's tastes in reading matter were genuinely unusual. Most of us prefer novels, biographies and memoirs. However, there are always those, like Malcolm X or Gabriel García Márquez, who see dictionaries as approachable texts and find magic in their method.

Having tantalized us, Macaulay amplifies his meaning: 'A leisure hour may always be very agreeably spent in turning over the pages.' In other words, he is talking not about close reading, but about perusal. This was the kind of approach that Coleridge had in mind when he labelled Johnson's work a 'most instructive and entertaining *book*', while confessing he would be surprised to hear 'but very qualified praises of it, as a *dictionary*'.[2] It was Coleridge's friend Charles Lamb who came up with the term '*biblia abiblia*' to denote those books that lack the essential bookish quality of actually being readable, yet have a certain appeal for audacious readers. The finished *Dictionary* is such a work – and more.

In the first place, it abounds with curious words: some amusing because of their sheer unusualness, others because they suggest ideas or practices that sound thoroughly droll. Some are funny because they seem ludicrous and overinflated; others are obsolete but rewardingly succinct ways of capturing a particular trait or malady – or indeed, as Johnson might put it, a 'dignotion' ('distinguishing mark'). So, for instance, an 'amatorculist' is 'a little insignificant lover'. A 'bellygod' is 'one who makes a god of his belly'. 'Deosculation' is 'the act of kissing', and, while we are on a deosculatory theme, a 'kissingcrust' is a 'crust formed when one loaf in the oven touches another'. Two words of more obvious everyday use outside breadmaking circles are the Shakespearian 'mouth-friend' – 'one who professes friendship without intending it' – and its relative 'mouth-honour', which is 'civility outwardly expressed without sincerity' (the word is used by Macbeth). A 'pointingstock' is 'something made the object of ridicule', which is surely more expressive than the durable 'laughingstock'.* A person described as 'potvaliant' is deemed to be 'heated with courage by strong drink'. 'Sciomachy' is 'battle with a shadow' – a useful term for students of politics, *X-Men* or *The Lord of the Rings*. A 'shapesmith' is 'one who undertakes to improve the form of the body', although it is hard to see bodybuilders defecting from the muscular *Flex* to a magazine with the title *Shapesmith*. To be 'subderisorious' consists of 'scoffing or ridiculing with tenderness and delicacy' – at the expense of an amatorculist, for instance. A 'vaticide' is 'a murderer of poets', while 'goldfinder' is a word 'ludicrously' used of those who empty lavatories. Besides such oddities, there are items like 'smellfeast' and 'bedswerver', which are delightfully graphic and hardly call for explanation. A 'suckingbottle' is 'a bottle which to children supplies the want of a pap'. A 'timbersow' is 'a worm in wood'. Johnson even lifts from Bailey the rare

---

* There is also 'gazingstock', 'a person gazed at with scorn or abhorrence'.

term 'goatmilker', apparently reserved for 'a kind of owl so called from sucking goats'.

But there is more to the *Dictionary* than a panoply of strange words, for it also teems with vignettes of strange phenomena. Under 'pincushion', Johnson quotes the dramatist William Congreve: 'Thou art a retailer of phrases, and dost deal in remnants of remnants, like a maker of *pincushions*.' Not unlike the maker of pincushions, Johnson takes scraps and offcuts and turns them into something new. In Eric Partridge's book *The Gentle Art of Lexicography*, there is a story about an elderly lady 'who, on borrowing a dictionary from her municipal library, returned it with the comment, "A *very* unusual book indeed – but the stories are extremely short, aren't they?"'[3] The anecdote may be apocryphal, but the old lady's judgement wasn't cracked. Dictionaries do contain sketches and miniature histories, and Johnson's, produced by a single man rather than by committee, is furbished with numerous spicy oddments and sugared nuggets. More than any other English dictionary, it abounds with stories, arcane information, home truths, snippets of trivia, and lost myths. It is, in short, a treasure house.

In an attempt to illustrate this point I have just opened the *Dictionary* at random – playing the *sortes Johnsonianae*. The first word I turn up is 'cheesevat', which is a 'wooden case in which the curds are confined when they are pressed into cheese'. Its sole supporting quotation is from Joseph Glanvill: 'His sense occasions the careless rustic to judge the sun no bigger than a *cheesevat*.' This is not quite what you would expect to find here. But glancing up a few lines I spot something altogether more improbable – the couplet 'Effeminate he sat, and quiet; / Strange product of a *cheesecake* diet.' Turning the page, I find the entry for 'cherry-tree', which reveals that the fruit was introduced to England in AD 55, and in the adjoining column I see the unfamiliar word 'cheslip', which is apparently the name of 'a small vermin, that lies under stones or tiles' (I later find out that it is actually a woodlouse). Moving on a few pages, I discover that 'chiminage' is the technical term for 'a toll for passage through a forest' and – under 'chink' – read that birds have no epiglottis, which makes me wonder for a moment how a bird stops food clogging up its larynx. I flick on another few pages, and the next word to leap out is 'chub', a river fish 'best in winter' which 'eats . . . not firm, but limp and tasteless' yet 'may be so dressed as to make him very good meat'. I am at a loss to know which would be less satisfactory, a diet of chubs or a diet of cheesecake.

The definitions and illustrative material are luxuriant with these sudden blooms. Readers may chance on the information that Alexander the Great drank from a cup which could hold fourteen pints, or on the old belief that hyenas can mimic the human voice. We learn, too, that in the eighteenth century a barrel of Essex butter contained 106 pounds, whereas one of Suffolk butter contained 256. We may sometimes be sceptical – did all barrels of herrings contain approximately 1,000 fish? – but we are amused, surprised and intrigued by what we find, even when it sounds unlikely.

Readers are encouraged to believe that millipedes swallowed whole are a convenient laxative, that bookbinders have traditionally used aqua fortis (nitric acid) to marble the covers of their books, and that at least one person has suffered as a result of assuming that 'aqua fortis' is 'strong water'. The calyx of the plant known as 'skullcap' looks like the heel of a slipper. Russian potash is stronger than Swedish. Windmills are twice as effective as watermills. Candied sea holly – also known as 'eryngo' – was once 'sent to London for medicinal use'. In Italy, the usual method for finding truffles or 'subterraneous mushrooms' involves tying a cord to the hind leg of a pig, taking him out into the fields, and observing where he rootles. Sugar cane in Tobago has been known to grow twenty-four feet high. The American frog 'brings forth young from her back'. Criminals in Turkey are dropped from high places 'upon hooks'. The backstaff, 'useful in taking the sun's altitude at sea', was invented by a Captain Davies. Cornish fishermen, fishing under the ice in winter, have on occasion come across swallows 'congealed in clods', and have taken them home and warmed them in their stoves in order to resuscitate them. The number of possible combinations of the letters of the alphabet is 1,391,724,288,887,252,999,425,128,493,402,200.*

At times Johnson seems to be indulging himself outrageously. For

---

* Johnson's peers considered the alphabet to have twenty-four letters, since *i* was not distinguished from *j*, nor *u* from *v*.

instance, he records that a 'twister' is 'one who twists; a ropemaker', and then subjoins 'some remarkable lines' which 'explain' the word 'in all its senses' – a twelve-line poem which includes the word 'twist', in various forms, more than thirty times. We hardly need this, but Johnson is enjoying his work: enjoying a funny little rhyme he has come across, and at the same time enjoying the mazy intricacies of syntax and the succulent richness of language.

This capacity of Johnson's for cherishing strangeness is apparent in the *Dictionary*'s preservation of beliefs and notions that were, even 250 years ago, remarkably backward. This is one of the *Dictionary*'s fascinations, and there is no better example of it than his extensive deployment of quotations from Sir Thomas Browne. Johnson admired Browne, and wrote a short biography of him, but to modern readers the works of this seventeenth-century physician seem mummified and bizarre. Browne was an amateur scientist, and loved to conduct experiments at his Norwich home. When he was visited by John Evelyn, the inquisitive diarist recorded that his house was a 'cabinet of curiosities'. Browne's writings have a similar quality.

A taste for Browne's exotic prose is conspicuous in the *Dictionary*. His importance as a stylist lies in his neologisms. Any writer with an enthusiasm for the outlandish will chafe against the boundaries of ordinary usage: to write about extreme experiences, you need to reach for vivid, unfamiliar vocabulary, or indeed to vault the limits of convention and invent your own words. Browne took great pleasure in doing this. His writings abound with terms that he dreamed up. A substantial part of his legacy has been lasting. He coined the words 'literary', 'insecurity', 'suicide', 'precarious', 'indigenous', 'medical' and 'electricity'. True, Johnson cites him as an authority for words we can scarcely believe existed: 'to australize' ('to tend towards the south'), 'bicipitous' ('having two heads'), 'extispicious' ('relating to the inspection of entrails in order to prognostication [*sic*]'), 'guttulous' ('in the form of a small drop'), 'latirostrous' ('broad-beaked'), 'rhabdomancy' ('divination by a wand'), 'suppedaneous' ('placed under the feet') and – a personal favourite, potentially useful for cricket commentators – 'anatiferous' ('producing ducks'). True, too, the scope of many of Browne's original coinages has altered since the seventeenth century: as we have seen, 'electricity' meant something different to him, and to Johnson, from what it meant to Faraday, and from what it means to us. Nevertheless, Browne's talent for confecting new and useful words was extraordinary.

Browne's matter is as unusual as his style, and by quoting him so often Johnson licenses a good deal of bizarre material. All bar three of the nearly 2,000 passages from Browne in the *Dictionary* come from a work called *Pseudodoxia Epidemica*, a giant compendium of popular misconceptions and antique thinking, first published in 1646 and expanded through five subsequent editions. In its overt concern with exactitude in matters of definition and terminology, together with its abundance of medical and pseudo-scientific language, *Pseudodoxia* was an ideal source for a lexicographer to quarry, but in Johnson's hands Browne's natural philosophy enjoys an afterlife as literature.

The real pleasure of the chosen illustrations is their weirdness. Browne was, after all, a man whose reaction to finding a death-watch beetle in the wainscot at home was to put it in a matchbox so he could observe the ticking noise it made. Its proboscis called to mind the beak of a tiny woodpecker. Once we know that he has tried to breed vipers and has fed dogs on powdered glass, we realize that in his world anything goes. So perhaps it is no surprise to read the quotation which Johnson provides to illustrate the noun 'cramp': 'Hares, said to live on hemlock, do not make good the tradition; and he that observes what vertigoes, *cramps*, and convulsions follow thereon, in these animals, will be of our belief.' It is possible, if one reads this quickly, to ignore its rather sinister implications. But read it again. Browne's 'he that observes' is a rhetorical trope designed to deflect attention away from him. Actually it is Browne who 'observes': in order to see whether it is true that hares can stomach hemlock, he feeds them the plant, and then observes their sufferings.

Pseudodoxia was useful to Johnson because it examined natural phenomena closely. This was an area in which he hoped to improve on his predecessors. We see how much room there was for improvement if we examine a contemporary work such as Benjamin Martin's *Lingua Britannica Reformata*. In Martin's dictionary 'badger' is defined as 'the name of a wild beast', 'beaver' as 'an amphibious animal, like an otter', 'elephant' as 'the biggest of all beasts', and 'hare' as 'a well known animal'. This is unhelpful. Yet, to put this into perspective, in

Ephraim Chambers's *Cyclopaedia* (the fifth edition, as worked on by the elder Macbean), none of these animal names even commands an entry. By contrast, Johnson's entries for animals and plants are charming and informative. A 'cat' is 'a domestic animal that catches mice, commonly reckoned by naturalists the lowest order of the leonine species'. A 'rhinoceros' is 'a vast beast in the East Indies armed with a horn in his front'. The shrew is 'generally supposed venomous' and 'is said to lame the foot over which she runs' – but Johnson is 'informed that all these reports are calumnious, and that her feet and teeth are equally harmless with those of any other little mouse'. The hedgehog is 'set with prickles, like thorns in an hedge', while the 'camelopard' (giraffe) is defined, a little alarmingly, as 'an Abyssinian animal, taller than an elephant, but not so thick'. A caterpillar is 'a worm which, when it gets wings, is sustained by leaves and fruits'. The fieldmouse 'burrows in banks, and makes her house with various apartments'.

Where the makers of modern dictionaries strive for uniformity, Johnson was quite happy to vary the size of his entries. Although some of his definitions of natural phenomena are lean, many are lengthy, even opulent, reflecting the contemporary love affair with unusual flora and fauna. Here more than anywhere he strays towards an encyclopedic approach, and the *Dictionary* begins to resemble, at least fleetingly, a herbal and a bestiary. He tends to rely heavily on earlier authors (the Jesuit *Dictionnaire de Trévoux*, Augustin Calmet's vast commentary on the Bible), but the texture of the entries is rich, and they contain many amusing titbits. An armadillo is 'a four-footed animal of Brazil, as big as a cat, with a snout like a hog, a tail like a lizard, and feet like a hedgehog'. The chameleon has a back that is 'jagged like a saw', and 'if it be put upon a black hat, it appears to be of a violet colour'. Of the crocodile we learn that 'when its bowels are taken out, or it is wounded, it smells very agreeably'. The woodlouse 'is a very swift runner'. Asbestos is 'almost insipid to the taste', while the seacow has 'flesh . . . white like veal, and very well tasted'.

Pseudodoxia was a valuable source of this kind of information. Especially valuable was its resistance to popular myth. Yet one of its defining traits is that it gives space to the very myths and misconceptions it aims to explode, and its most interesting part – certainly for the modern reader, and perhaps also for Johnson – is not its defeat of erroneous beliefs, but rather the errors themselves, which by turns amuse, horrify, seduce and bewilder. So, for example, Browne reminds us that people used to believe that badgers have legs longer on one side than the other, that a beaver will bite off his own testicles to evade capture, and that a female bear gives birth to young that resemble blobs of jelly, which she (literally) licks into shape.

It is from *Pseudodoxia* that Johnson gets his information about something called the 'boramez', a 'strange plant-animal or vegetable lamb of Tartary, which wolves delight to feed on . . . [and] affordeth a bloody juice upon breaking', as well as about how bad an 'ague' you can get if you sleep with Homer's *Iliad* under your head. Stranger still is the extract quoted under 'hedge-hog', in which Browne reproduces an ancient recipe for achieving night vision: all you have to do is pluck out the right eye of a hedgehog, boil it in oil, preserve the residue 'in a brazen vessel', and consume as required. No doubt Johnson was tickled to be able to reproduce Browne's diatribe against cucumbers, which, 'being waterish, fill the veins with crude and windy serosities, that contain little salt or spirit, and debilitate the vital acidity and *fermental* faculty of the stomach'. Johnson loathed cucumbers: he held with the old-fashioned view that 'a cucumber should be well sliced, and dressed with pepper and vinegar, and then thrown out, as good for nothing'.

Boiled hedgehog's eyes, asymmetric badgers, self-castrating beavers, hares intoxicated with hemlock, and the bloody juice of the boramez: these sound like a mixture of *Macbeth* and Hieronymus Bosch, with more than a touch of the erudite fantasies of Jorge Luis Borges. Such buried delights really do make the *Dictionary* a book with which to beguile a moment's leisure, and this is what Johnson had in mind when he explained that he had deliberately included some passages which might 'relieve the labour of verbal searches, and intersperse with verdure and flowers the dusty deserts of barren philology'. These words come from the Preface, which is most readers' point of entry to the *Dictionary*. Composed only after the rest of Johnson's work was done, it is a compelling statement of the *Dictionary*'s peculiarly Johnsonian temper.

To preface

To say something introductory

> 'Before I enter upon the particular parts of her character, it is necessary to *preface*, that she is the only child of a decrepit father' – *Spectator*

'The author of almost every book retards his instructions by a preface,' wrote Johnson, less than two years after the *Dictionary* was published. This was in an introductory essay for the New Year issue of Dodsley's evening paper the *London Chronicle*. Johnson was paid just one guinea for the piece, but, as was his wont, made the best of a job that others would have executed in more desultory fashion. He was a prolific author of prefaces and introductions, and was aware of the faults of the work he did in this strain. Prefaces, he knew, are usually attempts to avert criticism, or to respond to it. They are opportunities to improvise a few paragraphs of complacent autobiography. They are excuses to lambaste the deficiencies of other writers, or of the republic of letters, or of the world at large.

The preface that Johnson wrote for his *Dictionary* is all these things. Yet it is much more than this. It is not just for reasons of editorial convenience that it is the one part of the *Dictionary* that tends to be found in commercial editions of his works. Boswell claimed that 'there are few prose compositions in the English Language that are read with more delight'. We are likely to disagree with Boswell's choice of word: the Preface is not delightful, but lapidary and grave, and when it stirs our emotions it moves us to pity as often as to pleasure, chastening us more than it can truly be said to thrill or enchant us. Yet it is magisterial, noble, imperishable; and no one has ever written so acutely and at the same time so personally about the problems of language and lexicography.

The experience of writing the *Dictionary* had transformed Johnson's ideas about these subjects, and accordingly the Preface feels very different from the *Plan* of eight years before. Johnson is reconciled to the instability of language. He understands the importance of descriptive lexicography, and has renounced his more narrowly prescriptive notions. He thinks of his audience not as consumers and purchasers, but as readers and learners. He is almost a decade older, and a good deal more weary of the world, yet there is a clear sense of his self-confidence. Unlike the *Plan*, the Preface is not framed as a missive to Lord Chesterfield: it is a statement rather than an entreaty, as its language repeatedly shows. There is a naked vein of reference to Johnson's own judgement and experience: he emphasizes that this dictionary is *his* dictionary, and that it is precisely in this feature that its value inheres.

His rhetorical procedures for canonizing his achievement are complex. He begins by mocking his efforts of the past eight years. Picking up on his definition of 'lexicographer', he refers to the 'humble drudge' who compiles dictionaries. He deprecates his research, and confesses readily to the actual shortcomings of the *Dictionary*. In fact he exults in apology. Having acknowledged that his word-list is not completely up to date, he reflects that 'A large work is difficult because it is large, even though all its single parts might be singly performed with facility', and adds, 'nor can it be expected, that the stones which form the dome of a temple, should be squared and polished like the diamond of a ring'. A few lines on from this, he quells the suspicion that he ought to have examined the spoken word, rather than just written texts: 'sounds are too volatile and subtle for legal restraints', and attempting to 'enchain syllables' is as hopeless an undertaking as trying 'to lash the wind'.

These rebuttals of imagined and anticipated criticisms share space with a more general treatment of lexicography, in which Johnson expresses its promise and its pains. It is here that the Preface is memorably lyrical:

> When first I engaged in this work, I resolved to leave neither words nor things unexamined, and pleased myself with a prospect of the hours which I should revel away in feasts of literature, with the obscure recesses of northern learning which I should enter and ransack; the treasures with which I expected every search into those neglected mines to reward my labour, and the triumph with which I should display my acquisitions to mankind.

This, he admits, was delusional. But throughout his discussion of the pleasures and discontents of lexicography he maintains a richly metaphoric language which incarnates the drama of his labours. It is not just that words are 'the daughters of earth' and 'change their manners when they change their country': some are 'candidates' or 'probationers', others are 'fugitives' and 'intruders', and yet others, sliding from obscurity to oblivion, 'perish'. As so often, Johnson sounds as impressive when explaining his omissions as he does when recording his achievements.

Anyone who works seriously with language enjoys its slipperiness and versatility. It moves in a current of its own making. With this in mind, Johnson insists:

> It must be remembered, that while our language is yet living, and variable by the caprice of every one that speaks it, . . . words are hourly shifting their relations, and can no more be ascertained in a dictionary, than a grove, in the agitation of a storm, can be accurately delineated from its picture in the water.

Perhaps 'hourly' is an exaggeration, but Johnson is in poetic mood. He describes the process of research in terms that will ring true for anyone who has ever tried to hem in the edges of a large project:

> I saw that one enquiry only gave occasion to another, . . . that to search was not always to find, and to find was not always to be informed; and that thus to pursue perfection was, like the first inhabitants of Arcadia, to chase the sun, which, when they had reached the hill where he seemed to rest, was still beheld at the same distance from them.

In its final paragraphs the Preface becomes elegiac and deeply personal. Johnson has already made it clear that he thinks correct usage is buoyed by nationalism; he talks of recalling English from its deviation 'towards a Gallic structure and phraseology', proposes 'making our ancient volumes the ground-work of style', and, noting the long-established character of the Constitution, rallies his fellow patriots with the words 'let us make some struggles for our language'.[1] Now he cements this: 'I have devoted this book, the labour of years, to the honour of my country, that we may no longer yield the palm of philology without a contest to the nations of the continent.' He continues:

Whether I shall add anything by my own writings to the reputation of English literature, must be left to time: much of my life has been lost under the pressures of disease; much has been trifled away; and much has always been spent in provision for the day that was passing over me; but I shall not think my employment useless or ignoble if by my assistance foreign nations and distant ages gain access to the propagators of knowledge, and understand the teachers of truth.

Johnson really did believe that much of his life had been trifled away. We know that he had indeed 'lost' precious hours and days and weeks to illness and depression. Yet confidence in his achievement consoles him. 'It may repress the triumph of malignant criticism', he writes, 'to observe, that if our language is not here fully displayed, I have only failed in an attempt which no human powers have hitherto completed.' This is not hypersensitivity to the possibility of criticism, but a statement of self-certainty: Johnson is sure he has done as much as is humanly possible. In these closing lines his personality is vivid on the page.

The concluding sentence is the most memorable. 'I have protracted my work', Johnson attests, 'till most of those whom I wished to please have sunk into the grave, and success and miscarriage are empty sounds: I therefore dismiss it with frigid tranquillity, having little to fear or hope from censure or from praise.' Several critics have been suspicious of that deft assonance ('frigid tranquillity'): for a moment the language sounds disingenuously poised. But the sentiment is real. Johnson is mindful of his wife, dead these three years, and of his own ageing. No achievement, however large, can win back the dead; nor can it keep death's pale horse at bay – yet nor can any gust of critical hostility snuff out the light of life. By striking such a personal note where others would have been carefully impersonal, he presents the special character of his *Dictionary*.

Publication

1. The act of publishing; the act of notifying to the world; divulgation; proclamation

2. Edition; the act of giving a book to the publick

As the day of publication approached, Johnson lurched between pleasure at his achievement and anxiety for the work's reception. The pleasure was mixed with relief – something felt on both sides of the transaction. When the last sheet of copy was delivered, one of the booksellers, Andrew Millar, was heard to exclaim, 'Thank God, I have done with him.' On hearing of this, Johnson shot back, 'I am glad that he thanks God for any thing.' As for the anxiety, it was not misplaced. By the middle of the eighteenth century, books were commonplace objects. Their aura was much less potent than it had been a hundred years before. The expansion of print culture meant that new printed books, which had once automatically been sacred, now provided occasions for criticism. There was no conclusive way to indemnify books against critical malevolence. However, it was worth taking trouble over a work's presentation in order to ensure that it could not be lost in the ocean of new publications.

What, then, did the finished *Dictionary* look like? What kind of a feel did it have? It was, in the first place, a large, cumbersome item, weighing around twenty pounds – the same as a very big Christmas turkey. It was plainly intended to be bound in two volumes: at the end of the Grammar there were directions for the bookbinder, who was requested to bind the entries from *A* to *K* in one volume, and those from *L* to *Z* in a second. Some owners ignored this suggestion, possibly for aesthetic reasons, but more probably for practical ones. The handsome copy of the folio first edition I have before me as I write this (in the British Library) is bound in four volumes, and is still unwieldy. It is the sort of book that has to be rested on a table or a lectern; it is not easy to lift a volume one-handed, and only a basketball player

Rob.t Hildyard

A

DICTIONARY

OF THE

ENGLISH LANGUAGE:

IN WHICH

The WORDS are deduced from their ORIGINALS,

AND

ILLUSTRATED in their DIFFERENT SIGNIFICATIONS

BY

EXAMPLES from the beſt WRITERS.

TO WHICH ARE PREFIXED,

A HISTORY of the LANGUAGE,

AND

An ENGLISH GRAMMAR.

By SAMUEL JOHNSON, A.M.

In TWO VOLUMES.

VOL. I.

Cum tabulis animum cenſoris ſumet honeſti :
Audebit quæcunque parum ſplendoris habebunt,
Et ſine pondere erunt, et honore indigna ferentur.
Verba movere loco ; quamvis invita recedant,
Et verſentur adhuc intra penetralia Veſtæ :
Obſcurata diu populo bonus eruet, atque
Proferet in lucem ſpecioſa vocabula rerum,
Quæ priſcis memorata Catonibus atque Cethegis,
Nunc ſitus informis premit et deſerta vetuſtas.   HOR.

LONDON,
Printed by W. STRAHAN,
For J. and P. KNAPTON ; T. and T. LONGMAN ; C. HITCH and L. HAWES ;
A. MILLAR ; and R. and J. DODSLEY.
MDCCLV.

The title page of the first edition of the *Dictionary*

A GENERAL

DICTIONARY

OF THE

ENGLISH LANGUAGE.

A

A, The first letter of the European alphabets, has, in the English language, three different founds, open, and flender.

The broad found refembling that of the German *a* is found, in many of our monofyllables, as *all, wall, malt, falt*; in which *a* is pronounced as *au* in *caufe*, or *aw* in *law*. Many of thefe words were anciently written with *au*, as *fault, waulk*; which happens to be ftill retained in *fault*. This was probably the ancient found of the Saxons, fince it is almoft uniformly preferved in the ruftic pronunciation, and the Northern dialects, as *maun* for *man, haund* for *hand*.

A open, not unlike the *a* of the Italians, is found in *father, rather*, and more obfcurely in *fancy, faft*, &c.

A flender or clofe, is the peculiar *a* of the Englifh language, refembling the found of the French *e* mafculine, or diphthong *ai* in *pais*, or perhaps a middle found between them, or between the *a* and *e*, to this the Arabic *a* is faid nearly to approach. Of this found we have examples in the words, *place, face, wafte*, and all thofe that terminate in *ation*; as, *relation, nation, generation*.

A is fhort, as, *glafs, grafs*; or long, as, *glaze, graze*: it is marked long, generally, by an *e* final, *plane*, or by an *i* added, as, *plain*.

A, an article fet before nouns of the fingular number; *a man, a tree*; denoting the number *one*, as, *a man is coming*, that is, *no more than one*; or an indefinite indication, as, *a man may come this way*; that is, *any man*. This article has no plural fignification. Before a word beginning with a vowel, it is written *an*, as, *an ox, an egg*, of which *a* is the contraction.

A is fometimes a noun; as, a great *A*, a little *a*.

A is placed before a participle, or participial noun; and is confidered by Wallis as a contraction of *at*, when it is put before a word denoting fome action not yet finifhed; as, I am *a* walking. It alfo feems to be anciently contracted from *at*, when placed before local furnames; as, Thomas *a* Becket. In other cafes, it feems to fignify *to*, like the French *à*.

A hunting Chloe went.   *Prior.*

They go *a* begging to a bankrupt's door.   *Dryd.*

May pure contents for ever pitch their tents
Upon thefe downs, thefe meads, thefe rocks, thefe mountains,
And peace ftill flumber by thefe purling fountains !
    Which we may every year
Find when we come a fifhing here.   *Wotton.*

Now the men fell a rubbing of armour, which a great while had lain oiled ; the magazines of munition are viewed; the officers of remains called to account.   *Wotton.*

Another falls a ringing a Pefcennius Niger, and judicioufly diftinguifhes the found of it to be modern. *Addifon on medals.*

A has a peculiar fignification, denoting the proportion of one thing to another. Thus we fay, The landlord hath a hundred *a* year ; The fhip's crew gained a thoufand pounds *a* man.

The river Inn, that had been hitherto fhut up among mountains, paffes generally through a wide open country, during all its courfe through Bavaria ; which is a voyage of two days, after the rate of twenty leagues *a* day.   *Addifon on Italy.*

A is ufed in burlefque poetry, to lengthen out a fyllable, without adding to the fenfe.

Vol. I.

ABA

For cloves and nutmegs to the line-*a*;
And even for oranges to China.   *Dryden.*

A is fometimes, in familiar writings, put by a barbarous corruption for *be.*

A, in compofition, feems to have fometimes the power of the French *a* in thefe phrafes, *a droit, a gauche,* &c. and fometimes to be contracted from *at* ; as, *afide, ufflope, afoot, afleep, athirft, aware.*

If this, which he avouches, does appear,
There is no flying hence, nor tarrying here.
I gin to be *a weary* of the fun ;
And with the ftate of the world were now undone.
    Shakefpeare's Macbeth.

And now a breeze from fhore began to blow,
The failors fhip their oars, and ceafe to row ;
Then hoift their yards *a*-trip, and all their fails
Let fall, to court the winds, and catch the gales.
    Dryden's Ceyx and Alcyone.

A is fometimes redundant ; as, *arife, aroufe, awake* ; the fame with rife, roufe, wake.

A, in abbreviations, ftands for *artium*, or arts ; as, A. B. bachelor of arts, *artium baccalaureus* ; A. M. mafter of arts, *artium magifter* ; or, *annus* ; as, A. D. *anno domini.*

A B, at the beginning of the names of places, generally fhews that they have fome relation to an abbey.

ABA'CKE. *adv.* obfolete. Backwards.

But when they came where thou thy fkill didft fhow,
They drew *abacke*, as half with fhame confound,
Shepherds to fee them in their art outgo.   *Spenf. Paft.*

ABA'CTOR. n. f. [Lat. *abactor*, a driver away.] Thofe who drive away or fteal cattle in herds, or great numbers at once, in diftinction from thofe that fteal only a fheep or two, *Blount*.

A BACUS. n. f. [Lat. *abacus*.]

1. A counting-table, anciently ufed in calculations.

2. In architecture, it is the uppermoft member of a column, which ferves as a fort of crowning both to the capital and column.   *Dict.*

ABA'FT. *adv.* [of abæftan, Sax. Behind.] From the fore-part of the fhip, towards the ftern.   *Dict.*

ABAI'SANCE. *n. f.* [from the French *abaifer*, to deprefs, to bring down.] An act of reverence, a bow. *Obeyfance* is confidered by Skinner as a corruption of *abaifance*, but is now univerfally ufed.

To ABA'LIENATE. *v. a.* [from *abalienatus*, Lat.] To make that another's which was our own before. *Cocks. Lex. Jur.* A term of the civil law, not much ufed in common fpeech.

ABALIENA'TION. *n. f.* [Lat. *abalienatio*.] A giving up one's right to another perfon ; or a making over an eftate, goods, or chattels by fale, or due courfe of law.   *Dict.*

To ABA'ND. *v. a.* [A word contracted from abandon, but not now in ufe. See ABANDON.] To forfake.

Thofe foreigners which came from far
Grew great, and got large portions of land,
That in the realm, ere long, they ftronger are
Than they which fought at firft their helping hand,
And Vortiger enforced the kingdom to *aband.*
    Spenfer's Fairy Queen, b. ii cant. 10.

To ABANDON. *v. a.* [Fr. *abandonner.* Derived, according to *Menage*, from the Italian *abandonare*, which fignifies to forfake his colours, *bandum [vexillum] deferere. Pafquier* thinks

B   it

The first page of the *Dictionary*. Note the title: 'A General Dictionary . . .'

would be able to hold it up and open with a single hand. With its pages spread, it is almost twenty inches wide, and the pages are a foot and half in length; stacked, the four volumes make a pile nearly ten inches high. Johnson's finished tome was stately in appearance – '*Vasta mole superbus*' ('Proud in its great bulk'), as he beamingly described it in a letter to Thomas Warton.[1]

On the title page it is presented as 'A Dictionary of the English Language'.* Johnson's name, like the words 'English Language', is printed in red. Inside, the text is cleanly laid out on the page, without quite attaining elegance, and the presentation is much crisper than that of rival dictionaries. Its appearance owed a great deal to the influence of William Strahan. In the first place, Strahan was prudent in buying most of his type from the skilled type-founder Alexander Wilson, a scholarly figure who later became the first Professor of Practical Astronomy at Glasgow University and studied the 'spots' on the sun. In an age when type was often of poor quality, Wilson's was excellent. The Preface and headings were set in 4.6 mm 'English' type; the text in 3.5 mm pica, in double columns, with a generous margin. These were the two typefaces Strahan most frequently used, and were among the cheapest available, but they are easy on the eye. He bought his paper from the highly regarded stationer Stephen Theodore Janssen, who was later lord mayor of London, and it is thick, almost luxurious to the touch.

Strahan may have been a shrewd man, but his position, like that of any eighteenth-century printer, was precarious, because he was paid in arrears. The partners in the *Dictionary* made their payments in cash, with amounts rounded down to the nearest pound, and it was quite normal for there to be a six-month gap between the execution of a job and the receipt of payment. Of the partners, Andrew Millar was the most punctual, and the Knaptons were the least.

Fortunately, Strahan's business was expanding dramatically, and did not rely heavily on any one account. In 1746, when the contract for the *Dictionary* was signed, he paid out £378. 7s. 6d. in wages and received £1,337. 9s. in revenues; within four years his wage bill

---

* At the beginning of the entries for the letter *A* it is styled slightly differently – 'A General Dictionary of the English Language'.

trebled, and revenues, at a time of low inflation, climbed steeply. In November 1753 he wrote confidently to his friend David Hall, who had been an apprentice with him in Edinburgh and was now settled in Philadelphia, 'This twelvemonth past I have employed seven presses; and . . . could have kept two or three more.'[2] By February the following year he had a new printing house and nine presses. In August he wrote to Hall that 'trade has been slacker here this summer than I have known of it a long while', but by early November all his presses were busy, and he found himself paying out nearly £40 a week in wages.[3] The reason for this change was simple: Johnson had delivered the remaining part of his giant manuscript, and the business that convulsed Strahan's printing house during the winter months was translating it into printed copies of the *Dictionary*.[4]

Initially 2,000 copies were printed. Today this seems a modest figure, but the market was not huge: as late as the 1790s Edmund Burke estimated the reading public at below 100,000. Moreover, the *Dictionary* had been expensive to produce, and its price – £4. 10s. for a bound copy 'in boards' – reflected this. For all Johnson's avowedly pedagogic aims, his market consisted at first of affluent, educated readers.

Starting at the end of February 1755, and continuing throughout March, notices in the press announced that the volumes were at last to be published – and 'speedily'. On 1 March Dodsley distributed 1,500 copies of the *Plan*, which he had had reprinted, without the salutation to Chesterfield, in order to drum up interest in the *Dictionary*. These were given to prospective purchasers, but the gesture was insensitive: the *Plan* promoted a different idea of lexicography from Johnson's finished work. Dodsley was untroubled by this: his strategy was unapologetically commercial. He got Strahan to print fifty advertisements to be run in 'country papers', along with 250 showcards for booksellers' windows. Although none of this was expensive, the final account that Strahan presented was for more than £800, a sum that was not fully paid off until almost four years later.

The partners' repayments were inexcusably dilatory, yet Strahan was prepared to wait. The total cost of printing was £1,239. 11s. 6d. In addition to Johnson's £1,575, at least £1,500 was spent on paper – a large though not freakish figure, since the purchase of paper was usually reckoned to account for half the cost of publishing a book.

Still, this meant the outlay was in the region of £4,500. The partners stood to recoup £9,000, but the tedious progress of the work meant they were not disposed to think of this as a successful bit of business. Of all the partners, the Knaptons suffered by far the most: Paul died in June 1755, and his brother, John, was forced by bankruptcy and debts of £20,000 to sell his stock before the year was out.

The Knaptons' fate is cautionary. In the eighteenth century no single firm could finance a work on the scale of the *Dictionary*, but, while collaboration between booksellers could bring huge rewards, the most ambitious of publishing projects were always gruellingly protracted, and they demanded of their backers a mixture of sustained investment, patience and stamina. Johnson wrote in the Preface that 'no dictionary of a living tongue can ever be perfect, since while it is hastening to publication, some words are budding, and some falling away'; it is worth pausing to observe that while his own dictionary was moving, less than hastily, towards publication, some of the men who invested in it were also sinking into oblivion. The finished *Dictionary* is their memorial too.

We should note that one of Johnson's definitions of 'publication' is 'proclamation', and that another involves 'notifying . . . the world'. Not for him the reticence of the complaisant courtly author. After the years of toil – years in which he had wrestled with his melancholy, with his obligations to friends and supplicants, with the problems of his marriage and his wife's decline and death, with material anxiety and his strategies for defeating it, and above all with the trials of lexicography: the difficulties of finding materials and elucidating them, of arranging his findings and doing justice to the richness and complexities of English – he was done, and the flowers of his labours were at last arranged within a book. The achievement was remarkable, and Johnson wished it to be remarked.

Reception

1. The act of receiving

3. Admission of any thing communicated

6. Treatment at first coming; welcome; entertainment

When Boswell came to this part of Johnson's life, more than three decades later, he pronounced that 'the world contemplated with wonder so stupendous a work achieved by one man, while other countries had thought such undertakings fit only for whole academies'. He was in a position to review the range of responses the *Dictionary* had elicited, and although he was naturally disposed in its favour his summary is just. The critical reception was favourable. The *Dictionary* was a success.

One of the first responses came from Garrick, who wrote a poem in celebration of his former teacher's achievement. The poem appeared in the *Public Advertiser*, and was widely reprinted. It is neither a dignified nor a restrained piece of work, and concludes with the slightly silly couplet 'And Johnson, well arm'd like a hero of yore, / Has beat forty French, and will beat forty more!' In these lines Garrick is not just hymning his master's Herculean feats: he is also contrasting Johnson's English individualism with the bureaucratic absolutism and obsessive centralization which he, like most of his peers, identified with the French, their government and their administrative institutions. For Garrick, as for many of his social class, the publication of the *Dictionary* was an occasion to poke fun at France and the self-conscious elitism of Continental *philosophes*. In his case, it also offered an opportunity for self-promotion – something he rarely spurned. Many responses to the *Dictionary* had this flavour: an important cultural moment allows every commentator to grind his axe.

In the 1750s there was less reviewing of new books than there is today; brief notices were more common than detailed critique. Still, the *Dictionary* was enthusiastically written up in important periodicals such as the *London Magazine* and – none too surprisingly – the *Gentleman's Magazine*. In the latter it received an eight-page notice; appropriately enough, a few pages later there was an item about the different types of snail. These laudatory reviews were reprinted in other periodicals, and were joined by fresh tributes. However, praise was usually tempered by a few words of criticism. In a long piece for the *Monthly Review* consisting largely of quotations from the Preface, an anonymous contributor (Sir Tanfield Leman) applauded 'a performance that will be received with gratitude by those who are sincerely zealous for the reputation of English literature'. He declined to point out 'what appear to us as defects', on the grounds that 'most of them will be obvious' and he had no wish 'to feed the malevolence of little or lazy critics'.[1]

Naturally, the little and lazy critics had their say, but of the less positive assessments the only properly judicious one came from Adam Smith in the pro-Whig *Edinburgh Review*. Smith began courteously by conceding that 'when we compare this book with other dictionaries, the merit of its author appears very extraordinary', yet he wished that Johnson 'had oftener passed his own censure upon those words which are not of approved use, though sometimes to be met with in authors of no mean name'. Furthermore, Johnson's approach was not 'sufficiently grammatical': Smith proposed improvements.[2] In this case as in others, the suggested amendments were impracticable, and a more realistic consensus held that the *Dictionary*, despite its faults, was a handsome achievement, while its 'author' had proved himself an outstanding scholar and public benefactor. Dissent was rare, and those who did voice doubts tended to have personal motives. There was no louder opponent of Johnson than an Irish cleric and philologist called John Maxwell, who excoriated the *Dictionary* in an essay on its 'character'.[3] Two and a half centuries later, Maxwell's diatribe looks comically self-serving: it was the rancorous howl of a man mortified by Johnson's success, having spent a decade toiling on a rival work of his own.

The plaudits were not short-lived. Nine months after the *Dictionary* was published, the poet Christopher Smart wrote in the *Universal Visiter* that Johnson's creation was something 'which I look upon with equal pleasure and amazement, as I do upon St Paul's Cathedral; each the work of *one* man, each the work of an *Englishman*'.[4] This is an unfortunate analogy: the design of St Paul's may have been entirely the work of Christopher Wren, but no one could pretend that Wren was exclusively responsible for the design's *execution*. The *Dictionary*, however, can legitimately be thought of as Johnson's single-handed feat, even though he did draw on other writers' specialist knowledge of medicine and zoology, law and etymology, as well as on earlier dictionaries, commentaries and compendia. Perhaps too it would not have been begun without the encouragement of the partners, nor compiled without the help of the amanuenses, nor completed without the efforts of Strahan its printer. Nevertheless, the tone of Smart's encomium was valid. The *Dictionary* was considered, from the moment of its inception, to be Johnson's, and from the time of its completion it was *Johnson's Dictionary* – his book and his property, his monument, his memorial.

We should not imagine, however, that its completion allowed Johnson to indulge in some self-congratulatory clambake. When Charles Burney wrote to him praising his achievement, he dolefully replied that 'Yours is the only letter of goodwill that I have yet received, though indeed I am promised something of the sort from Sweden.' This two and a half years after the *Dictionary*'s publication! He told Burney that 'among all my acquaintance there were only two who . . . did not endeavour to depress me with threats of censure from the publick, or with objections learned from those who had learned them from my own preface'. Indeed, where the finished draft has the word 'censure', he originally wrote the more vivid 'abuse'.[5]

One may infer a small exaggeration: Johnson would hardly be the first person to remember hostility more readily than praise. But the completion of the *Dictionary* did not bring him happiness. Nor did it even ease his worries. He was ill. In the winter months of 1755 he suffered bronchitis and acute conjunctivitis. On 29 December he wrote to Lewis Paul, an inventor whose machine for spinning wool he was attempting to promote, stating that he had had a 'cough so violent that I once fainted under its convulsions'. 'I have been pretty much dejected,' he tells him. The next day sees him writing to the flagging Hill Boothby as a 'poor helpless being reduced by a blast of wind to weakness and misery'.[6] During this period he had to be bled three times; on one occasion he gave up fifty-four ounces of blood. Without the *Dictionary* to occupy him, he was at the mercy of his melancholy. He became aware of a rumour that he had died. And, as ever, there were problems with money. Humiliatingly, on 16 March 1756 he was arrested for a debt of £5. 18s., which he was able to settle only by borrowing from Samuel Richardson – although he was so confident of his friend's help that before the money arrived he sent out for a pint of wine to share with the bailiff.

Johnson's finances were imperilled by his familiar generosity. By this time his household included an especially trying case, the blind poet Anna Williams. She was the daughter of Zachariah Williams, a Welsh doctor and inventor. Zachariah had travelled to London more than thirty years before to compete for a £20,000 prize, sponsored by the government, for the first person to devise a means of accurately calculating longitude at sea ('accurately' meaning, for these purposes, to within half a degree). Williams's scheme was unsuccessful – the prize was not won until 1773 – but Johnson learned of the case and was impressed by Williams's findings. Aware that the old man was dying, he attempted to salvage some final respect for him by distilling his work in a pamphlet that was published under Williams's name. This pamphlet characterized him as 'a kind of stranger in a new world' and 'the single votary of an obsolete science, the scoff of . . . puny philosophers', while asserting the typical Johnsonian moral that 'no man is more in danger of doing little, than he who flatters himself with abilities to do all'.[7] Williams died three months after the *Dictionary* was published, and his daughter, peevish and severe, from this time relied increasingly on Johnson. Having initially moved to Gough Square to convalesce after an eye operation, she remained his companion for thirty years.★

Responsibilities to others weighed on Johnson's conscience, and, while many of his literary designs were anything but commercial, it was always necessary to write for money. Accordingly, during the

---

★ Johnson even persuaded Garrick to allow a benefit performance of Aaron Hill's play *Merope* at Drury Lane, which raised £260 for Ms Williams. Several of his letters from January 1756 see him urging tickets on his correspondents.

second half of the 1750s he found it necessary to augment his income by penning a prodigious assortment of prefaces, reviews and essays. Much of this was Grub Street work. For instance, he produced a preface for Richard Rolt's new dictionary of trade and commerce, although he had never met the author, nor even read him; and, while he took apiculture seriously, we are still surprised to find him reviewing a book about 'Collateral Bee-boxes', much as we are surprised to find him presenting a digest of William Borlase's *Observations on the Ancient and Present State of the Islands of Scilly*.

Nothing Johnson wrote was frothy; even his lightweight miscellanea are spiced with the odd pinch of perspicacity. But of all the productions he ran off in the years immediately following the *Dictionary*, the most enduring is his short novel *Rasselas*. In January 1759 his mother died, and legend has it that he wrote *Rasselas* during the evenings of a single week in order to defray the expenses of her funeral. In fact he wrote it in the week leading up to her death: the prospect of her passing heightened his moral sensitivity, and the anticipated costs – of doctors, of her burial, and of settling her debts – obliged him to convert this moral sensitivity into something publishable.

It is usually suggested that Johnson was too poor to visit his mother as she lay dying. In truth it was a case of reluctance, not poverty. A journey to Lichfield would not have been costly. Inconvenient perhaps, but not unfeasible. The real deterrent was the sheer horror of renewing relations with his estranged parent, whose affections he had once ineffectually struggled to win, and whom he had not seen in as many as twenty years. In the letters he wrote to her during her final days he professes himself her 'dutiful' son, and refers to her as 'honoured Mother' or 'honoured Madam'. Their relationship had always been formal and strained, and it seems that his conscience now repulsed all sentiment, staving off the possibility of some last tear-stained reconciliation. Instead he performed his filial duty by writing *Rasselas*, for which he was paid £100.

This is not the place to talk at length about Johnson's one sustained work of narrative fiction. It will suffice to say that *Rasselas* is a critique of optimism – a doctrine that had come under heavy attack since the Lisbon earthquake of November 1755, which had killed 30,000 people in six minutes. In its mellow consideration of the mind's capacities and its careful debunking of specious theories, *Rasselas* shows Johnson's expressive gifts at their most vital, but despite its profusion of aphorisms it is curiously open-ended. The utterances of its narrator, a poetic sage by the name of Imlac, are often mistakenly assumed to be the author's personal opinions. It is tempting to read Imlac's words in this way: his maxims seem peculiarly applicable to Johnson, to his perspectives, and to his principles. Taken out of context, these *bons mots* are deceptive, but there is a true parallel: *Rasselas* is the story of a pilgrimage, and Johnson's was a life in transit. He was proud of his achievements, but agonizingly conscious of how little they had secured for him. Before him lay a desert of scholarly inconsequence; he had to galvanize his enthusiasm for the world, in order to keep it from corroding. 'To talk in public,' says Imlac, 'to think in solitude, to read and to hear, to inquire, and to answer inquiries, is the business of a scholar.' 'Do not suffer life to stagnate,' he advises, since 'it will grow muddy for want of motion'. Instead, 'commit yourself again to the current of the world'.

The image of Johnson racing to write *Rasselas* to pay for his mother's funeral, romantic hyperbole though it is, conveys the precariousness of his existence, almost four years after his work on the *Dictionary* was done. His financial uncertainties continued. He gave up the house in Gough Square in March 1759, probably for lack of funds, but possibly after pressure on the landlord from neighbours who complained that Johnson disturbed them at night by walking around chuntering to himself. In the next few years he would switch addresses frequently. His friend William Fitzherbert claimed that he once called on him during this time and found him without pen, ink or paper. This was still his general way of living: to deny himself even his most basic needs. As Boswell would observe, 'there lurked about him a propensity to paltry saving'.

Yet just as Johnson was plunging into another trough of despondency, the reputation of the *Dictionary* at last brought reward. Since its publication, he had increasingly found himself the recipient of other people's hospitality, but his income had shrivelled. Now help came from an unexpected quarter: in July of 1762 Johnson was granted a state pension of £300 a year by the twenty-four-year-old monarch, George III.

Triumphant

1. Celebrating a victory
2. Rejoicing as for victory
3. Victorious; graced with conquest

The *Dictionary*'s definition of 'pension' meant that the King's generosity was not without its embarrassments. Johnson had damningly explained that 'in England it is generally understood to mean pay given to a state hireling for treason to his country'. Although the pension was ostensibly awarded in recognition of the *Dictionary*, and was secured through the influence of William Strahan's friend Alexander Wedderburn, a noted Scottish lawyer and Member of Parliament, there were more powerful political forces at work. The Prime Minister, Lord Bute, had been censured for excessive patronage of his fellow Scots, and by granting Johnson a pension he was able both to suggest the reversal of this trend and to discourage Johnson's periodic blasts of public agitation. Johnson was assured that no favours were expected of him, but his critics were openly suspicious. John Wilkes was especially scathing, and his recurring attacks on both pensioner and government provoked Johnson to declare that 'instead of applying to my Lord Chief Justice to punish him, I would send half a dozen footmen and have him well ducked'. As for the promiscuous clamour of criticism, he told Boswell, 'I wish my pension were twice as large, that they may make twice as much noise.'

Johnson may be thought to have sacrificed principle to expedience in accepting the pension, but the award was a key moment in his life. His existence took on a new grandeur; the pension did not make him rich, but it ensured he would no longer have to grub around for the odd guinea. As late as 1764 the painter Ozias Humphry could visit Johnson in Inner Temple Lane and find him breakfasting at one o'clock in the afternoon, dressed like a derelict. This absurd figure in 'an old black wig' and faded breeches was easily mistaken for a 'madman'; Humphry recorded that 'he denies himself many conveniences, though he cannot well afford any, that he may have more in his power to give in charities'.[1] Yet Humphry had never met Johnson before, and could not realize how far he had come: while the habits of poverty lingered, the poverty itself was a thing of the past. Money could not tranquillize his melancholy – when in 1768 he spent seventeen guineas on his first pocket watch, its dial-plate was inscribed with a verse from the Greek New Testament meaning 'The night cometh' – but at last he was able to maintain himself.

Johnson in sociable mode – *A Literary Party at Sir Joshua Reynolds's*, by D. George Thompson, published by Owen Bailey, after J. W. E. Doyle. Left to right: Boswell, Johnson, Reynolds, Garrick, Edmund Burke, the Corsican patriot Pasquale Paoli, Charles Burney, Thomas Warton, Oliver Goldsmith

The Johnson of legend is Johnson the pensioner, free to ramble, idle and adventure, to travel with Boswell to the Hebrides and sleep on hay in his riding coat, to try hunting (which he did not enjoy) and impersonating a kangaroo (which he did), to 'have a frisk' with his much younger friends and dine on veal pie with plums and sugar, to investigate ghosts, to teach himself Dutch, and to laugh uninhibitedly 'like a rhinoceros'. Within weeks of being granted the pension he saw the sea for the first time – a symbolic testament to his broadening horizons – when he travelled to Devon with Sir Joshua Reynolds (and was shamed by his incorrect definition of 'pastern'). In May the following year he met Boswell, the architect of the

James Boswell by Sir Joshua Reynolds, 1785

Johnson myth. The famous Club was formed in 1764. In 1765 he met the Thrales, and moved to the aptly named Johnson's Court, where he lived for nearly eleven years.★ It was in that year too that he became 'Dr Johnson', when Trinity College, Dublin, made him an honorary Doctor of Laws.

Furthermore, starting in about 1765, Johnson began to receive considerable coverage in the press. This can be attributed in part to the growth of British newspapers and magazines, but is also an index

---

★ Johnson's Court was named for Thomas Johnson, an Elizabethan tailor.

of Johnson's growing reputation. By the late 1760s he had become a celebrity. In an average month in 1750 his name appeared in the press once or twice. This was still the case a decade later. However, by 1765 it was appearing about ten times a month. By 1770 the average had gone up to fifteen. And in 1775 his name appeared on average forty times a month.[2] 'I believe there is hardly a day in which there is not something about me in the newspapers,' Johnson informed Boswell in the summer of 1781, and he was right. The numbers may not sound large, but the press was less preoccupied with fame and the famous than it has since become. By the standards of the period, Johnson was supereminent – a representative Englishman, the cynosure of British letters, a cultivated John Bull, the archetype of the sociable scholar. Sometimes the coverage was unflattering: on one occasion he demanded that a particularly viperous item be read aloud to him in its entirety, and when it was finished exclaimed, with a perfect sense of theatre, 'Are we alive after all this satire!'

Johnson's achievements chimed not only with the growth of the British press, which buttressed an idea of national identity, but also with the contemporary growth of the middle classes, and with their emerging self-consciousness. He was, after all, the embodiment of the middle-class professional, a writer who thought of writing as a job, and who played up the banality of his labours in order to seem more humane and approachable. (The individuals who have been most prominent in shaping what we call modern standard English have with few exceptions come from outside the ruling class: besides Johnson, one thinks of Caxton, Shakespeare, Tyndale and Wyclif.) The *Dictionary* was not a success with the *bon ton*, but it appealed to the newly affluent and the upwardly mobile. Its creator, like them, was a self-made man. It is the self-made and the self-aggrandizing who tend to surround themselves with artefacts designed to attest to their respectability and seriousness. The *Dictionary* succeeded thanks in no small part to the shift from Restoration elitism to a more middle-class Britain, characterized by a mercantile consciousness.

What Johnson could not have foreseen was that English would become a global phenomenon, a mainstay of the British economy and an international currency. A third of the world's population now have some command of English, and it is the language that the other two-thirds most commonly aspire to learn. Entertainment, finance, scientific innovation and the IT revolution have made English – and specifically American English – the world's dominant tongue. Johnson spoke disparagingly of 'the American dialect, a tract of corruption';[3] he would have been horrified to discover that most of the significant contributions to his academic afterlife would be made by Americans.

The *Dictionary* equipped Johnson well for his next projects, with which he cemented his reputation as a magisterial polymath and a national treasure. One of these was the edition of Shakespeare he had first projected in the early 1740s. Jacob Tonson, whose claim to the copyright in Shakespeare had frustrated Johnson's ambitions a decade before, now agreed a contract with him. But this was to be another slow-cooked confection, and the terms of the contract meant that Johnson would be paid not in ready money, but with free copies of the finished work, which he could sell to subscribers.

This was the sixth major edition of Shakespeare in half a century, yet because of the *Dictionary* Johnson was thought capable of improving on the editions of Rowe, Pope, Theobald, Warburton and Hanmer. The experience of carefully reading the dramatist for the *Dictionary* made him a credible editor; he had already glossed most of the troublesome words in the plays, and had unpicked the knottier passages. When he published his *Proposals for Printing by Subscription the Dramatic Works of William Shakespeare*, in June 1756, he emphasized that his purpose would be 'to correct what is corrupt, and to explain what is obscure'. An important part of the eight-volume edition that resulted, nine years later, was its detailed attention to the apparent difficulties of the dramatist's language, which Johnson briskly, brilliantly elucidated in his notes. About a quarter of his commentary can be traced back pretty clearly to the *Dictionary*.[4] His criticism of Shakespeare's entire œuvre, in his preface to the edition, is supremely confident because, no matter how general it appears to be, it is anchored by his close reading of the plays. Furthermore, in reproducing earlier commentators' often divergent readings, he repeats one of the achievements of the *Dictionary*: he presents a genealogy of opinions which evokes the endless contests of scholarship and literature.

The *Dictionary* also prepared Johnson for his work on the *Lives of the Poets*, his last indispensable publication. The *Lives* were written as critical prefaces to be inserted into a fifty-eight-volume collection of English poetry. Here once again he turned an occasional project, backed by the booksellers, into a statement of national identity. Trenchant, opinionated and often deeply personal, the *Lives* propose not so much a canon of essential authors as a continuation of the *Dictionary*'s unfurling of intellectual history. Moreover, unlike modern biographers, Johnson separates the events of his subjects' lives from their achievements in poetry, rather than braiding them ingeniously. One of the results is a particular attention to writing per se: instead of extrapolating psychological points from the texts he examines, Johnson considers them as feats of language. It was above all his critical intelligence, sharpened during the *Dictionary* years, which was to be the guarantee of the *Lives*' usefulness. Significantly, the bound sets bore the title 'Johnson's Poets' on their spines. This ruse, guaranteed to invite publicity and entice purchasers, was offensive to the man himself, who had very little say in which poets were included. Nevertheless, the fact that his name bulked much larger than those of his subjects was an indication of how far he had come: of the critical authority with which the *Dictionary* had endowed him, and of the crucial, lasting transmutation of that critical authority into an incontestable, irresistible personal authority.

Ubiquity

Omnipresence; existence at the same time in all places

'Could they think that to be infinite and immense, the *ubiquity* of which they could thrust into a corner of their closet?' – Robert South

Its excellence notwithstanding, the *Dictionary* was not an instant best-seller. At £4. 10s., it was beyond the means of all but the most prosperous readers. This, after all, was the price of a year's dental care or an everyday suit of clothes. So within months a second edition was appearing in weekly numbers; its availability as a part-work was intended to attract those who could not afford to purchase the entire text in one go. The scheme was hardly a success: 2,300 copies of the early parts were published, but Strahan reduced this to 768 for the second volume because of declining demand. Serialization would work for Chambers's *Cyclopaedia*, and a hundred years later the public would rush out to buy the latest instalment of a new novel by Dickens or Mrs Beeton's *Household Management*, but it did not work for the *Dictionary*. Even though the part work spread the cost, the edition was still dear: the run of 165 instalments would have cost £4. 2s. 6d., and the purchaser would then have had to meet the further expense of having the set bound.★ Johnson's only recorded comment on the subject is in a letter to Warton, written in June, four days before the first part of the second edition became available. 'Dodsley is gone to visit the Dutch,' he writes. 'The Dictionary sells well. The rest of the world goes on as it did.'[1]

It was almost ten years before there was a third edition, which was

---

★ Today, even though first editions of the *Dictionary* are not scarce, they fetch relatively high prices. A superior copy might sell for as much as £20,000, and you would be fortunate to find one for less than £5,000. By contrast, a good copy of Bailey's dictionary can be had for as little as £100.

published in October 1765 to coincide with Johnson's edition of Shakespeare; 1,024 copies were printed, and eight years then elapsed before a further new edition. This was the revised fourth edition, which was issued in a run of 1,250 copies, still at £4. 10s., a price that was maintained for the fifth (1784) edition too. The fifth was the last two-volume folio edition and was printed in a run of 1,000 copies. In other words, at the time of Johnson's death in 1784, and thirty years after its first publication, there were about 6,000 copies of the complete English editions of the *Dictionary* in circulation, in addition to a few hundred copies of two limited Dublin issues of 1775 and 1777.

This is not a great number. But the folio was an extravagance, and Johnson grasped that many consumers wanted a work that simply gave them the meanings of words and their correct spelling. So, in 1756, the first abridged edition of the *Dictionary* was printed. It retained the Grammar but dropped the History, abbreviated some definitions, left out a number of the more recondite words, and omitted the illustrative quotations, although the names of the authorities were retained. Reduced to a conveniently sized octavo volume, it circulated widely; the price was a more affordable ten shillings. By the time Johnson died the abridgement had gone into a seventh edition.

Indeed, in its reduced format the *Dictionary* became an instrument of cultural imperialism. Johnson's version of Englishness was widely exported. In the nineteenth century a miniature edition of the *Dictionary* was published by the Glasgow printer George Fulton, for use in schools. Between 1821 and 1866 more than 90,000 copies were sold.[2] A good many of these were shipped to Australia and New Zealand, where the edition gained currency in the schoolroom.

The abridgements were not just Johnson's in name: they preserved the tenor of his definitions and his choice of language. However, anyone inspecting the octavo will find that Johnson's great Preface is gone; in its place is an introduction less than two pages long, obviously his in its cadences and manner, but with none of the melancholic or philosophic ingredients. Johnson simply appeals to the judgement of 'common readers' seeking a degree of knowledge suitable to the 'common business of life', denigrates the efforts of his rivals, and talks up his own achievements ('the words of this dictionary . . . are more diligently collected, more accurately spelled, more faithfully explained, and more authentically ascertained').

While the folio assured the prestige of Johnson's work, the abridgement ensured that, in epitome at least, it reached a mass audience. Moreover, the success of the octavo encouraged the belief that there was a market for a cheaper folio edition. By the time the copyright expired, in 1783, rivals to the original band of booksellers had decided that the commercial potential of the *Dictionary* was ripe for exploitation. The London firm of James Harrison began publishing it in folio in weekly instalments in October 1785. This edition, in 100 numbers, was set to cost £2. 10s. A month later, the *Dictionary*'s shareholders retaliated with a similar serial edition; it would appear in eighty-four weekly instalments, costing a total of £2. 2s. Even this comparatively low price was unlikely, however, to make it widely affordable. In his sparkling history of the *Oxford English Dictionary*, Simon Winchester asserts of its eighteenth-century predecessor that 'by the end of the century every educated household had, or had access to, the great book. So firmly established did it swiftly become that any request for "The Dictionary" would bring forth Johnson and none other.' 'One asked for The Dictionary,' writes Winchester, 'much as one might demand The Bible.'[3]

In time this proved the case, but at first the popularity of Bailey's octavo dictionary outstripped that of Johnson's. When eventually Johnson did overtake Bailey, it was in unauthorized and often bastardized forms. The reputation of Johnson's *Dictionary* was disseminated not so much through the rich intelligence of the folio as through the publication of a swarm of miniature versions. Several hundred of these appeared during the nineteenth century, their titles ranging from *Johnson's Diamond Dictionary* and *The Young Lady's and Young Gentleman's Pocket Dictionary* to *Johnson's Bijou Dictionary* and *The Smallest English Dictionary in the World* – the last of which was thoughtfully issued in a tiny tin box with a reading glass set in the lid.[4]

These compact versions of the *Dictionary* were matched by a number of attempts to expand it. The first of these was begun in the 1780s by Sir Herbert Croft, who had once contributed a biography of the poet Edward Young to Johnson's *Lives of the Poets*.[5] But Croft's archive of more than 20,000 words missed by Johnson was never published, and the first supplements to reach the press did not come out until the first quarter of the nineteenth century. While some, such as John Seager's of 1819, were respectful, others, notably George Mason's of 1801, were contemptuous. However, in all cases the motive for extending the scope of the work was the feeling that Johnson had not done justice to the full range of English vocabulary.[6] This mood was summed up in 1818, when a Kentish vicar, Henry John Todd, presented a revised edition of the full *Dictionary*.

Todd's edition, sometimes referred to as Todd-Johnson, was printed by Andrew Strahan, youngest son of Johnson's printer. While it was true to the spirit of Johnson's enterprise, not all Todd's additions and amendments were helpful – there is a good deal of quibbling ('Dr Johnson says . . .', or 'Dr Johnson has not noticed . . .') – but his revision was widely adopted as a replacement for Johnson's unadulterated lexicon. It was soon abridged by Alexander Chalmers, an energetic journalist who edited Gibbon and Fielding among others, and Chalmers was in his turn edited by the American Joseph Worcester. In the same year that Todd's enlarged *Dictionary* came out, the first American edition, based on the eleventh London edition, was published by a debt-ridden Philadelphia bookseller called Moses Thomas, whose premises in Chestnut Street were appropriately known as 'Johnson's Head'.* In these and other forms the *Dictionary* flourished, and its influence fanned out through the United States, throughout the rest of the English-speaking world, and beyond it.

---

* This was one of several costly ventures on Thomas's part – another was the expensively produced *Analectic Magazine*, edited by Washington Irving. His taste for such extravagances eventually ruined him.

Variety

1. Change; succession of one thing to another; intermixture of one thing with another.

4. Variation; deviation; change from a former state

5. Many and different kinds

'He now only wants more time to do that *variety* of good which his soul thirsts after' – William Law

Johnson's main intervention in the afterlife of the *Dictionary* was the revision he undertook for the fourth edition. He was persuaded to do this by its proprietors, and was paid £300 for his work. Assisted again by the shabby Mr Peyton, and possibly by the younger of the brothers Macbean, he started the job in the late summer of 1771, and it occupied him for much of 1772. But he had been revising his *magnum opus*, or at least considering ways to do so, ever since its first publication. Rather than working to a carefully plotted programme, he amended the *Dictionary* as inclination took him, with the spontaneous energy of a scholar, not the mechanical indifference of a drudge.

In the 'Advertisement' that preceded the finished edition in 1773, Johnson claimed that he had decided on revision only on 'finding the *Dictionary* about to be reprinted'. He explained that 'Many faults I have corrected, some superfluities I have taken away, and some deficiencies I have supplied.' Yet, lest purchasers of earlier editions worry that they had wasted their money, he promised that 'the student . . . will not, without nice collation, perceive how . . . [the editions] differ, and usefulness seldom depends upon little things'. In private he was even more modest about the improvements he had made. In a letter to Boswell he noted that 'a new edition of my great Dictionary is printed', but, 'having made no preparation, I was able to do very little'. 'The main fabrick of the work remains as it was,' he wrote, and as he looked over its pages he concluded it was 'as often better, as worse, than I expected'.[1]

As we have seen before, Johnson belittles his own industry. He expended more time and more thought on the changes than either the Advertisement or the letter to Boswell suggests. In his account of this period in Johnson's life, Boswell passes briskly over the *Dictionary*. He concentrates instead on the sociable Johnson, who professes his love for Bologna sausages, sends Peyton to the shops to buy him an ounce of vitriol, joshes a man who spends seven or eight minutes relating the prevalence of fleas in Shrewsbury, and fantasizes about removing to St Kilda to live on a diet of fish, books and dried tongue. But in private Johnson was furiously busy, vamping up his lexicon.

The amendments he made show him actively seeking not just to mend and polish his work, but to elevate it. He added quotations, removed quotations, augmented some definitions, condensed others, altered etymologies, discriminated new senses, and added completely new definitions.[2] The experience of editing Shakespeare – and of revising the edition, with George Steevens, at the same time that he was revising the *Dictionary* – resulted in a number of changes in his notes on Shakespearian usage. At the same time he relaxed his rule about excluding his contemporaries, and quoted several of his friends – Sir Joshua Reynolds and Arthur Murphy among them – as well as one of his enemies, Lord Chesterfield. Johnson's erstwhile patron is the sole authority for the newly admitted word 'ridiculer', furnishing the sentence 'The *ridiculer* shall make only himself ridiculous.'

'Ridiculer' was one of a modest number of new headwords. The total number of entries in the fourth edition is 43,279, an increase of barely more than 1 per cent. But in all Johnson made about 15,000 changes to his text. A few examples should give a flavour of them. For instance, he adds for the new edition that the word 'dozen' is 'seldom used but on light occasions'. Of the noun 'glister' ('an injection into the anus'), which he believes should be spelt 'clyster', he adds the comment 'It is written wrong even by Brown' – a reference to Sir Thomas Browne, that favourite source of forensic language. Under 'sword' there is a magnificent new quotation, more than ten lines long, from Book VI of *Paradise Lost*.[3] Under 'generally' there is an extra quotation from the poet and physician Richard Blackmore:

'*Generally* speaking, persons designed for long life, though in their former years they were small eaters, yet find their appetites encrease with their age.' Blackmore is one of several authors whose works Johnson seems to have examined closely since making the first edition. Another is the clergyman Walter Harte, who had once been 'bear-leader' to Lord Chesterfield's son, and whose poem *The Amaranth* (1767) provides more than 100 fresh illustrations. There is new material, too, from James Beattie, a friend of Boswell and Strahan, and author of an *Essay on Truth* (1770) which was an important counterblast to the sceptical metaphysics – so rebarbative to Johnson – of David Hume.

To create space for this new material Johnson had to make cuts elsewhere. The greatest savings could be achieved by clipping or compressing illustrative quotations, and some were savagely reduced. The most aggressive treatment was reserved for Philip Miller's *Gardener's Dictionary* and the poems of James Thomson. Johnson pruned the quotations from Miller to make them more pointed and succinct, but his decision to eradicate many of the passages he had taken from Thomson's popular poem *The Seasons* reflected his changing tastes. In the fourth edition Thomson's mannered, painterly sensibility gives way to the religious gravity of Milton and the High Church divines.[4]

This change in the illustrative material is not instantly noticeable. However, it suggests Johnson's renewed commitment to making the *Dictionary* a work of moral tutelage. In the process, it became more old-fashioned. Although space was limited and precious, he found extra room for the orthodox values of the Church of England, which he believed to be under attack. To this end he quotes from Charles Leslie's *The Case of the Regale and of the Pontificate* (1700), which insisted on the Church's right to self-government, and from Francis White's *Treatise of the Sabbath Day* (1635), a stout defence of Anglicanism's Articles of Faith. He quotes, too, from John Kettlewell's practical guide to the Christian communion, and from a biography of Henry Hammond, the most distinguished seventeenth-century expert on the New Testament. It is probable that some of these and the many other theological texts he mined for the fourth edition became known to him only after 1755. Yet equally we may infer his

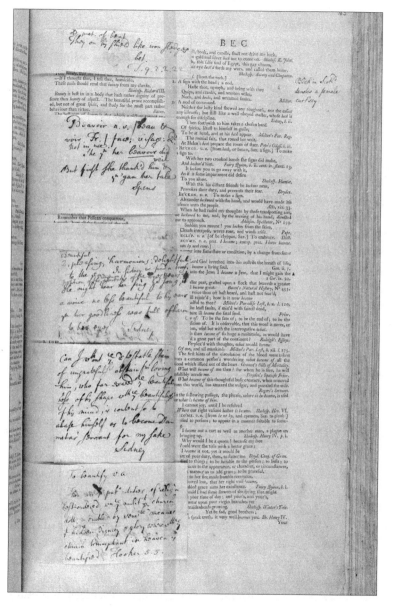

A page of the Sneyd-Gimbel copy of the *Dictionary* at Yale University. The slips contain material transcribed by one of Johnson's amanuenses for inclusion in the fourth edition

increasing determination, in maturity, to make the *Dictionary* a pious, educational and exemplary book, full of good moral counsel and Christian doctrine that might be imbibed by its users.

The decision to deploy quotations from William Law, a brilliant exponent of Christian mysticism, typifies this. Johnson encountered Law's *Serious Call to a Devout and Holy Life* while a 'rude and violent' undergraduate; it was the first book that compelled him to think in earnest about religion. Law was still alive when Johnson compiled the first edition of the *Dictionary*, and Johnson felt able to include no more than a couple of snippets from his work. However, by the time of the fourth edition Law was dead, and Johnson, striving to defend Anglican practices, introduced almost 200 quotations from the *Serious Call*. Law was not only a persuasive spokesman for the Church of England, but also an advocate of women's rights, and so we find, from the *Serious Call*, passages such as this: 'The church has formerly had eminent saints in that [i.e. the female] sex; and it may *reasonably* be thought, that it is purely owing to their poor and vain education, that this honour of their sex is for the most part confined to former ages.'

Crucially, too, Law's politics dovetailed with Johnson's. After a long period of abstinence from political controversy, in the first half of the 1770s Johnson wrote a series of pro-government pamphlets. The fourth edition suggests his political sympathies, identifying him with nonjurors such as Law, and renewing his opposition to Whiggery, which he associated with religious nonconformism.[5] While the new passages do not bulk large, they insinuate Johnson's political values – and especially his attitude to ecclesiastical politics – into the body of the *Dictionary*. Law more than any other quoted author can be thought of as a spokesman for Johnson's most cherished views. It is worth pointing out, then, that the quotation from Law which appears at the head of this chapter is one of those added for the fourth edition; unintended though the effect may be, we can take it as a summary of Johnson's moral and educative intentions as he worked on revising the *Dictionary*.

Johnson completed his revisionary labours in October 1772. Two months later he reflected on his achievement in a Latin poem. Dated 12 December, it was probably composed in his head during a bumpy coach journey down from Lichfield the day before. Its title, *Gnothi*

Seauton, is the Greek for 'Know Thyself' – the advice inscribed above the entrance to the temple of Apollo at Delphi. The poem is a poignantly gloomy production, fifty-four lines of trundling hexameter. Melancholic and introspective, it recalls the mood of the Preface. Johnson likens himself to the sixteenth-century scholar Joseph Justus Scaliger, whose reaction to completing his own 'lectionary' (of Arabic and Greek) was a mixture of boredom and self-contempt. He suggests that tasks like theirs should be reserved as punishment for criminals, and broods that his achievement has inspired only bad dreams and a fear of the gulf of time opening up in front of him. The poem exploits a vast, almost ostentatious, array of classical precedents, yet appears woundingly heartfelt – a true image of the pains of his endeavour.[6] His friend Arthur Murphy believed it 'left a picture . . . drawn with as much truth, and as firm a hand, as can be seen in the portraits of Hogarth or Sir Joshua Reynolds'.[7] Whatever he may have pronounced in public, it is clear that the revision of the *Dictionary* was another arduous chapter in its making, and that Johnson's investment in the art of lexicography never ended.[8]

Weightiness

1. Ponderosity; gravity; heaviness

2. Solidity; force

3. Importance

The influence of the *Dictionary* was sweeping. Johnson established both a methodology for how dictionaries should be put together and a paradigm for how entries should be presented. Anyone who sought to create a dictionary, post-Johnson, did so in his shadow. One of the more startling examples of this was William Kenrick's *New Dictionary of the English Language* (1773), which plagiarized Johnson's errors as well as his beauties. Despite having been spectacularly rude about Johnson in the past, Kenrick felt able to define 'pastern' as 'the knee of an horse', 'cough' as 'a convulsion of the lungs, vellicated by some sharp serosity' and 'embryo' as 'the offspring yet unfinished in the womb'. In a droll understatement, he explained that 'the reader will find I have generally followed the celebrated dictionary of the learned Dr Johnson'. Where Kenrick's debt was total, others were more circumspect in their borrowings, but the legacy of Johnson still loomed large. It was one of the authors most frequently cited in the *Dictionary*, John Milton, who wrote that books 'contain a potency of life in them to be as active as that soul was whose progeny they are',[1] and Johnson's great book has inspired, invigorated, provoked and chafed far more people than its notoriously combative author ever dreamed of affecting.

In the year Johnson died, Robert Nares, who would later become Keeper of Manuscripts at the British Museum, published a work entitled *Elements of Orthoepy*, a survey of English pronunciation. Nares believed that Johnson had provided mankind with 'one acknowledged standard to recur to', and reflected that 'the English Dictionary appeared; and as the weight of truth and reason is irresistible, its authority has nearly fixed the external form of our language; and from its decisions few appeals have yet been made'.[2] There were plenty who agreed with this entirely, but the afterlife of the *Dictionary* has proved much more turbulent than Nares anticipated.

From an early stage there were noisy detractors. Perhaps the loudest of them was John Horne Tooke. The son of a London turkey merchant, Tooke was educated at Eton and Cambridge, before embarking on an erratic career as a curate, political agitator, lawyer and Member of Parliament for the pocket borough of Old Sarum. His philological interests began in earnest only in his thirties, but culminated in the two hefty volumes that make up *The Diversions of Purley* – which took its odd name from the Surrey village where it was written. James Sledd and Gwin Kolb have described him as 'one of the most systematically frantic etymologists who ever lived'.[3] His vivisection of the *Dictionary* was as furious as his etymologies. Not content to pronounce it 'imperfect and faulty', he complained that it was 'one of the most idle performances ever offered to the public', that its author 'possessed not one single requisite for the undertaking', that its grammatical and historical parts were 'most truly contemptible performances', and that 'nearly one third . . . is as much the language of the Hottentots as of the English'.[4] He was not alone. James Gilchrist, a grammarian influenced by Tooke, spoke of Johnson's 'Babylonish lexicography' as 'a Babel of absurdity', adding that 'I should consider that man as having a weak, short-sighted understanding, who after studying the subject would deny that Johnson was absolutely a blind lexicographer.'[5] Another of Tooke's disciples, Charles Richardson, produced a *New Dictionary of the English Language* on 'philosophical principles'. It included bitter complaints about almost every aspect of Johnson's lexicography; his notion of what constituted a definition was branded 'very lax and imperfect', and Richardson, despite admitting that Johnson was capable of 'most admirable precision and completeness', went to considerable lengths to point out his predecessor's gift for 'absurdity'.[6]

Tooke, Gilchrist and Richardson were all students of language, and disparaged Johnson in order to exalt their own theories. So did the first editor of the *Encyclopaedia Britannica*, a young Scottish printer called William Smellie. In his entry under 'dictionary', he acknowledged

Johnson's 'masterly manner', but spent five pages outlining his own ideas of how Johnson's methods – specifically, his methods of definition – could be improved. Non-specialists did likewise. A curious though comparatively minor voice among these scorners of Johnson's efforts was that of Archibald 'Horrible' Campbell, a ship's purser of apparently fabulous ugliness. Campbell found himself during a long voyage with nothing to read but the *Rambler*; the result of the experience was a work entitled *Lexiphanes* (1767), a dialogue in which he caricatured Johnson wickedly. The Johnson of *Lexiphanes* is a grandiloquent bore, who requires his interlocutor to 'expulse' all 'agglomerated asperities' lest they 'obthurate the porches of your intelligence with the adscititious excrement of critical malevolence'. He refers to Scots as 'risible Oat-consumers', and warns that whoever dares criticize him shall feel his cudgel, which 'with reiterated repercussions . . . shall soon disseminate, by a rapid eventilation, the brains in his pericranium, blood in his pericardium, marrow in [his] periosteum, and intestines in his peritoneum'. This elaborate menace is provoked by the suggestion that Johnson wrote the *Rambler* 'to make a dictionary necessary, and afterwards compile[d] his dictionary to explain his *Ramblers*'.[7]

All Johnson's adversaries complained about the *Dictionary*'s copious selection of pedantic terms 'smelling of the inkhorn'. Jemima, Marchioness Grey, a prolific correspondent of the period, spoke for most of her class in complaining that they 'really break my teeth'.[8] Johnson would have enjoyed this: his Latinisms were, in part, a requital of lazy patrician slang. On his trip to the Hebrides with Boswell in 1773, he used the word 'depeditation' in reference to the actor Samuel Foote, who had suffered a broken leg. Like a Scrabble player, Boswell challenged this, and Johnson admitted he had made the word up, before adding mischievously 'that he had not made above three or four in his Dictionary'.

Horace Walpole summed up for the unbelievers when he pronounced, at the end of the eighteenth century, 'I cannot imagine that Dr Johnson's reputation will be very lasting.' His dictionary was 'a surprising work for one man', but 'the task is too much for one man, and . . . a society should alone pretend to publish a standard dictionary.'[9] Walpole's reservations notwithstanding, the admirers outnumbered the detractors, and the reputation of the *Dictionary* was repeatedly boosted by other philologists, lexicographers, educationalists and word detectives. In a letter to Samuel Richardson, written while still at work on his *magnum opus*, Johnson referred casually to 'this age of dictionaries'.[10] His words were to prove not so much a diagnosis of the condition of the times, as a vision of what was to come.

The intellectual life of the half-century that followed the *Dictionary* gave birth to a host of disquisitions on the philosophy of language. As one scholar of the period judiciously observes, 'There is more of almost everything linguistic in the second half of the eighteenth century than in the first: more grammars and more kinds of grammar, more theories of language, more sorts of questions asked about language.' In addition, there were 'more dictionaries, spelling books, proposals for reordering pedagogy, and more languages taught'.[11] The names of those who contributed to this extraordinary escalation of linguistic learning are rarely meaningful to us now (who remembers the once-formidable Anselm Bayly or L. D. Nelme?), but, en masse, they initiated the modern science of linguistics, and in their writings Johnson is a constant presence, be it explicitly or implicitly. His interest in the functions of language, and his perception that the mutability of language guaranteed its vitality, inspired the study of its dynamic and social aspects; and the *Dictionary*, in its tacit disavowal of prescriptive lexicography in favour of a more descriptive method, redirected language studies in the English-speaking world.

Furthermore, Johnson's influence extended beyond Britain and beyond English. The president of the Florentine Accademia declared that the *Dictionary* would be 'a perpetual Monument of Fame to the Author, an Honour to his own Country in particular, and a general Benefit to the Republic of Letters'.[12] This was no empty commendation. Johnson's work served as a model for lexicographers abroad. It is no surprise that his friend Giuseppe Baretti chose to make the *Dictionary* the model for his Italian–English dictionary of 1760, and for his Spanish dictionary nearly two decades later. But there are numerous examples of influence beyond Johnson's own circle. His work was translated into French and German. It was a capital resource for the lexicographers of the Netherlands, Sweden and Portugal, and formed the basis of a dictionary of Cornish by an itinerant curate,

John Bannister. In 1777, when Ferdinando Bottarelli published a pocket dictionary of Italian, French and English (the three languages side by side), his authorities for the French and Italian words were the works of the French and Italian academies: for the English he used Johnson. In Germany, the *Dictionary* was essential to Gotthold Lessing's experiments in lexicography, and to the more decisive labours of the grammarian Johann Christoph Adelung. When John Mendies of Serampore wrote a Bengali–English dictionary, he used Johnson as his model, and as late as 1851, when the Baptist Mission Press in Calcutta brought out an improved edition, it was billed as 'a companion to Johnson's Dictionary'.

Even the weaker parts of the *Dictionary* were imitated or reproduced. One notable example occurs in the supplement to the French *Encyclopédie*, where the entry for '*Anglois*' follows the History closely. Evidently its author, Jean-Baptiste Robinet, condensed his account from Johnson's. Furthermore, Robinet applauds the *Dictionary* as '*le plus régulier, le plus complet, le plus savant, que nous ayons en Anglois*', and considers the author a '*philosophe profond, littérateur solide, écrivain poli & correct*'. Johnson's achievement is '*le fruit d'une lecture immense*'. The author sounds but one note of caution, suggesting that Johnson seems '*un peu trop attaché à l'antiquité*'.

More enduringly significant than the European influence of the *Dictionary* was its influence across the Atlantic. The American adoption of the *Dictionary* was a momentous event not just in its history, but in the history of lexicography.* For Americans in the second half of the eighteenth century, Johnson was the seminal authority on language, and the subsequent development of American lexicography was coloured by his fame.

America's two great nineteenth-century lexicographers, Noah Webster and Joseph Worcester, argued fiercely over Johnson's legacy. Webster, a Connecticut lawyer and schoolteacher, was a reformist and a nationalist, a strong advocate of his newly constituted country's cultural independence, yet also an inheritor of the values espoused by the

---

* Things would have been very different, of course, if France had won the Seven Years War; America would have become a French colony, and presumably therefore French-speaking, with little use for Johnson and his *Dictionary*.

Pilgrim Fathers, who identified linguistic propriety with religious rectitude. In 1789 he declared that 'Great Britain, whose children we are, and whose language we speak, should no longer be *our* standard; for the taste of her writers is already corrupted, and her language on the decline.' 'She is,' he argued, 'at too great a distance to be our model, and to instruct us in the principles of our own tongue.'[13]

The process of divorce had already begun. Webster helped effect it with his influential *American Spelling Book* (1783), which was priced at fourteen cents a copy and soon outsold everything save the Bible. There followed *A Compendious Dictionary of the English Language* (1806), in which he repudiated the authority of Johnson and set out a wide range of reforms. It is to Webster more than anyone else that we owe the American preference for the spellings 'color', 'ax', 'theater' and 'traveler'. He was in the vanguard, too, of the American rebellion against the clipped pronunciation of patrician British English. In 1828 he published *An American Dictionary of the English Language*. It comprised 70,000 entries, and was dedicated, not without a touch of self-aggrandizement, to God. Webster retained plenty of Johnson's authorities, yet added quotations from many specifically American ones: from George Washington, Benjamin Franklin and John Quincy Adams, from the historian Jeremy Belknap, the preacher Ichabod Spencer and the poet William Clifton; and especially from American writers on scientific subjects, such as Benjamin Silliman, Amos Eaton, Parker Cleaveland and Thomas Say. When a second edition was published, he sent a copy to Queen Victoria, and told Andrew Stevenson, the diplomat who carried it to her, that 'Our common language is one of the ties that bind the two nations together; I hope the works I have executed will manifest to the British nation that the Americans are not willing to suffer it to degenerate *on this side of the Atlantic*.'[14]

Webster loathed Johnson's *Dictionary*, although he conceded that its author was 'one of the greatest men that the English nation has ever produced'. Johnson's work was in Webster's jaundiced view 'extremely imperfect and full of error'. There were too many obsolete words, and too few terms of science. The etymologies were wayward, the definitions steeped in starchy Englishness. Some of the words Johnson included were 'too low to deserve notice', and a few 'no more belong to the English language than . . . Patagonian words'. 'It was most injudicious in Johnson', wrote Webster, 'to select Shakespeare as one of his principal authorities. Play-writers in describing vulgar scenes and low characters use low language, language unfit for decent company.' He castigated Johnson's 'injudicious' selection of illustrative material: the quotations were, he felt, 'one of the most exceptionable parts of his performance', not only because many of the selected writers 'did not write the language with purity', but also because 'a still larger portion of them throw not the least light on the definitions'.[15]

Webster was a dry, humourless man, whose character we can deduce, I think, from the title of his *Essay on the Necessity, Advantages and Practicability of Reforming the Mode of Spelling, and of Rendering the Orthography of Words Correspondent to the Pronunciation.* Yet even Webster had to concede that 'Johnson's writings had, in Philology, the effect which Newton's discoveries had in Mathematics.'[16] In truth, his work owed a great deal to his famous English predecessor: he lifted hundreds of definitions in their entirety, reproduced others with minor alteration, and glossed Johnson's more sententious entries with a sententiousness all of his own. Thus, for mere example, he allowed his definition for 'network' to include the words 'reticulated' and 'decussated', and explained that 'oats' formed 'a considerable and very valuable article of food for man in Scotland'.[17] Exemplifying the word 'second', he wrote that 'Dr Johnson was second to none in intellectual powers, but second to many in research and erudition.' Johnson had considered 'wabble' a 'low, barbarous word'; Webster, engaging with the terms of condemnation, pronounces it 'neither low nor barbarous'. According to Johnson 'shabby' is 'a word that has crept into conversation . . . but ought not to be admitted into the language'. Webster argues that 'For the idea expressed by *shabby*, there is not a better word.' Here and elsewhere, it is as if he is in conversation with his eminent forerunner, striving to score points.

Where Webster found fault with Johnson, Joseph Worcester saluted him. Worcester was, like Webster, a schoolteacher; he grew up in a Calvinist family in New Hampshire, one of fifteen children. His first foray into lexicography was in 1827, when he edited Todd-Johnson. In 1846 he completed his *Universal and Critical Dictionary of the English Language*. He defended Johnson's work, arguing that 'from the time of its first publication, [it] has been, far more than any other, regarded as a standard for the language'. He quoted John Walker, author of the influential *Critical Pronouncing Dictionary and Expositor of the English Language* (1791), in his claim that Johnson's endeavours had been 'deemed lawful plunder by every subsequent lexicographer'.[18] Yet, not long after Worcester reflected that 'the publication of this Dictionary formed a greater era in the history of the language than that of any other work', and insisted that 'no other dictionary has had so much influence', plans were being hatched to replace it.

In 1857, London's august Philological Society decided that a new English dictionary was needed. The subject had been brought up several years before by the Cambridge polymath William Whewell, but decisive action was taken only after the Dean of Westminster, Richard Chenevix Trench, read a persuasive paper 'On Some Deficiencies in our English Dictionaries'. At first the Society gave serious consideration merely to revising Johnson. But this strategy was deemed to be a false economy, and a year after Dean Trench's paper the Society passed a resolution to create what they called *A New English Dictionary on Historical Principles*.

Work began in earnest on 12 May 1860. Its final fruit was, of course, the celebrated *Oxford English Dictionary*, but progress was wretchedly slow, and it took forty years to get as far as the end of the letter *F*. Even after sixty-eight years and the efforts of numerous brilliant men and women, including an army of helpers (my favourite among the many names is that of the Wolverhampton schoolmaster Gustavus Adolphus Schrumpf), the finished product was unsatisfactory in its treatment of slang, common idioms and regional variations. It went far, far beyond the scope of Johnson's work, but we do not have to look at the *OED* for long to see the imprint of his unique legacy. James Murray worked with Johnson's *Dictionary* open on the table beside him in his Scriptorium; it was an invaluable point of reference as he steered a course through the deep waters of English. Murray acknowledged that a good number of Johnson's explanations were adopted without change, for 'When his definitions are correct, and his arrangement judicious, it seems to be expedient to follow him. It would be mere affectation or folly to alter what cannot be improved.' In the end the *OED* reproduced around 1,700 of Johnson's definitions, marking them simply 'J.'. His layout and method of definition were also followed. These debts are palpable, and the giant collaborative achievement of the *OED* impresses on us the extraordinary richness of Johnson's largely unaided endeavour.

Further testimony to Johnson's influence is submerged in the literature of the hundred years that followed the *Dictionary's* first publication. The best-known example is the one cited in my opening chapter: Becky Sharp defenestrating her presentation copy of Johnson on Chiswick Mall. Later in *Vanity Fair* the less than erudite Rawdon Crawley subscribes to the very authority Becky repudiates, using Johnson as a tool to help him compose a letter. And in another of Thackeray's novels, *Pendennis*, we are told that 'public consent' is 'quite as influential as "Johnson's Dictionary"' in shaping the meaning of words. Even though Thackeray's intention is to play down the influence of Johnson, this is really quite a robust tribute.

Similar references litter other novels of the eighteenth and nineteenth centuries. In *Tristram Shandy*, a novel of which Johnson was openly suspicious, there is an episode in which a hot chestnut rolls off a table and falls 'perpendicularly into that particular aperture of Phutatorius's breeches, for which, to the shame and indelicacy of our language be it spoke, there is no chaste word throughout all Johnson's dictionary'. A century later the *Dictionary* is still a touchstone for Mr Gibson in Elizabeth Gaskell's *Wives and Daughters*, albeit for slightly insulting reasons: when he reads Mr Coxe's impassioned love letter to his daughter Molly, he concludes that it is dangerous to have the works of Shakespeare in the library at his surgery, and decides that he had better have a copy of the less inflammatory *Dictionary* instead. In *Moby-Dick*, Ishmael explains that in describing the whale's form he is compelled to use 'the weightiest words of the dictionary': 'And here be it said, that whenever it has been convenient to consult one in the course of these dissertations, I have invariably used a huge quarto edition of Johnson, expressly purchased for that purpose; because that famous lexicographer's uncommon personal bulk more fitted him to compile a lexicon to be used by a whale author like me.'

Dickens refers several times to the *Dictionary*, in works ranging from the early short story 'Mrs Lirriper's Legacy' to *David Copperfield* and *Nicholas Nickleby*. Wackford Squeers, the cruel proprietor of Dotheboys Hall, reflects with pleasure on his insistence that a dying pupil be given a copy of the 'best' dictionary (namely Johnson's) on which to lay his head. It pops up in all sorts of lesser-known novels. On the first page of Lord Lytton's *The Caxtons*, for instance, the narrator invokes Johnson's definition of 'boy', and in Disraeli's satirical *Vivian Grey*, published when he was just twenty-one, a character is found 'complaining bitterly of the imperfections of Johnson's Dictionary'.* In Wilkie Collins's *Hide and Seek* the sherry-drinking Mr Goodworth complains of pious Mr Thorpe's verbosity, 'You can't fob me off with long words, which I don't understand, and which I don't believe you can find in Johnson's Dictionary.' In George Meredith's *Evan Harrington* the Countess, a woman convicted early on of 'a languid alien accent', says that she understands the word 'renegade' because she 'saw it in Johnson's Dictionary, or an improvement on Johnson, by a more learned author'. Her sister decides not to question 'her intimacy with the most learned among lexicographers'.

One unblushing admirer of the *Dictionary* was Jane Austen's father, who assembled a substantial collection of books by Johnson, by his friends and associates, and about both the man and his circle. Inspired by her father, Austen relished Johnson's writing – especially the moral essays, with their crusade against foppishness, fashion and superficial thinking. She shared, too, his taste for abstract nouns: one has only to think of the titles of her novels to see this. It is no surprise, then, to find reference to Johnson in her published works. Fanny Price loves his *Idler* essays, and has clearly read *Rasselas*. But a more explicit reference appears in *Northanger Abbey*: when Henry Tilney queries Catherine Morland's use of the word 'nicest', his sister advises her that 'You had better change it as soon as you can, or we shall be overpowered with Johnson.'

The *Dictionary* has also played its part in the law, especially in the United States. Legislators are much occupied with ascertaining 'first

---

* In the same novel the publisher John Murray, with whom Disraeli had lately fallen out, is wickedly caricatured as a drunken marquess – 'servile, and pompous, and indefatigable, and loquacious'.

meanings', with trying to secure the literal sense of their predecessors' legislation. Sometimes it is a question of what Dickens's Sam Weller enquired when presented with a subpoena: 'What's that in English?' Often it is a matter of historicizing language: to understand a law, you need to understand what its terminology meant to its original architects.

The most eye-catching citation of recent years came in the proceedings of a federal lawsuit in February 2000 (*Campbell* v. *Clinton*, 203 F.3d 19, 340 US App. D.C. 149, D.C. Cir., Feb 18 2000). The action was brought by seventeen members of the US Congress, who sought 'declaratory relief' that President Bill Clinton had no constitutional right to continue air strikes against the Federal Republic of Yugoslavia without the explicit authorization of Congress. The plaintiffs argued, specifically, that he had failed to obtain 'a declaration of war', and that he had thereby deprived them of their constitutional right and duty to play a part in choosing whether to commit their country to war or refuse their assent. Approximately 4,500 air strikes had been launched during a five-week period in the spring of 1999. The US Constitution (Article I, Section 8, Clause 11) gives Congress exclusive power to declare war. President Clinton, it was argued, had violated this constitutional principle. One of the issues at stake was the meaning of 'declare': was a declaration of war synonymous with military engagement, or was it simply a recognition of the prerequisites for conflict? Equally, what was meant in the Constitution by the word 'war'? The decision was made to consult the dictionary which would have been the standard authority at the time when the Constitution was drawn up in 1787. That standard authority was of course Johnson.

The *Dictionary* has been cited many other times in debates over the Constitution in American courts. In *Kohler* v. *Bank of Bermuda (New York) Ltd* (F. 3d 187, 2nd Cir., Sept. 28 2000), Johnson's definition of 'subject' was introduced to clarify the constitutional distinction between subjects and citizens. In *US* v. *Wisenbaker* (14 F.3d 1022, 73 A.F.T.R. 2d 94-1309, 5th Cir. (Tex.), Feb. 9 1994) the judge cited the *Dictionary*'s scathing definition of 'excise' – a definition to which Houston M. Wisenbaker, Jr, whose company had evaded vast sums of Federal Motor Fuel Excise Tax, apparently subscribed.

It is strange to reflect that, as long as the American Constitution remains intact, Johnson's *Dictionary* will have a role to play in American law. Its author might not have been pleased by this. Once, when a man had left the room after a disagreement, Johnson was asked for an explanation and eventually observed that 'he did not care to speak ill of any man behind his back, but he believed the gentleman was an *attorney*'.

X

X is a letter, which, though found in Saxon words, begins no word in the English language⋆

In most of the cases I have just described, lawyers turned to Johnson's *Dictionary* because they were aware of discrepancies between eighteenth-century English and modern usage. While the language of the mid eighteenth century is close to our own, readers of the *Dictionary*, leafing through its creamy pages, will come across numerous entries that point up the difference. These propel us back in time, obliging our sympathies to turn somersault, yet they also engage our sense of the rich and particular linguistic moment in which we live, for what now seems stable will quite soon seem stale or antiquarian.

Languages, we know, do not stand still. New words are borrowed or invented. Others become obsolete. Morphology alters. So does pronunciation. Words are tools we use in order to communicate; they bend to suit our needs. Many change their meanings. Some acquire a more specialized use, while others extend their range; some acquire prestige, and others are degraded. There are well-known examples, such as 'nice', 'broadcast' and 'silly', which has translated, over a period of 600 years, from 'fortunate' via 'innocent' to a lightweight synonym for 'foolish'.† In the novels of Jane Austen, 'intelligence' means 'news'. 'Office' used to mean a job, but now it usually refers to a place.[1]

At first sight Johnson's claim that 'no word in the English language' begins with an *X* sounds wayward. Xylophones and the Xerox

---

⋆ This is not the only letter to elicit an unlikely statement from Johnson. Apparently, *R* 'is called the canine letter, because it is uttered with some resemblance to the growl or snarl of a cur', and of the letter *S* he writes that it 'has the same hissing sound as in other languages, and unhappily prevails in so many of our words that it produces in the ear of a foreigner a continued sibilation'.

† Johnson does not define 'broadcast' at all, while his opening definitions of both 'nice' and 'silly' suggest their most etymologically correct (and now rare) meanings.

machine were of course beyond his purview, and we can forgive him for knowing nothing of the small three-masted ship known as a xebec. But in the first edition of Bailey, with which he was closely familiar, there were more than twenty words beginning with X. Surely Johnson ought to have registered some of these.

On closer inspection, the X words in Bailey turn out to be hopelessly obscure. Even the most erudite seventeenth-century reader would have struggled to find a use for 'xenodochy' (kindness to strangers), 'xerophagy' ('the eating of dry meats'), 'xochitotle' ('the hang-nest of *America*, a bird like a sparrow') or 'xyster' (a surgical instrument, used for scraping bones).★ Johnson refused to recognize these words as proper English. Instinctively, we may feel that he was right to do so, but this feeling is followed by the knowledge that what was true for Johnson is true no longer. X begins more than a few English words, and some of them are pretty useful, because they denote things that are essential to our culture – the X-ray, for one.

From the perspective of the modern reader, the *Dictionary* abounds with evidence of language's pliancy. We may be surprised, for instance, to find that Johnson defines 'to womanize' as 'to emasculate; to effeminate; to soften'. He adds that the verb is 'proper, but not used'. We may also be surprised to see that 'maudlin' means 'drunk', as opposed to 'tearfully sentimental'; Johnson explains that the word is a corruption of the name of Mary Magdalene, whose many representations show her 'with swoln eyes, and [a] disordered look' – and thus rather like a drunkard.[2] 'Penguin' is not just a bird, but also a kind of fruit. 'Clientele', meaning 'the condition or office of a client', is 'a word scarcely used'. 'Smug' is defined as 'nice; spruce', although when Johnson adds that it can imply 'dressed with affectation of niceness' he suggests the beginnings of its modern meaning. The entry for 'slut' explains that it is 'a word of slight contempt to a woman': two and a half centuries on, calling someone a 'slut' is unlikely to be taken slightly, and the term has extended to include men as well as women.

★ One's immediate reaction may be 'What about "xenophobia"?' In fact, rather surprisingly, the word 'xenophobia' dates only from the early twentieth century.

There is, of course, a plethora of definitions we cannot expect to resemble those we would find in a modern dictionary. 'Car' is 'a small carriage', not the term for an automobile. A 'penthouse' has yet to become a luxurious top-floor apartment: to Johnson it is still just 'a shed hanging out aslope from the main wall'. A 'urinal' is merely 'a bottle, in which water is kept for inspection'. 'Ascii' is a long way from being spelt entirely in upper-case letters to signify the American Standard Code for Information Interchange: to Johnson's classically educated contemporaries it is the name of 'those people who, at certain times of the year, have no shadow at noon'. A 'plumber' is 'one who works upon lead'; in those few places where there was something approaching the modern mains water supply, it was conveyed by means of lead pipes, but in the eighteenth century plumbers more often worked on guttering and windows.

Some definitions now require a critical gloss. What, for instance, are we to make of the second sense of the verb 'to blanket', which is 'to toss in a blanket, by way of penalty or contempt'? There is a clue in the supporting quotation: it comes from Alexander Pope's poem *The Dunciad*. Pope refers to the fate that befell his arch-enemy, the unscrupulous bookseller Edmund Curll, who was tossed in a blanket by the scholars of Westminster School after publishing without authority part of a funeral sermon by their head boy. What looks at first to be not just a lost meaning, but a reflection of some weird and punitive civilization, is in fact a reference to a single episode. Johnson includes it in the *Dictionary* because, as much as anything, it may prove helpful to readers of *The Dunciad*. Still, the sense is obscure, and it is unlikely to be revived; the definition is a memento of Grub Street and its manic politics.

Less trivially, we can discern in Johnson's time-worn explanations the shifting boundaries of literary genre. A 'satire', he writes, is 'a poem in which wickedness or folly is censured'. His perception of the genre, shaped by his reading in Dryden and Pope, is conditioned by his own experience as a satirist, in his poems *London* and *The Vanity of Human Wishes*. For Johnson, and for most of his peers, satire is a mode inherited from Juvenal and Horace, rather than from Petronius, and its necessary vehicle is formal verse.

Again, it may pique the modern reader to find the novel defined as 'a small tale, generally of love'. This is inadequate as a description of *Robinson Crusoe* or *Clarissa*, *Tom Jones*, *Don Quixote* or *La Princesse de Clèves*. But most other novels of the period were inconsiderable things, and Johnson could find little enthusiasm for such flimsy articles; he preferred old-fashioned narratives of a sort he termed 'the fictions of romantick chivalry', and many works which we would call novels he considered 'romances'. The novel was still quite a new phenomenon in Britain at this time, and not an entirely respectable one. Johnson had misgivings about realistic fiction, which seemed less morally pregnant than his preferred prose forms, the sketch, the essay and the allegory. The 'small' of his definition is a comment on the novel's consequence, not its physical dimensions. Yet his depreciation of the genre is a reflection less of personal taste than of a more general contemporary distrust of the novel: its critics found it vacuous and disposable, and were concerned lest a sybaritic appetite for novels cause readers to neglect more serious books. We can read the definition as further evidence of 'Johnson the opinionist', but it is better understood as evidence of semantic flux – and of its engine, a wider cultural flux. The value of the novel was debatable. The *Dictionary* reflects the currency of this debate.

Here is a list of a few other words that have undergone a sharp change in meaning since 1755.

anecdote	something yet unpublished; secret history
asinine	belonging to an ass
barbecue	a hog dressed whole, in the West Indian manner
calculus	the stone in the bladder
choppy	full of holes, clefts, or cracks
contrite (1)	bruised; much worn
cruise	a small cup
devotee	one erroneously or superstitiously religious; a bigot
drug (2)	any thing without worth or value; any thing of which no purchaser can be found
empiricism	dependence on experience without knowledge or art; quackery
fake	a coil of rope

fireman (2)	a man of violent passions
to garble	to sift; to part; to separate the good from the bad
high-flier	one that carries his opinions to extravagance
lavatory	a wash; something in which parts diseased are washed
mufti	the high priest of the Mahometans
nice (1)	accurate in judgement to minute exactness; superfluously exact
orgasm	sudden vehemence
paddock	a great frog or toad
paraphernalia	goods in the wife's disposal
parlous	keen; sprightly; waggish
pedant (1)	a schoolmaster
pencil (1)	a small brush of hair which painters dip in their colours
pet (2)	a lamb taken into the house, and brought up by hand
pompous	splendid; magnificent; grand
pug	a kind name of a monkey, or any thing tenderly loved
recipe	a medical prescription
riffraff	the refuse of any thing
sinus	a bay of the sea; an opening of the land
sleazy	weak; wanting substance
soho	a form of calling from a distant place★
tabby	a kind of waved silk
tradition (2)	any thing delivered orally from age to age
urinator	a diver; one who searches under water

Two final definitions that can hardly be allowed to escape mention are those of 'jogger' and 'rapper'. One need not be told that Johnson doesn't think a 'rapper' is a hip-hop musician, but his definition – 'one who strikes' – seems an accidentally prescient judgement on a musical genre that has often been associated with violence and makes

---

★ In fact it was a hunting cry, and the London neighbourhood of this name was once a popular destination for hunters.

use of strong rhythmical language. And 'jogger', a word which will surely suggest to many readers of this book an image of healthy living at its most purgatorial, is reassuringly glossed by Johnson as 'one who moves heavily and dully'.

Zootomy

Dissection of the bodies of beasts

The final word in Johnson's *Dictionary*, less familiar than any of those in the preceding chapter, is 'zootomy'. An adequate modern dictionary might include another score or two of words: items such as 'zounds' and 'zucchini', 'Zulu' and 'zydeco', 'zygote' and – perhaps – 'Zyklon B'. But 'zootomy' seems an appropriate place for the *Dictionary* to end; applied metaphorically, the word is, near enough, a synonym for 'biography'. Johnson has been dissected many times: his carcass has been dismembered by a string of biographers, the corpus of his works microscopically picked apart by critics, students and fans. The *Dictionary*, however, has only lately begun to command the exacting attention it deserves. 'Zootomy' may be where it ends, but submitting it to this kind of intimate examination is the beginning of a new kind of understanding of its author and the world he inhabited.

Johnson continually sketched out ideas for books he hoped, aspired or intended to write. These included a history of criticism, a set of biographies of the great philosophers 'written with a polite air', a history of Venice, a prayer book, a dictionary of ancient mythology, editions of Chaucer and Bacon, a compendium of proverbs, a collection of epigrams, a history of the 'revival of learning' in Renaissance Europe, a cookbook laid out 'upon philosophical principles', a history of his melancholy, and an autobiography (these last two surely very much the same). None was ever written. But the *Dictionary* is at least some of these things.

It is doughty, authoritative, wide-ranging; lavish in its citations and self-consciously literary; patriotic, pious, and politically charged; sometimes quirky, often elegant, and occasionally obscure; keenly attentive to many of the age's new developments, yet negligent of others; an extension and refinement of existing lexicographic traditions, but also a starting point for new ones; and the culmination of an extraordinary, strenuous labour which both degraded and en-nobled its author.

More than any other reference work of its size, it repays perusal, inspection and investigation. We have seen that its pages continually offer up unexpected jewels – strange facts and pithy explanations, oddments of philological wisdom, and thought-provoking quota-tions. We have seen, too, that they tell a story about their maker, about his society, and about the subtlety and plasticity of language. Two hundred and fifty years after its completion, the *Dictionary* remains not merely readable, but vital. It is the best memorial of Samuel Johnson and his age.

James Boswell liked to think otherwise. In the advertisement to the second edition of his *Life of Johnson*, he declared, 'I have *Johnsonised* the land; and I trust they will not only *talk*, but *think*, Johnson.' The *Dictionary* shows us how this really came about, and also why Johnson should be *read*.

In my first chapter I mentioned Robert Browning, who chose to do just this, working his way right through the *Dictionary* in order to equip himself for a literary career. He thought of its contents as a sort of poem. Its appeal was threefold: it contained a vast amount of poetic language, provided definitions that were often sumptuously lyrical, and comprised tens of thousands of quotations from a wide variety of authors, many of whom were forgotten but worthy of recall, and whose writings, as presented by Johnson, bodied forth a history of human psychology. Browning's attention to the *Dictionary* was exceptionally dedicated, but suggests the range of uses to which it could be put.

No sooner had Johnson finished his labours than the *Dictionary*, so long a figment of his busy mind, took on a new life, or rather an assortment of new lives, as an object of often furious critical scrutiny, a tool of education, a touchstone for language scholars, an upmarket commodity, and a crucially important point of reference in what were to prove increasingly heated debates about Englishness and Britishness, the emergence of Empire, the changing structures of politics and class, and the idea of a national character. Johnson's was an astonishing feat of endurance and of literature. What he could not have anticipated, however, was the scope of its legacy.

Acknowledgements

Anyone writing about Samuel Johnson is indebted to the labours of his or her predecessors. In the interests of concision, I have attempted to keep my book's end matter to a minimum, and after some reflection I have chosen not to include a bibliography of works consulted. A full and detailed bibliography would have considerably increased the book's size, and – to paraphrase Johnson – I was wary lest the bulk of this volume fright away potential readers. On the other hand, an abbreviated bibliography could not have done justice to the wealth of scholarship relating to Johnson and his age. I have therefore chosen to discharge specific intellectual debts in my notes.

It is appropriate, however, to acknowledge here the contributions of a small number of scholars. In 1955 James Sledd and Gwin Kolb published the first full-length study, *Dr Johnson's Dictionary: Essays in the Biography of a Book*. Their scholarship has been valuably augmented by Robert DeMaria's *Johnson's Dictionary and the Language of Learning* and by Allen Reddick's *The Making of Johnson's Dictionary*. More recently, Anne McDermott's CD-ROM of the *Dictionary* (Cambridge: Cambridge University Press, 1996) has become a key tool for anyone wishing to study it closely.

There is no substitute, however, for perusing Johnson's work in hard copy. Readers wishing to purchase one of the full-size folio editions of the *Dictionary* are likely to be disappointed: eighteenth-century copies are expensive, as indeed are modern facsimiles. Fortunately, Jack Lynch has put together an attractive edition of the *Dictionary* (London: Atlantic Books, 2004), which faithfully reproduces more than 3,000 entries from Johnson's original. I recommend this unreservedly.

In the course of writing this book, I have incurred many debts of gratitude. Those who have guided or assisted me include Richard Arundel, Michael Bundock, David Crystal, Bob Davenport, Robert DeMaria, Sam Gilpin, Gesche Ipsen, Rachel Kennedy, Frank Lynch, Jack Lynch, Natasha McEnroe, Fred Nicholls, Sonja Peasey, Ellena Pike, Rowan Routh, James Scudamore, Anthony Strugnell, Amelia Wakeford and Matthew Wright. My thanks, also, to the staff of the British Library, London; the Public Record Office, Lichfield; Dr Johnson's House, Gough Square; the Samuel Johnson Birthplace Museum, Lichfield; the Tate Collection, London; the National Portrait Gallery, London; and the Beinecke Rare Book and Manuscript Library, Yale University.

I would like especially to thank Tony Nuttall, who first encouraged my interest in Samuel Johnson; John Mullan, an invigoratingly sceptical reader of my work; Robert Macfarlane, who persuaded me to write about the *Dictionary*; my agent, Peter Straus, who instinctively understood how and why I wanted to do so; and my editor at John Murray, Anya Serota, whose enthusiasm for the book has been at once unflagging and judicious.

Notes

Endnotes are not supplied for my numerous quotations from James Boswell's *The Life of Samuel Johnson, LL.D., with a Journal of a Tour to the Hebrides*, ed. George Birkbeck Hill and revised by L. F. Powell (6 vols., Oxford: Clarendon Press, 1934–64). Nor have I supplied detailed references for quotations from dictionaries, from Johnson's *London*, *Plan of an English Dictionary* and *The Vanity of Human Wishes*, or from the *Encyclopédie* of Diderot and d'Alembert. In addition, endnotes are not given for quotations from primary texts by authors other than Johnson, except when extended use is made of a particular source.

Adventurous

1. The best account of this attempt to set the arts in order is Lawrence Lipking, *The Ordering of the Arts in Eighteenth-Century England* (Princeton: Princeton University Press, 1970).
2. Robert Burchfield, *Unlocking the English Language* (London: Faber and Faber, 1989), xi.
3. Frederik N. Smith, *Beckett's Eighteenth Century* (Basingstoke: Palgrave, 2002), 199, n. 9. The words mean, respectively, 'reprehension; chiding', 'union by conjunction of the extremities' and 'to blow the nose'.
4. The British critic Walter Raleigh argued that 'when we pretend to laugh at our national character, we call it John Bull; when we wish to glorify it, we call it Samuel Johnson' (*Six Essays on Johnson* (Oxford: Clarendon Press, 1910), 32). Thomas Carlyle described Johnson as 'one of our great English souls', 'the largest soul that was in all England' and 'a Prophet to his people' (*On Heroes, Hero-Worship, and the Heroic in History* (1841), ed. Michael K. Goldberg, Joel J. Brattin and Mark Engel (Berkeley: University of California Press, 1993), 153–7).
5. *The Yale Edition of the Works of Samuel Johnson*, gen. eds. Allen T. Hazen

and John H. Middendorf (16 vols., New Haven: Yale University Press, 1958–), II, 434. Hereafter *Yale*.

Amulet

1. *Yale*, III, 321.
2. *Johnsonian Miscellanies*, ed. George Birkbeck Hill (2 vols., Oxford: Clarendon Press, 1897), I, 129. Hereafter *JM*.
3. James L. Clifford, *Young Sam Johnson* (New York: McGraw-Hill, 1955), 65
4. See *Johnsonian Gleanings*, ed. Allen Lyell Reade (11 vols., London: privately published, 1909–52), X, 161–82.
5. Ibid.
6. *JM*, II, 418–19.
7. *Yale*, I, 4.
8. Johnson writes that his father went to the fair at Chester 'when I had the small pox' (*Yale*, I, 176).
9. Washington Irving, *Little Britain* (London: Sampson Low, Marston, Searle & Rivington, 1880), 6.
10. *JM*, I, 149.

Apple

1. *Yale*, I, 17.
2. *JM*, I, 328, 160, 314, 163.
3. *Thraliana: The Diary of Mrs Hester Lynch Thrale (later Mrs Piozzi) 1776–1809*, ed. Katharine C. Balderston (2nd edn, Oxford: Clarendon Press, 1951), 161.

Bookworm

1. Sir John Hawkins, *The Life of Samuel Johnson, LL.D.* (2nd edn, London: J. Buckland et al., 1787), 2, n.
2. *JM*, I, 154.
3. *The Lives of the English Poets, by Samuel Johnson, LL.D.*, ed. George Birkbeck Hill (3 vols., Oxford: Clarendon Press, 1905), II, 261. Hereafter *Lives*.

4. *Yale*, XVI, 95 (*Rasselas*).
5. John Wain, *Samuel Johnson* (London: Macmillan, 1974), 39–40.

Commoner

1. Douglas Macleane, *A History of Pembroke College* (London: Oxford Historical Society Publications, 1897), 167–75.
2. *Yale*, I, 26 (the translation is Boswell's, from Johnson's Latin).
3. Clifford, *Young Sam Johnson*, 124.

Darkling

1. *JM*, II, 427.
2. Wain, *Samuel Johnson*, 64.
3. *Yale*, II, 457.
4. Ibid., 458.
5. Thomas Babington Macaulay, *Samuel Johnson LL.D.* (London: The Traveller's Library, 1856), 41. This is a single-volume reprint of Macaulay's review of James Boswell, *The Life of Samuel Johnson LL.D.*, ed. John Wilson Croker (5 vols., London: John Murray, 1831).
6. *Yale*, V, 128–9.

To decamp

1. *Yale*, I, 39–40.
2. *The Letters of Samuel Johnson: The Hyde Edition*, ed. Bruce Redford (5 vols., Oxford: Clarendon Press, 1992–4), I, 206. Hereafter *Letters*.
3. Crime declined as the century continued. Johnson's friend Giuseppe Baretti noticed a distinct improvement between 1750 and 1760. A general pattern of betterment was noted by many other observers, including the city magistrate Sir John Fielding and the social reformer Francis Place. See M. Dorothy George, *London Life in the Eighteenth Century* (3rd edn, London: London School of Economics and Political Science, 1951), 17–18.
4. Of these words only 'footpad' is defined in the *Dictionary*, but Johnson records plenty of other terms associated with criminals and criminality, such as 'thief-taker', 'lurkingplace', 'pickpurse', 'to shark' and 'incendiary' ('one who sets houses or towns on fire in malice or for robbery').

5. James Boswell, *London Journal, 1762–1763*, ed. Frederick A. Pottle (London: Heinemann, 1950), 83–4.
6. This statistic is taken from Roy Porter, *London: A Social History* (London: Hamish Hamilton, 1994), 171.
7. According to Porter (p. 134) Georgian Londoners also consumed 14,000,000 mackerel, 700,000 sheep and lambs, and 115,000 bushels of oysters every year.
8. *JM*, I, 380.

To dissipate

1. *Lives*, II, 431.
2. Ibid., 398–9.
3. Richard Holmes, *Dr Johnson and Mr Savage* (London: Hodder & Stoughton, 1993), 50.
4. *Lives*, II, 380, 400.
5. Holmes, *Dr Johnson and Mr Savage*, 171.
6. *Thraliana*, 178.

English

1. *Second Factum pour Messire Antoine Furetière, abbé de Chalivoy, contre quelques-uns de l'Académie française* (Amsterdam: Henry Desbordes, 1688), 32 (my translation).
2. Swift also complained, in a letter to the *Tatler* on 28 September 1710, that 'all new affected Modes of Speech, whether borrowed from the Court, the Town, or the Theatre, are the first perishing Parts in any Language'.
3. Richard Mulcaster, *The First Part of the Elementarie* (London: T. Vautroullier, 1582), 164–6.
4. Steven Pinker, *Words and Rules: The Ingredients of Language* (London: Weidenfeld & Nicolson, 1999), 12.

Entrance

1. Of these, the Knaptons, Longman and Hitch were frequent collabor-ators. In the 1740s they were shareholders in Bailey's *Universal*

Etymological Dictionary, as well as sharing in the publication of a number of other works that included commentaries on Virgil, Caesar and the Old Testament. Hitch was later joined in partnership with Charles Hawes, while Shewell and Longman broke their partnership in 1748.

2. For a full account of Dodsley's influence within the eighteenth-century book trade, see Harry M. Solomon, *The Rise of Robert Dodsley: Creating the New Age of Print* (Carbondale, Ill.: Southern Illinois University Press, 1996).

3. An excellent summary of the cost of living is provided by Liza Picard, in *Dr Johnson's London* (London: Weidenfeld & Nicolson, 2000), 293–8. I have taken several of my statistics from this source.

4. It seems likely that Johnson acquired Hodge only after leaving Gough Square. Boswell, who first met Johnson several years after he had moved from that address, definitely knew Hodge: 'I am,' he recorded, 'unluckily, one of those who have an antipathy to a cat . . . and I own, I frequently suffered a good deal from the presence of this same Hodge.'

5. Thomas Carlyle, 'Boswell's Life of Johnson' (1832), in *English and other Critical Essays* (London: Dent, 1964), 45–6, n.

Factotum

1. *Letters*, IV, 336.
2. Ibid., I, 41.
3. British Library Add. MS 38729, fol. 131.
4. *Letters*, II, 315.
5. Already, some forty years after the Act of Union, Scottish booksellers and printers were playing a large role in the British publishing business. In the nineteenth century this role would increase, with the rise of firms such as Constable, Collins, A. & C. Black, Oliver & Boyd, and Macmillan.

To gather

1. British Library Add. MS 35397, fol. 67.
2. Johnson refers to Ainsworth 584 times, and to Bailey 197 times. In addition, there are some 1,144 references to 'Dict.', which is Johnson's shorthand for something along the lines of 'I have found this word in an earlier dictionary.' His references to 'Dict.' are especially common in

the first few letters. In many cases, though not a majority, 'Dict.' appears to be an alternative form of reference to Bailey. A detailed survey of Johnson's use of these sources has been made by Catharina M. de Vries, in her study *In The Tracks of a Lexicographer: Secondary Documentation in Samuel Johnson's Dictionary of the English Language* (Leiden: LED, 1994).

3. Hawkins, *The Life of Samuel Johnson*, 175.

4. *Letters*, III, 127.

Higgledy-piggledy

1. The thirteen copy texts known to be extant are: the third volume of *The Works of Francis Bacon* (1740); Bryan Duppa, *Holy Rules and Helps to Devotion* (1675); one volume of an anthology entitled *Works of the most Celebrated Minor Poets* (1749), which includes poems by Thomas Tickell, George Stepney and Samuel Garth; Matthew Hale's *Primitive Origination of Mankind* (1677), bound in one volume with the eighth edition (1676) of Burton's *Anatomy of Melancholy*; John Norris, *A Collection of Miscellanies* (1699); seven of the eight volumes of William Warburton's edition of the *Plays of William Shakespeare* (1747); the second volume of Robert South's *Twelve Sermons* (1694); the second volume of Christopher Pitt's translation of Virgil's *Aeneid* (1740); Izaak Walton's *Life of Dr Sanderson* (1678); the eighth edition of Isaac Watts's *Logick* (1745); and – consulted for the fourth edition, but not for the first – Michael Drayton's *Works* (1748) and Walter Harte's *The Amaranth* (1767).

2. One amanuensis, who favoured a single vertical stroke when crossing out the letters in the margin, must have been disappointed to discover that as few as 5 per cent of the passages he transcribed found their way into the *Dictionary* (compared to a figure of 80 or 90 per cent for his colleagues). The most plausible explanation is that his slips were accidentally destroyed.

3. The marginalium also includes the name Davies – presumably a reference to Sir John Davies's *Discourse of the True Reasons Why Ireland Has Never Been Entirely Subdued* (1612). It follows that Johnson read Davies before reading Hale. For a detailed examination of Johnson's use of Hale, see Daisuke Nagashima, 'How Johnson Read Hale's *Origination* for his Dictionary: A Linguistic View', *The Age of Johnson* 7 (1996), 247–97.

4. See Eugene J. Thomas, 'A Bibliographical and Critical Analysis of Dr

Johnson's *Dictionary* with Special Reference to Twentieth-Century Scholarship' (Ph.D. dissertation, University of Wales Institute of Science and Technology, Aberystwyth, 1974), 142.

5. This was an enduring concern. When Johnson came to writes his *Lives of the Poets*, thirty years later, he expressed in his diary the hope that they be 'written . . . in such a manner, as may tend to the promotion of Piety' (*Yale*, I, 294).

6. According to Janine Barchas, in her recent study *Graphic Design, Print Culture, and the Eighteenth-Century Novel* (Cambridge: Cambridge University Press, 2003), 'Samuel Johnson's *Dictionary* . . . confirms the existence of a long-standing rhetorical prejudice against the dash in mid-eighteenth-century print culture', and authors including Johnson, Fielding and Swift 'unanimously objected' to 'Grubstreet application of the dash', which was felt to be 'lower-class and ephemeral' (pp. 165–6).

7. This excellent example is borrowed from Robert DeMaria, *Johnson's Dictionary and the Language of Learning* (Chapel Hill, NC: University of North Carolina Press, 1986), 17.

8. Hawkins, *The Life of Samuel Johnson*, 545.

9. *JM*, I, 292.

10. Hawkins, *The Life of Samuel Johnson*, 396, 400.

11. *Yale*, VI, 314–15.

12. There may be a covert reference to Johnson's financial cares in his definition of 'necessaries' ('things not only convenient but needful; things not to be left out of daily use'), which ends with the poignant Latin motto *Quibus doleat natura negatis*, loosely meaning 'If you're denied these things, life is hard.'

Lexicographer

1. Isaac Watts, *Logick* (8th edn, London: T. Longman and T. Shewell, 1745), 105–8.

2. Roy Porter, *Flesh in the Age of Reason* (London: Allen Lane, 2003), 7. For a full treatment of Johnson's use of Locke, see James McLaverty, 'From Definition to Explanation: Locke's Influence on Johnson's Dictionary', *Journal of the History of Ideas* 47 (1986), 377–94, and Elizabeth Hedrick, 'Locke's Theory of Language and Johnson's Dictionary', *Eighteenth-Century Studies* 20 (1987), 422–44.

3. In *Rambler* 125 (*Yale*, IV, 300), Johnson notes that one of the maxims of civil law is that 'definitions are hazardous'. 'Definition is . . . not the

province of man,' he argues, and 'the works and operations of nature are too great in their extent, or too much diffused in their relations, . . . to be reduced to any determinate idea'. A great many things 'are scarcely to be included in any standing form of expression', since 'they are always suffering some alteration of their state'. The human imagination 'has always endeavoured to baffle the logician, to perplex the confines of distinction, and burst the inclosures of regularity'.

4. The best treatment of Johnson's etymologies is in Daisuke Nagashima, *Johnson the Philologist* (Osaka: Intercultural Research Institute, Kansai University of Foreign Studies, 1988), 149–205.

5. Robert DeMaria and Gwin Kolb, 'Johnson's *Dictionary* and Dictionary Johnson', *The Yearbook of English Studies* 28 (1998), 25–6.

6. In fact 'spider' derives from the Old English *spithra*, related to the verb 'to spin'. 'Dor' or 'dorr' is 'a kind of flying insect, remarkable for flying with a loud noise'. For a detailed assessment of Johnson's etymology of 'gibberish', see Robert DeMaria and Gwin Kolb, 'Dr Johnson's Etymology of Gibberish', *Notes & Queries* 243 (1998), 72–4.

7. The image is not unique to the definition of 'lexicographer'. In an earlier chapter I quoted Johnson's reference in the *Plan* to 'drudgery for the blind'; it appears again in an *Adventurer* essay dating from 1753 (*Yale*, II, 348), where he describes 'the low drudgery of collating copies, comparing authorities, digesting dictionaries'.

Library

1. Johnson's labelling of his sources is inconsistent. Much of the time the sources *are* clearly identified: as 'Shakespeare's Hamlet' or 'Knolles's History of the Turks' or 'Stillingfleet's Defence of Discourses on Romish Idolatry'. When the name of the work is not given, the name of the author is commonly supplied. But the names of authors and of their works are often abbreviated, and at their most curt the abbreviations need deciphering. If it's not immediately obvious that 'Po. Ra. Locke' means Pope's *Rape of the Lock*, or that 'M.' means Milton and 'Dr.' Dryden, it is a deal less obvious who is meant by 'Br.' or 'W____n.' or 'P. Fletch.'. Besides, Johnson is not consistent in his use of such labels. This is partly a function of print-setting; names are reduced to allow economies of space. But it does seem a little cranky that Shakespeare is frequently 'Shakesp.' or 'Shakes.' or 'Shak.', and a few dozen times 'Sha.', though only once 'Shake.'. In most cases it is not hard to work

out that the abbreviation denotes the author of *The Tempest* and *King Lear*. What, however, are we to make of the quotations simply labelled 'Brown'? This can mean several different people – most of them really called Browne. Very occasionally, just to confuse matters, the name recovers its final *e*.

2. Many of the quotations from Shakespeare are incorrectly attributed. The responsibility for these errors probably lay with the amanuensis who transcribed the passages Johnson marked in his copy of Warburton's edition.

3. For a full discussion of this subject, see Daisuke Nagashima, 'The Biblical Quotations in Johnson's *Dictionary*', *The Age of Johnson* 10 (1999), 89–126.

4. Boswell says of Bolingbroke's writings that 'The wild and pernicious ravings, under the name of "Philosophy", which were thus ushered into the world, gave great offence to all well-principled men.' Johnson pronounced their author 'a scoundrel, and a coward: a scoundrel for charging a blunderbuss against religion and morality; a coward, because he had not resolution to fire it off himself'. A small number of quotations from Bolingbroke do survive despite Johnson's apparent commitment to excluding him. These may be the accidental contribution of his amanuenses, or they may show that Johnson could not pass up an opportunity to expose Bolingbroke's affected diction.

5. *Thraliana*, 34.

6. *The Early Biographies of Samuel Johnson*, ed. OM Brack, Jr, and Robert E. Kelley (Iowa City: University of Iowa Press, 1974), 82.

7. Umberto Eco, *Semiotics and the Philosophy of Language* (London: Macmillan, 1984), 46–86.

8. DeMaria, *Johnson's Dictionary and the Language of Learning*, 37.

Melancholy

1. *Letters*, I, 42–4.

2. Hawkins, *The Life of Samuel Johnson*, 230.

3. Ibid., 87, 250.

4. *Yale*, III, xxxii. Even if the *Dictionary* suggests an ambivalence about Greek and Latin learning, it is rich in references to authors such as Homer, Virgil, Horace and Plato, as well as to lesser figures – the didactic poet Lucretius, for instance, and the pre-Socratic philosopher Anaxagoras.

5. A brilliantly learned account of the development of this kind of language, and of Johnson's part in it, is W. K. Wimsatt's *Philosophic Words: A Study of Style and Meaning in the Rambler and Dictionary of Samuel Johnson* (New Haven: Yale University Press, 1948). My examples are drawn from Wimsatt.

6. This subject is dealt with in detail by Geoffrey Cantor, in his essay 'The Rhetoric of Experiment' in David Gooding, Trevor Pinch and Simon Schaffer, eds., *The Uses of Experiment: Studies in the Natural Sciences* (Cambridge: Cambridge University Press, 1989). Cantor describes the role of scientific prose as an 'instrument of persuasion' (p. 161), and suggests that the rhetorical features of scientific discourse make it 'a discourse of power'.

7. *Yale*, V, 150.

8. Ibid., I, 43–4.

9. Ibid., II, 60.

10. *Letters*, I, 57.

11. *Yale*, IV, 300; XVI, 151.

12. Ibid., III, 221; V, 44; II, 228, 476; V, 235; III, 217. Johnson informed Boswell that 'Whatever philosophy may determine of material nature, it is certainly true of intellectual nature, that it abhors a vacuum: our minds cannot be empty.'

Microscope

1. *JM*, I, 207.

2. *Yale*, III, 131–3.

3. *JM*, I, 306.

4. *Gentleman's Magazine* 24 (1754), 113.

Nicety

1. *Lives*, III, 440.

2. Hawkins, *The Life of Samuel Johnson*, 219, 258.

3. *JM*, II, 390.

To note

1. Robert McCrum, William Cran and Robert MacNeil, *The Story of English* (3rd edn, London: Faber and Faber, 2002), 137.
2. *Yale*, V, 318–19.
3. In the *Dictionary* Johnson defines 'to receive' as 'to embrace intellectually', 'to allow' and 'to admit'. 'Received' is not separately defined, but 'receivedness' is defined as 'general allowance'. When he states that the word 'opiniatry' is 'not yet received', he presumably means that the word's existence has yet to be allowed by other arbiters of correctness.
4. Until the middle of the following century, most Britons had their literacy assessed only when they signed the marriage register, and in most parts of Britain women were less likely to be literate than men were. For a full treatment of this subject, see David Vincent, *Literacy and Popular Culture: England 1750–1914* (Cambridge: Cambridge University Press, 1989).
5. As Catharina de Vries has observed, the *Dictionary*'s 'country' terms are often drawn from Ainsworth, Bailey and Edward Phillips. She notes that a word taken by Johnson from Ainsworth will typically have 'a dialectal flavour' and 'has a high chance of being the English name of a plant, a fish, a bird, an insect, an animal or a mineral . . . or pertains to country life in its widest sense . . . or refers to low life' (*In The Tracks of a Lexicographer*, 46). Thus for instance 'frogbit', 'hedge-nettle', 'hogsmushrooms', 'hurlbat', 'madgehowlet', 'mermaid's trumpet', 'muskcherry', 'swordgrass' and 'weaverfish'. A word drawn by Johnson from his examination of Bailey also 'has some chance of . . . rural connections' (p. 113). Examples might include 'gerfalcon', 'to gip', 'recheat' and 'swinebread'. A personal favourite is 'poupicts', which is apparently 'a mess of victuals made of veal stakes [*sic*] and slices of bacon'. Finally, Phillips's *New World of Words*, edited by John Kersey, is the source of rustic words such as 'burrock', 'churrworm' and 'ciderkin'.
6. A useful analysis of the *Dictionary*'s place in Anglo-Scottish relations can be found in Janet Sorensen, *The Grammar of Empire in Eighteenth-Century British Writing* (Cambridge: Cambridge University Press, 2000), 63–103.

Opinionist

1. See Lane Cooper, 'Dr Johnson on Oats and Other Grains', *Publications of the Modern Language Association of America* 52 (1937), 785–802.

2. *Lives*, I, 169.

3. The subject of Johnson's politics has provoked considerable debate. This is not the place to enter the fray: while the *Dictionary* contains traces of political opinion, it is hardly a sustained work of political thought. The first place to look for detailed evidence of Johnson's politics is, naturally, in his political writings. The best guide to these is still Donald Greene's *The Politics of Samuel Johnson* (2nd edn, Athens, Ga.: University of Georgia Press, 1990). Among several recent counterblasts the most vigorous is Jonathan Clark's *Samuel Johnson: Literature, Religion and English Cultural Politics from the Restoration to Romanticism* (Cambridge: Cambridge University Press, 1994).

4. His definition of 'caitiff' is rounded off with a superfluous Greek epigram that damns the practice of slavery.

5. For a full discussion of this, see Robert DeMaria, 'The Politics of Johnson's *Dictionary*', *Publications of the Modern Language Association of America* 104 (1989), 64–74. Another definition, of 'renegade', originally contained a similarly scathing aside, at the expense of the Tory-turned-Whig John Leveson Gower. But Johnson struck it out, on the advice of Strahan.

6. South is also the voice of temperance. In his entry for 'alehouse' Johnson quotes him: 'One would think it should be no easy matter to bring any man of sense in love with an *alehouse*; indeed of so much sense, as seeing and smelling amounts to; there being such strong encounters of both, as would quickly send him packing, did not the love of fellowship reconcile to these nuisances.' A rather different perspective on temperance is offered by Swift, in this quotation under 'porpoise' (spelt 'porpus' by Johnson):

> Parch'd with unextinguish'd thirst,
> Small beer I guzzle till I burst;
> And then I drag a bloated corpus
> Swell'd with a dropsy like a *porpus*.

7. *JM*, I, 249–50.

8. Ibid., 250.

9. Hawkins, *The Life of Samuel Johnson*, 327.

10. Ibid., 316.

11. *Yale*, I, 52–3.

12. Ibid., III, 97.

13. Ibid., IV, 11.

14. Ibid., I, 50.

15. *Letters*, I, 73. Bruce Redford, the admirable editor of Johnson's letters, explains that 'Strahan seems to have complained that the text sent to the printing house was not written as closely or arranged as economically as it should have been. If . . . [Johnson] were paid a set sum for each sheet of MS copy, but the sheets were not written tightly or the quotations pasted closely, then one MS sheet would no longer equal one printed sheet and . . . [he] would be overpaid.' Redford also speculates that the illustrative quotations 'may have sprawled beyond the stipulated limits', complicating Strahan's job further still.
16. *Yale*, III, 339.

Opulence

1. Paul Langford, *A Polite and Commercial People: England 1727–1783* (Oxford: Oxford University Press, 1989), 6–7.
2. James Hanway, *A Journal of Eight Days Journey . . . To which is added, An Essay on Tea* (London: H. Woodfall, 1756), 204.
3. John Brewer, *The Pleasures of the Imagination: English Culture in the Eighteenth Century* (London: HarperCollins, 1997), 35–7.
4. The debate was lively. John Brown's *Estimate of the Manners and Principles of the Times*, published two years after the *Dictionary*, was a popular bestseller. A critique of 'luxury' in all its ramifications, it expressed particular anxiety about the increasing effeminacy of luxury's male devotees.
5. *Gentleman's Magazine* 13 (1743), 486.
6. Robert J. Mayhew has helpfully pointed out that Johnson's 'definitions of aesthetic terms relating to landscape . . . appear less reactionary when viewed in the context of the tradition of English lexicography', and that his 'careful discrimination of shades of meaning gave a far richer lexicon of landscape than had previously existed' (*Landscape, Literature and English Religious Culture, 1660–1800: Samuel Johnson and the Languages of Natural Description* (Basingstoke: Palgrave, 2004), 147). It is worth noting, then, that the *Dictionary* does not define the term 'picturesque', which was to be another keyword in the aesthetic theories of the period, but that in the fourth edition one definition of 'prospect' is 'a picturesque representation of a landscape'. This definition is supported with a quotation from Sir Joshua Reynolds, which mentions the work of the quintessentially picturesque painter Claude Lorrain.
7. I have borrowed this elegant formula from Morris Golden's study *The*

Self Observed: Swift, Johnson, Wordsworth (Baltimore: Johns Hopkins University Press, 1972), 85.

8. *Yale*, III, 21.

Pastern

1. *JM*, II, 278.
2. See Sarah Markham, *John Loveday of Caversham 1711–1789: The Life and Tours of an Eighteenth-Century Onlooker* (Salisbury: Michael Russell, 1984), 433.
3. *JM*, II, 308.
4. At one point Johnson brackets together three separate entries – 'hogs-beans', 'hogsbread', 'hogsmushrooms' – and provides a single definition: 'Plants'. The next entry is 'hogsfennel'. His definition of this is 'a plant'.
5. *Gentleman's Magazine* 23 (1753), 433.
6. See David Boyd Haycock, *William Stukeley: Science, Religion and Archaeology in Eighteenth-Century England* (Woodbridge: Boydell, 2002), 72–4.
7. While Boswell reports that Wilkes's piece appeared in the *Public Advertiser*, it has not been traced in that journal, and Boswell is more likely to have seen a reprinted version in the *European Magazine*.
8. See David Crystal, *The Stories of English* (London: Allen Lane, 2004), 316–17.
9. Simon Winchester, *The Meaning of Everything: The Story of the Oxford English Dictionary* (Oxford: Oxford University Press, 2003), xxiii–xxiv.
10. Goldsmith reflected, after the Club had been in existence for more than twenty years, that 'there can now be nothing new among us: we have travelled over one another's minds'. Johnson jabbed back, 'Sir, you have not travelled over my mind, I promise you.'
11. *Letters*, IV, 379. This was probably meant to call to mind Alexander Pope's lines in his *An Essay on Criticism* (1711): ''Tis with our judgements as our watches, none / Go just alike, yet each believes his own.'

Patron

1. *World* 100 (28 November 1754), 599–604.
2. Ibid., 101 (5 December 1754), 605–10.
3. *Yale*, IV, 194; V, 100–106, 317.

4. Ibid., VI, 99.
5. *JM*, I, 405.
6. *Letters*, I, 95–7.
7. In his rewarding study *Samuel Johnson and the Impact of Print* (Princeton: Princeton University Press, 1989), Alvin Kernan calls the letter 'the Magna Carta of the modern author, the public announcement that the days of courtly letters were at last ended' (p. 105).
8. One of Johnson's lesser known biographers, writing in the year after his death, records his equally damning judgement that 'All the celebrated qualities of Chesterfield . . . are like certain species of fruit which is pleasant enough to the eye, but there is no tasting it without danger' (William Shaw, *Memoirs of the Life and Writings of the Late Dr Samuel Johnson*, ed. Arthur Sherbo (Oxford: Oxford University Press, 1974), 25–6).

Philology

1. Nevertheless, the links between Warton's history of English and Johnson's have drawn little comment. The chief exception is Gwin Kolb and Robert DeMaria, 'Thomas Warton's *Observations on the "Faerie Queene" of Spenser*, Samuel Johnson's "History of the English Language", and Warton's *History of English Poetry*: Reciprocal Indebtedness?', *Philological Quarterly* 74 (1995), 327–35.
2. *Letters*, I, 109.
3. Ibid., I, 82.
4. Johnson made a few small changes to the Grammar for later editions, and to the History for the fourth edition only. The Preface was very slightly altered for the second and fourth editions.
5. *Letters*, I, 92.

Pleasureful

1. Macaulay's *Life of Johnson*, ed. John Downie (London: Blackie & Son, 1918), 22.
2. Samuel Taylor Coleridge, *Biographia Literaria*, ed. James Engel and Walter Jackson Bate (2 vols., Princeton: Princeton University Press, 1983), I, 237–8.
3. Eric Partridge, *The Gentle Art of Lexicography* (London: André Deutsch, 1963), 14.

To preface

1. It is worth noting at this point that Johnson does not define 'national-ist' or 'nationalism' in the *Dictionary*: the words did not acquire currency until the nineteenth century. 'Patriot' is defined in the first edition as 'one whose ruling passion is the love of his country', and he would have been happy to think of himself in these terms. However, in the years that followed it took on a negative sense. Johnson notices this in the fourth edition: 'It is sometimes used for a factious disturber of the government.' The historian John Cannon explains that Johnson came to equate 'patriotism' with 'the noisy and insincere rhetoric of a man who made a trade out of his concern for his country' – a man such as the insolently self-promoting John Wilkes, whose political agitations struck Johnson as disgustingly artificial (*Samuel Johnson and the Politics of Hanoverian England* (Oxford: Clarendon Press, 1994), 215).

Publication

1. *Letters*, I, 100.
2. Quoted in J. A. Cochrane, *Dr Johnson's Printer: The Life of William Strahan* (London: Routledge & Kegan Paul, 1964), 102.
3. Strahan's workers were marshalled by another Scot, Archibald Hamilton, who had fled Edinburgh after the Porteous riots some twenty years before. Although Hamilton's efficiency was questioned by Johnson, the business flourished under his stewardship. Strahan's revenues for 1755 exceeded £4,000, and in 1756 they totalled £5,634. 12s. 6d. – more than four times the figure of a decade before.
4. This view is corroborated by Allen Reddick's authoritative study *The Making of Johnson's Dictionary* (rev. edn, Cambridge: Cambridge University Press, 1996).

Reception

1. *Monthly Review* 12 (April 1755), 322.
2. *Edinburgh Review* 1 (January–July 1755), 54–5.
3. *A Letter from a Friend in England to Mr Maxwell . . . with a Character of Mr Johnson's English Dictionary, Lately Published, and Mr Maxwell's Justification of Himself* (Dublin: S. Powell, 1755).

4. *Universal Visiter* 1 (January 1756), 4.

5. *Letters*, I, 157.

6. Ibid., 116–17.

7. Zachariah Williams, *An Account of an Attempt To Ascertain the Longitude at Sea, by an Exact Theory of the Variation of the Magnetical Needle* (London: Robert Dodsley, 1755), 16.

Triumphant

1. *JM*, II, 400–402.

2. For these statistics I am indebted to Helen-Louise McGuffie's *Samuel Johnson in the British Press, 1749–1784: A Chronological Checklist* (New York: Garland, 1976).

3. *Yale*, X, 202.

4. For this figure I am indebted to Arthur Sherbo, *Samuel Johnson, Editor of Shakespeare* (Urbana, Ill.: University of Illinois Press, 1956).

Ubiquity

1. *Letters*, I, 109.

2. See J. D. Fleeman, 'Johnson in the Schoolroom: George Fulton's Miniature *Dictionary* (1821)', in Harvey Ross, Wallace Kirsop and B. J. McMullin, eds., *An Index of Civilisation: Studies of Printing and Publishing History in Honour of Keith Maslen* (Clayton, Vic.: Centre for Bibliographic and Textual Studies, Monash University, 1993), 163–71.

3. Winchester, *The Meaning of Everything*, 32.

4. J. D. Fleeman explains that 'No Miniature edition of Johnson's Dictionary has any authoritative relationship with the Dictionary proper: only the folio text deriving from 1755 . . . and the abridged versions in octavo dating from 1756 . . . have that status. Nevertheless a great many pocket editions began to appear towards the end of the eighteenth century, claiming in some way to be "Johnson's"' (*A Bibliography of the Works of Samuel Johnson, Treating his Published Works from the Beginnings to 1984*, prepared for publication by James McLaverty (2 vols., Oxford: Clarendon Press, 2000), I, 556).

5. In his enjoyable book *Chasing the Sun: Dictionary-Makers and the Dictionaries They Made* (London: Jonathan Cape, 1996) Jonathon Green describes Croft as 'an earnest if eccentric figure', whose writings

'included a number of bizarre publications, among them a proposed new system of punctuation, . . . and *Love and Madness*, which was based on letters written by the suicidal poet Thomas Chatterton, which to his shame Croft had obtained through trickery' (pp. 228–9).

6. One of the words Mason wishes to add is 'patronless', for which he cites, from Shaftesbury's 'Advice to Authors', the sentence 'The arts and sciences must not be left *patronless*.'

Variety

1. *Letters*, II, 8–9.
2. Only quite small changes were made to the front matter. However, Johnson's changes in the Grammar do show that he had read and digested Robert Lowth's recently published *Short Introduction to English Grammar*.
3. Part of this quotation had appeared, under another headword, in the first edition. Allen Reddick, in his study *The Making of Johnson's Dictionary*, explains that during the process of revision Johnson consulted his old manuscript and looked for quotations that could be recycled under different headwords. Reddick is especially valuable as a guide to the changes made by Johnson for the fourth edition, to which he devotes three of his eight chapters.
4. I was first alerted to this by Reddick's *The Making of Johnson's Dictionary*.
5. Reddick notes (p. 154) that 'the only purely political work' from which Johnson quotes new passages in the fourth edition is Charles Davenant's 'aggressively anti-Whig' *Discourse upon Grants and Resumptions* (1700), which inveighed against Whig ministerial corruption and the imposition of excise duties.
6. For a detailed treatment of Johnson's classical references in the poem, see Barry Baldwin, *The Latin and Greek Poems of Samuel Johnson* (London: Duckworth, 1995), 78–86.
7. *JM*, I, 409.
8. The sixth and seventh editions, published after Johnson's death, incorporate a few hundred further revisions. These were based on his annotations in a copy of the fourth edition which was bequeathed to Sir Joshua Reynolds.

Weightiness

1. John Milton, *Areopagitica* (London, 1644), 4.

2. Robert Nares, *Elements of Orthoepy* (London: T. Payne & Son, 1784), 269–70.

3. James H. Sledd and Gwin J. Kolb, *Dr Johnson's Dictionary: Essays in the Biography of a Book* (Chicago: University of Chicago Press, 1955), 183.

4. John Horne Tooke, *Epea Pteroenta. Or, The Diversions of Purley*, Part I (2nd edn, London: J. Johnson, 1798), 223, n.

5. James Gilchrist, *Philosophic Etymology, or Rational Grammar* (London: Rowland Hunter, 1816), 128, 160.

6. Charles Richardson, *A New Dictionary of the English Language* (2 vols., London: William Pickering, 1836–7), 37–40.

7. Archibald Campbell, *Lexiphanes: A Dialogue* (London: J. Knox, 1767), 6, 35, 107–9.

8. Quoted in James L. Clifford, *Dictionary Johnson: Samuel Johnson's Middle Years* (London: Heinemann, 1979), 80.

9. *Walpoliana*, ed. John Pinkerton (2 vols., London: R. Phillips, 1799), I, 34.

10. *Letters*, I, 79.

11. Murray Cohen, *Sensible Words: Linguistic Practice in England 1640–1785* (Baltimore: Johns Hopkins University Press, 1977), 78.

12. Quoted in Sledd and Kolb, *Dr Johnson's Dictionary*, p. 110.

13. Noah Webster, *Dissertations on the English Language* (Boston: Isaiah Thomas, 1789), 20–21.

14. Noah Webster, *A Letter to Dr David Ramsay . . . Respecting the Errors in Johnson's Dictionary* (New Haven: Oliver Steele & Co., 1807), 6.

15. Ibid.

16. Letter to Andrew Stevenson, 22 June 1841. Quoted in Richard M. Rollins, *The Long Journey of Noah Webster* (Philadelphia: University of Pennsylvania Press, 1980), 127. Emphasis added.

17. For a detailed discussion of Webster's debt to Johnson, see Joseph H. Friend, *The Development of American Lexicography 1798–1864* (The Hague: Mouton, 1967), 38–46, together with Joseph W. Reed, Jr, 'Noah Webster's Debt to Samuel Johnson', *American Speech* 37 (1962), 95–105.

18. Joseph E. Worcester, *A Universal and Critical Dictionary of the English Language* (Boston: Wilkins, Carter & Co., 1846), lxiv.

X

1. These two examples are taken from John Honey, *Language is Power: The Story of Standard English and its Enemies* (London: Faber and Faber, 1997), 145.
2. Anyone interested in the history of artistic and literary representations of Mary should consult Susan Haskins's *Mary Magdalen: Myth and Metaphor* (London: HarperCollins, 1993).

Picture Acknowledgements

The author and publishers wish to thank the following for permission to reproduce illustrations: pp. 26, 57, 193 and 194, the Trustees of Dr Johnson's House Trust; pp. 26, 51, 55, 112, 205 and 206, the National Portrait Gallery, London; p. 74, the British Library, London (shelfmark C.28.g.9); p. 169 © Tate, London, 2005; p. 217, the Beinecke Rare Book and Manuscript Library, Yale University.

The illustrations on pp. 17, 36 and 38 are taken from *The Complete Works of William Hogarth* (London: The London Printing and Publishing Company, 1870).

General Index

Writings by Samuel Johnson (SJ) appear directly under title; other writings under author's name

Index of Words

The words listed are those from the *Dictionary* defined or mentioned in the text